IMAGES
of America

LOST INDIANAPOLIS

IMAGES
of America

LOST INDIANAPOLIS

John P. McDonald

ARCADIA
PUBLISHING

ISBN 978-0-7385-2008-7

Published by Arcadia Publishing
Charleston, South Carolina

Printed in the United States of America

Library of Congress Catalog Card Number: 2002107389

For all general information contact Arcadia Publishing at:
Telephone 843-853-2070
Fax 843-853-0044
E-mail sales@arcadiapublishing.com
For customer service and orders:
Toll-Free 1-888-313-2665

Visit us on the Internet at www.arcadiapublishing.com

To Tamara, and to Katelyn, Zachary, and Riley: May you grow to appreciate the reminders of those who came before you.

Images and stories of select people, places, and companies that once were part of the heart of Indianapolis, but are now only shadows of the past.

Contents

ACKNOWLEDGMENTS

The author gratefully acknowledges the help of many individuals and resources, including:

Travis S. Little
Claude Baker
Paul Browning
Samantha Gleisten
Jack Hartigan
Indiana Historical Society
Indiana State Library
Sheila Kavanaugh
Pat and Betty McDonald
Rick Patton
Susan Sutton
Frank Thomas, Jr.
Robert Wildman

These stories are drawn from information in the *Indianapolis Star* and *Indianapolis News*, from *Encyclopedia of Indianapolis*, from eyewitness accounts, and from the Internet.

Introduction

"Suwarrow" might have been the name for Indianapolis.

Exactly how a Polynesian atoll might have lent its name to the 12th largest city in the United States is a small part of the rich history of Indianapolis—a history that leaves behind many faded reminders for us to ponder today.

Back in 1816, the U.S. Congress decided to give the newly formed State of Indiana four square miles of land to lay out a capital city. At the time, the capital was in Corydon, having moved there in 1813 from Vincennes, which was the capital since the state's beginnings in 1801. The first Territorial Governor was William Henry Harrison, who would later become the ninth President of the United States.

Coincidentally, Vincennes had also been the first "capital" of an Indian nation lead by the great Shawnee chief, Tecumseh, who later moved his base to a camp along the Tippecanoe River north of present-day Lafayette. Harrison's troops defeated Tecumseh's men in the Battle of Tippecanoe in 1811—which in turn became the source of Harrison and John Tyler's campaign slogan: "Tippecanoe and Tyler, Too."

With the land in hand, where would the state's leaders decide to place the new capital city? In 1820, the legislature sent ten commissioners to meet up with early settler William Conner to survey the land near the center of the state. Starting at Conner's home near present-day Fishers, Indiana, they searched along the White River until they came upon the mouth of Fall Creek. By a vote of three to two, the spot was set, though for some reason five of the commissioners did not vote.

The legislature quickly drafted a bill to make it official, but they left a blank line for the name of the new city. The committee in charge debated for days. They considered and rejected many Indian names. One legislator even proposed "Tecumseh," which Harrison surely would have opposed had he been there. As the days wore on, they started to get tired. One committee member suggested "Suwarrow," the name given to a small atoll in the Cook Islands discovered two years earlier by the crew of a Russian ship named the "Suvorov." Maybe he was just reading a newspaper to pass the time and saw the story, but thankfully, the legislature rejected the option.

Intending to break the stalemate, Jeremiah Sullivan proposed "Indianapolis" one evening to another committee member, Samuel Merrill. The next day Sullivan brought up the name in debate and it did not gather much of a response. To everyone's surprise, however, Merrill seconded the motion, causing the lawmakers to sit up and take notice. It became the center of debate, and because the weary lawmakers were at the bottom of the creative barrel, they adopted a word that translated literally means "Indiana City."

The new city got off to a bad start, despite the highest hopes and a planned grid of streets and avenues converging on a glorious circular plaza at its center. During the first summer mosquitoes breeding in the White River spread malaria that killed one-eighth of the population. The city was badly isolated, and even after the capital officially moved there in 1824, there were few takers for the land. It took almost 20 years for the state to sell all of the initial plots.

Looking to connect the state and its capital with the outside world, the legislature considered two alternatives: build a system of canals that would link the city into the growing canal transportation system launched by the success of the Erie Canal, or invest in the new steam engine technology and the railroads that were starting to spread across the East. Seeking to reach a compromise, Governor Noah Noble signed the "Mammoth Improvement Bill" in 1836 to build both railroads and canals—at the same time.

Work began immediately and continued until the bills started to mount. In just three years, Indiana ran up over $14 million in debt—equivalent to $38 billion today. The state declared bankruptcy, and work halted.

Progress could not be stopped however, and by 1855, seven different private railroad lines converged in the city, making Indianapolis one of the key rail hubs for the expanding country. In that decade, the population doubled and retail stores, now connected with supplies of goods from the East, flourished. Indianapolis also became a manufacturing and wholesale center. Giant hotels sprang up, including the opulent Bates House—later sold to Henry Claypool who would build a new grand hotel on the same site. That same decade would also see the city's first University, Northwestern Christian, eventually renamed for its primary benefactor, Ovid Butler.

By the Civil War, the city stood ready to serve as a gear in the machinery of war. Training camps sprouted across the city as volunteers streamed in from the countryside. Food processors and manufacturers along the rail lines met the needs of the soldiers at home and in the field. As industry boomed, so did the population, and soon interurban trolleys were connecting quiet suburban bedroom communities like Woodruff Place to the burgeoning downtown. After the war, Indianapolis saw large central department stores formed from by entrepreneurs like Lyman S. Ayres and William H. Block. By 1910, a quarter million people called Indianapolis home. The Merchants Bank Building "skyscraper" on the southeast corner of Meridian and Washington rose in 1912, and it would remain the city's tallest building for 50 years.

At about this time, the automobile craze hit Indianapolis, and with its manufacturing capacity and easy rail links to sources of materials and parts, it became an early home of the automobile industry. Indiana would eventually produce over 70 different makes of cars, including Indianapolis-based Stutz Motor Company. Several automotive moguls including Carl Fisher, who operated what was one of the first automobile dealership in the world, later went into partnership to build a proving ground for these automobile manufacturers, giving birth to the Indianapolis Motor Speedway and the world-famous 500-Mile Race.

Under the firm control of the powerful mayor, Thomas Taggart, the city undertook several beautification and park projects, including the popular Riverside Park. When World War I broke out, Indianapolis boomed again, as manufacturers competed for war production contracts. At the close of the war, the Legislature elected to build a grand five-block memorial to Indiana's fallen heroes; it is still one of the largest war memorials in the country.

During the roaring twenties, Indianapolis became a center for jazz music, launching the careers of legends like Hoagy Carmichael from the clubs along Indiana Avenue. Anchoring the block was the giant Madame Walker Theater, named for a prominent black female entrepreneur, Madam C.J. Walker. Companies like RCA relocated to the city, but with the stock market crash, Indianapolis sank into the Great Depression, rescued only by increased war production for World War II. By the end of the 1940s, manufacturing production in the city multiplied by almost ten times.

The 1950s brought the freedom of the car culture and suburban sprawl. Developers built shopping malls like Glendale Center, and drive-ins like the Tee Pee drew their teenage customers. Some, like Burger Chef, would grow to become national chains based in Indianapolis. By the 1960s, like so many other urban centers, this sprawl had caused the inner core of the city to start to fade. The city gained the reputation of being a boring place, and got an unwanted moniker to match—"naptown."

City leaders decided that it was time for a change, and decided to hitch their future to sports. Business leaders launched a franchise of the fledgling ABA, the Indiana Pacers, and built them a new stadium, Market Square Arena, in a public-private partnership that would become the pattern for future projects. By the 1980s, the city had a domed stadium, the Hoosier Dome (now RCA Dome), and would lure the Baltimore Colts to the new facility. The city hosted the 1980 NCAA Final Four, one of the first large national sporting events held in the city outside of the Indianapolis 500. In 1987, the city hosted the 10th Pan American Games, an Olympic-style event that required organizers to construct numerous sports venues around the city.

The Final Four would be held in Indianapolis again in 1991, 1997, and 2000, at which time the NCAA announced that it would move its headquarters to the new White River State Park on the west side of downtown. They would join a new ballpark, Victory Field, which replaced the venerable Bush Stadium, a new Indianapolis Zoo, which replaced the old one originally in Riverside Park, and a host of new museums, hotels, and restaurants clustered around the expanded Indiana Convention Center and RCA Dome.

Truly, the city has accomplished much in its short history, but as time marches on, reminders of our past are fading away. Companies, buildings, parks, and places that were once centers of city life stand crumbling or as shadows of their former glory. Some are gone forever, swept into fading photographs in dusty closets. This book attempts to tell the story of some of these markers of our past, reminding us of what we once were—and what is now "Lost Indianapolis."

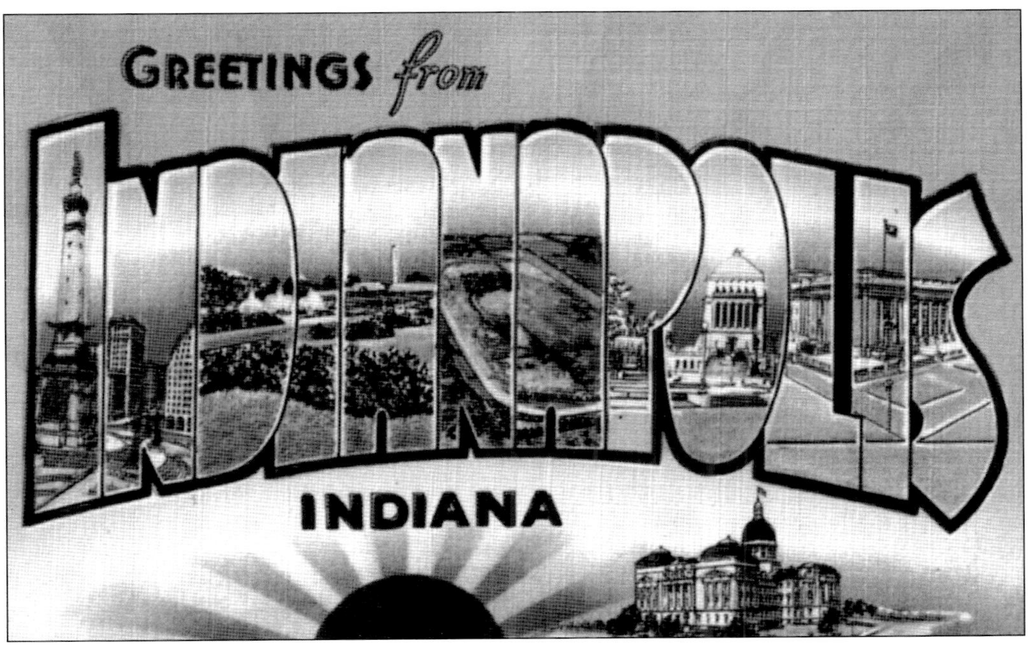

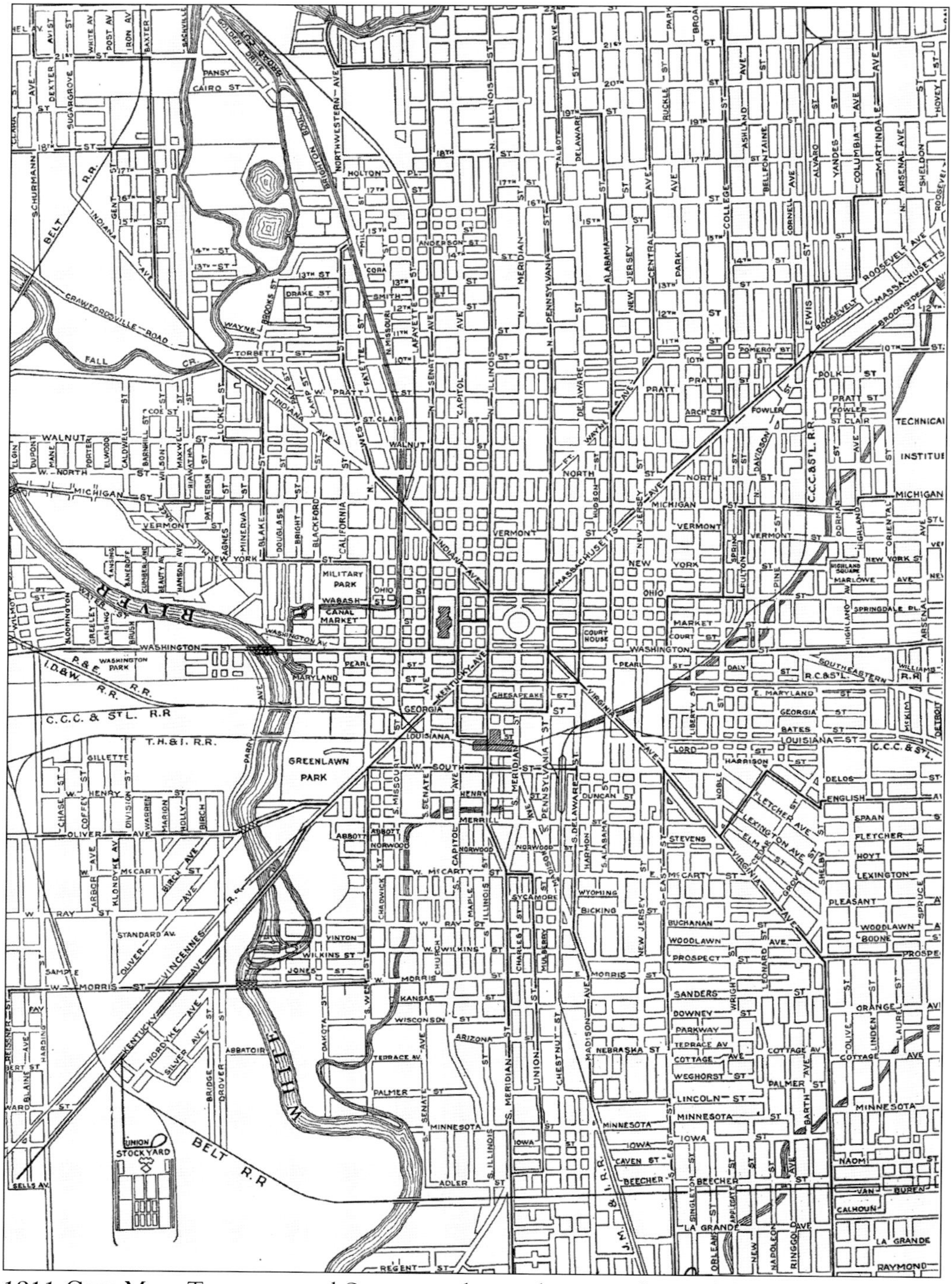

1911 City Map. Twenty-second Street was the northernmost limit of the city near the turn of the century.

One

The Central Canal

Governor Noah Noble is remembered for two things: the fact that residents named Noblesville for him, and that on January 27, 1836, he signed a law that would issue bonds to build a transportation infrastructure for the new State of Indiana. Unfortunately, only one of these two things would work out well: Noblesville lives on, but by 1839, the state would go bankrupt under the crushing debt generated by the transportation program.

In Noah's day, politicians put much thought into ways to connect landlocked towns and cities to the rest of America. There were two competing technologies: railroads, which were still new and unorganized, and canals, which would create shipping lanes linked to major rivers and waterways. In 1825, the Erie Canal was completed, and its success caused many states to jump onto the canal bandwagon and plan ambitious projects of their own. The process for choosing the path of a railroad or a canal was often highly political, with legislators looking to "bring home" something for their constituents.

The Indiana project was no different, except that rather than attempt to choose between the two technologies, they decided to pursue both. Ignoring economic realities, the bond issue authorized by the governor on that day was set up to fund all projects simultaneously. Anxious to get started, politicians returned home to begin building "their part" of the system—and many small projects along the paths began all at once.

The Central Canal was to be a major part of Indiana's new canal system, linking the "Wabash and Erie Canal" to the "Cross-Cut Canal," creating a pathway across the state that would link the Ohio River to Lake Erie and beyond. Work began on several sections at once, with the primary digging occurring in the middle portion of the Central Canal, or the "Indianapolis division," among other reasons to show lawmakers that progress was occurring on their plan.

The dig, which was about 24 miles in length, began at Broad Ripple and ended at "Port Royal," a lost town near Waverly, Indiana. By early 1839, the first section from Broad Ripple south to a creek called Pleasant Run opened, with water tapped from the White River northeast of Broad Ripple. Almost immediately, businesses sprang up along its banks, using the flowing water as power for milling and machinery. A small amount of transportation traffic started, mostly moving goods up and down the path from business to business, as well as some recreational traffic.

Soon, though, financial disaster struck and work stopped. Other parts of the Central Canal crawled north from Evansville, eventually becoming part of the reworked Wabash and Erie Canal. Most other sections were filled in. By 1850, the legislature ordered the completed and watered portion through Marion County sold, as it was losing money in its operation. After passing through a series of private owners, it was finally handed over to the Indianapolis Water Company who used it to power turbines that pumped water to its customers. Throughout the century, residents strolled along parts of the canal north of downtown, while the section of canal in the city would at times become an open sewer.

By the 1960s, construction of the downtown interstate system forced some of the flowing water underground where it emerged on the west side of downtown to flow for some distance towards the White River. In the mid-1970s, the Indianapolis Water Company turned over the section south of Sixteenth Street to the city for a revitalization project that saw the canal re-dredged and lined with concrete. This new canal project marked one of the first major downtown beautification projects, which in turn stimulated growth of new residential and retail buildings along its path. The redeveloped downtown canal now winds its way through part of the White River State Park, with memorials and museums lining its banks.

The northern portion near Broad Ripple remains much as it was when it was first dug, complete with towpaths along its edge. The source of the canal is still on the east side of Westfield Boulevard north of Broad Ripple Avenue. The canal flows southwest under several bridges behind the rows of shops to emerge on the west side of College Avenue and run along Westfield Boulevard to the southwest. Along with its redeveloped counterpart downtown, these sections of the Central Canal remain easily visible, if unnoticed as residents hurry about their daily lives.

In contrast to the days when the canal was a slow-flowing inconvenience, today it winds through the heart of the revitalized downtown museum, retail, and residential districts. Though the original purpose of the canal never really came to be, one can still walk along its banks and imagine what this small piece of lost Indianapolis was like in the days before rail and roads linked the city to the rest of the world.

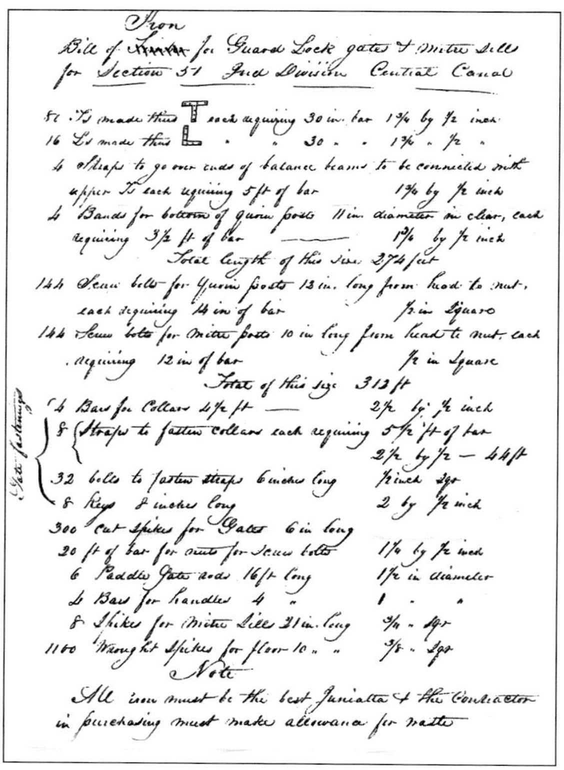

Iron
Bill of ~~Lumber~~ for Guard Lock gates & Mitre Sills
for Section 51 Ind Division Central Canal

80 T's made thus T each requiring 30 in. bar 1 1/2 by 1/2 inch
16 L's made thus L " 30 " 1 1/2 " 1/2 "
4 Straps to go over ends of balance beams to be connected with upper T's each requiring 5 ft of bar 1 1/2 by 1/2 inch
4 Bands for bottom of quoin posts 11 in. diameter in clear, each requiring 3 1/2 ft of bar —— 1 1/2 by 1/2 inch
Total length of this size 274 feet
144 Screw bolts for quoin posts 13 in. long from head to nut, each requiring 14 in of bar 1/2 in Square
144 Screw bolts for mitre posts 10 in long from head to nut each requiring 12 in of bar 1/2 in Square
Total of this size 312 ft
Gate fastenings:
4 Bars for Collars 4 1/2 ft —— 2 1/2 by 1/2 inch
8 Straps to fasten collars each requiring 5 1/2 ft of bar 2 1/2 by 1/2 — 44 ft
32 bolts to fasten straps 6 inches long 1/2 inch sqr
8 Keys 8 inches long 2 by 1/2 inch
300 Cut spikes for Gates 6 in long
20 ft of bar for nuts for screw bolts 1 1/4 by 1/2 inch
6 Paddle gate rods 16 ft long 1 1/2 in diameter
4 Bars for handles 4 " 1 " "
8 Spikes for Mitre Sill 21 in. long 3/4 " sqr
1100 Wrought Spikes for floor 10 " " 3/8 " sqr
Note
All iron must be the best Juniatta & the Contractor in purchasing must make allowance for waste

BILL OF IRON FOR GUARD LOCK GATES AND MITER SILLS FOR SECTION 51 INDIANAPOLIS DIVISION CENTRAL CANAL. This document is essentially an order form for various types of iron connectors, braces, and bars for the construction of lock gates, including "80 T's made thus each requiring 30 in. bar $1\frac{1}{2}$ by $\frac{1}{2}$ inch." along with a drawing of the design for the connector. Sailors use locks to raise or lower a vessel on a canal from one elevation to another. A set of lock gates close in front of and behind a boat, and pumps move water in or out to raise or lower the level to match the next segment of the canal. Attendants open the forward gate and the boat proceeds. (Miami County Historical Society.)

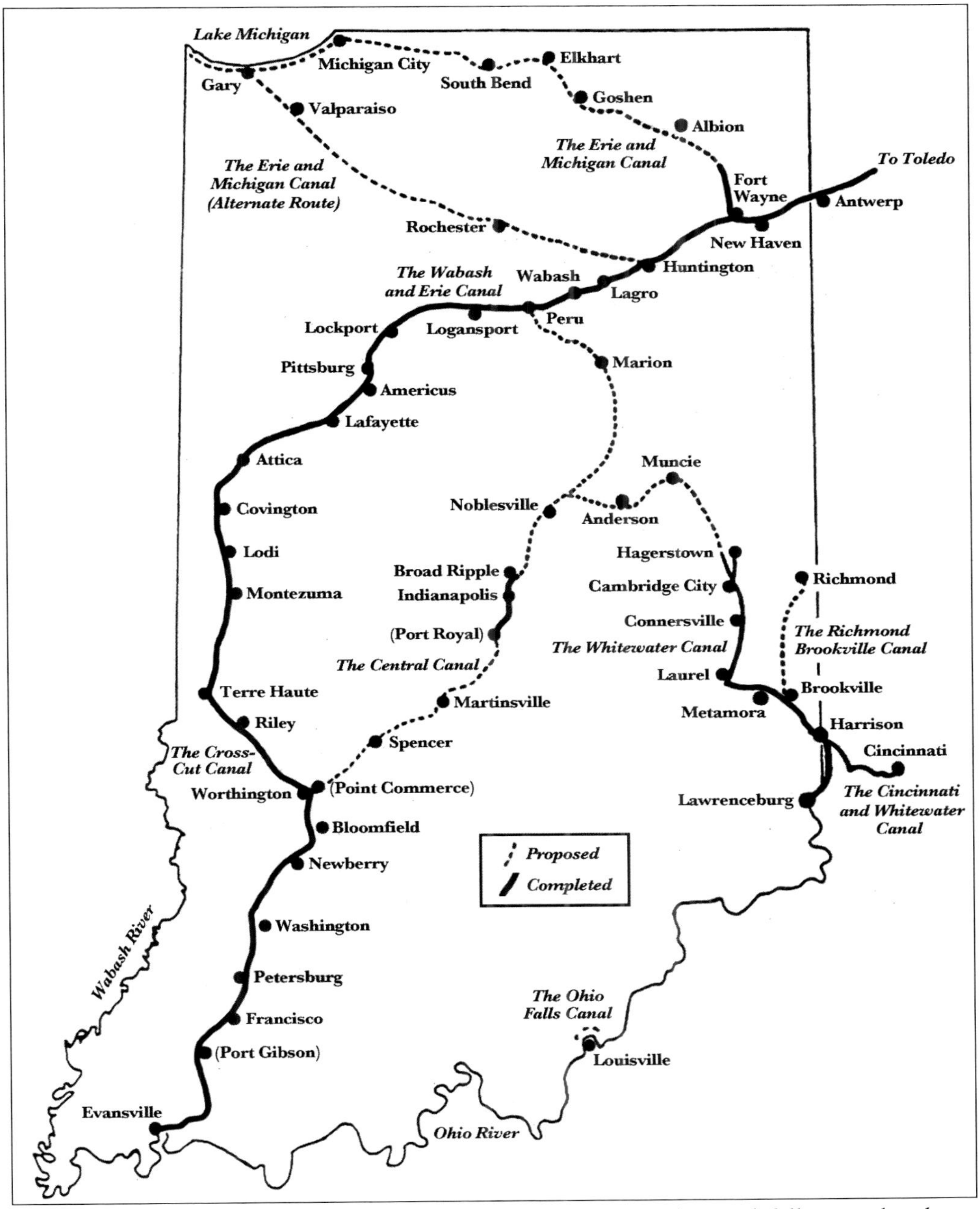

INDIANA'S CANAL SYSTEM. Of the 1,000-mile system, the only canal fully completed was the Wabash and Erie Canal. Originally designed to link the Maumee in Fort Wayne with the Wabash, the owners rerouted it in the late 1840s to pick up abandoned portions of the Central Canal north of Evansville and the Cross-Cut Canal south of Terre Haute. When fully opened in 1853, it was 468-miles long, was the longest canal in the United States, and it linked the Ohio River with Lake Erie and eventually the Atlantic Ocean. Just seven years later, the railroads forced the closure of the route south of Terre Haute, and by 1876, most of the rest of the canal route had been auctioned off.

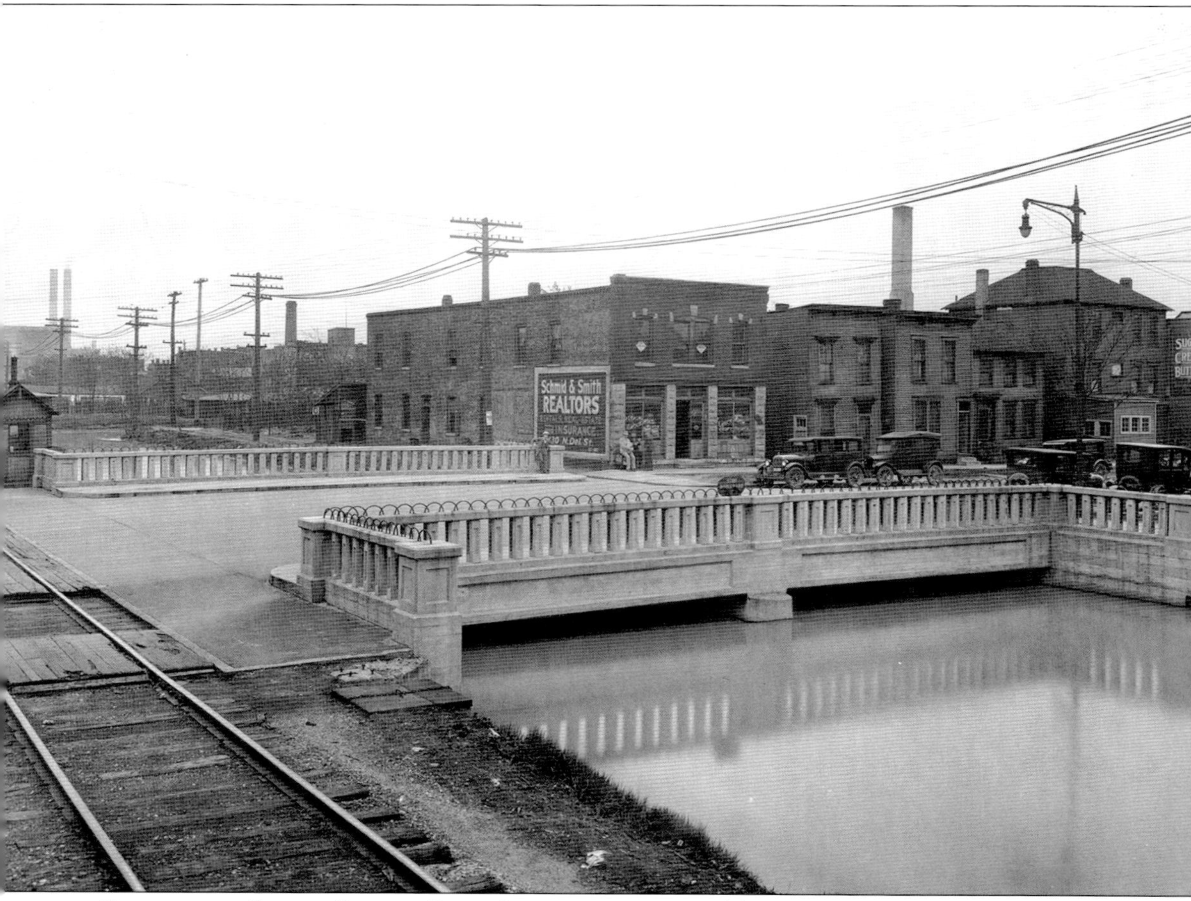

THIRTEENTH STREET BRIDGE OVER CANAL—1927. A rail line occupies the towpath along this section of the Central Canal. (Indiana Historical Society Bass Photo Collection #201885.)

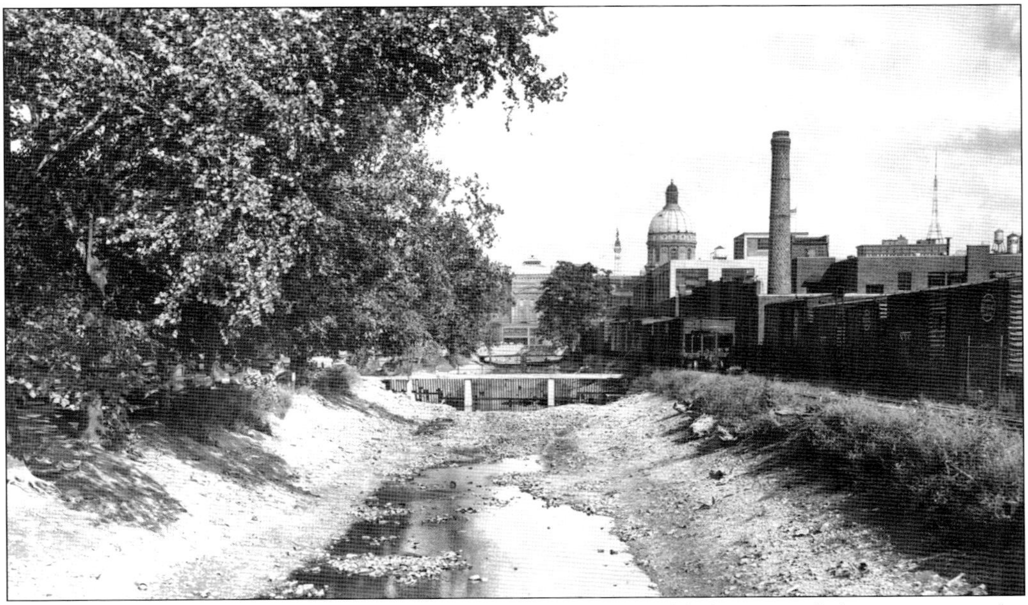

CANAL LOOKING EAST. Though undated, the photographer likely snapped this picture in the early 1950s, as one can see in the distance what is likely WFBM's first broadcast tower atop the Merchants Bank Building. (Indiana Historical Society Bass Photo Collection.)

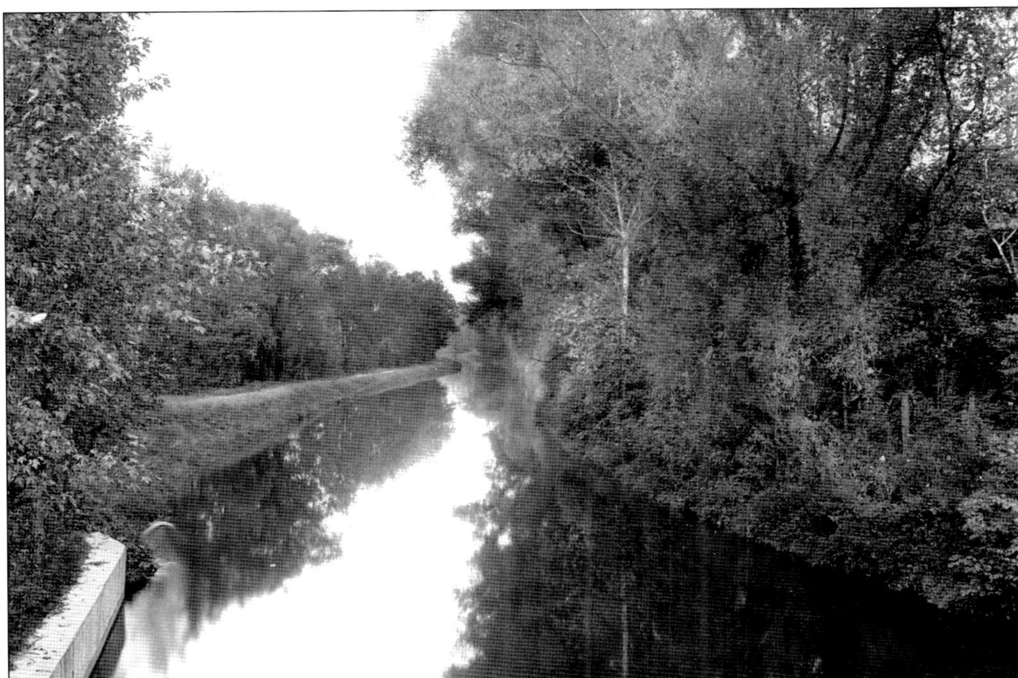

NEAR NORTHWEST AVENUE—1926. This photograph shows what the canal looked like throughout most of its life—a beautiful natural setting along which residents might enjoy a Sunday afternoon. (Indiana Historical Society Bass Photo Collection #99846F.)

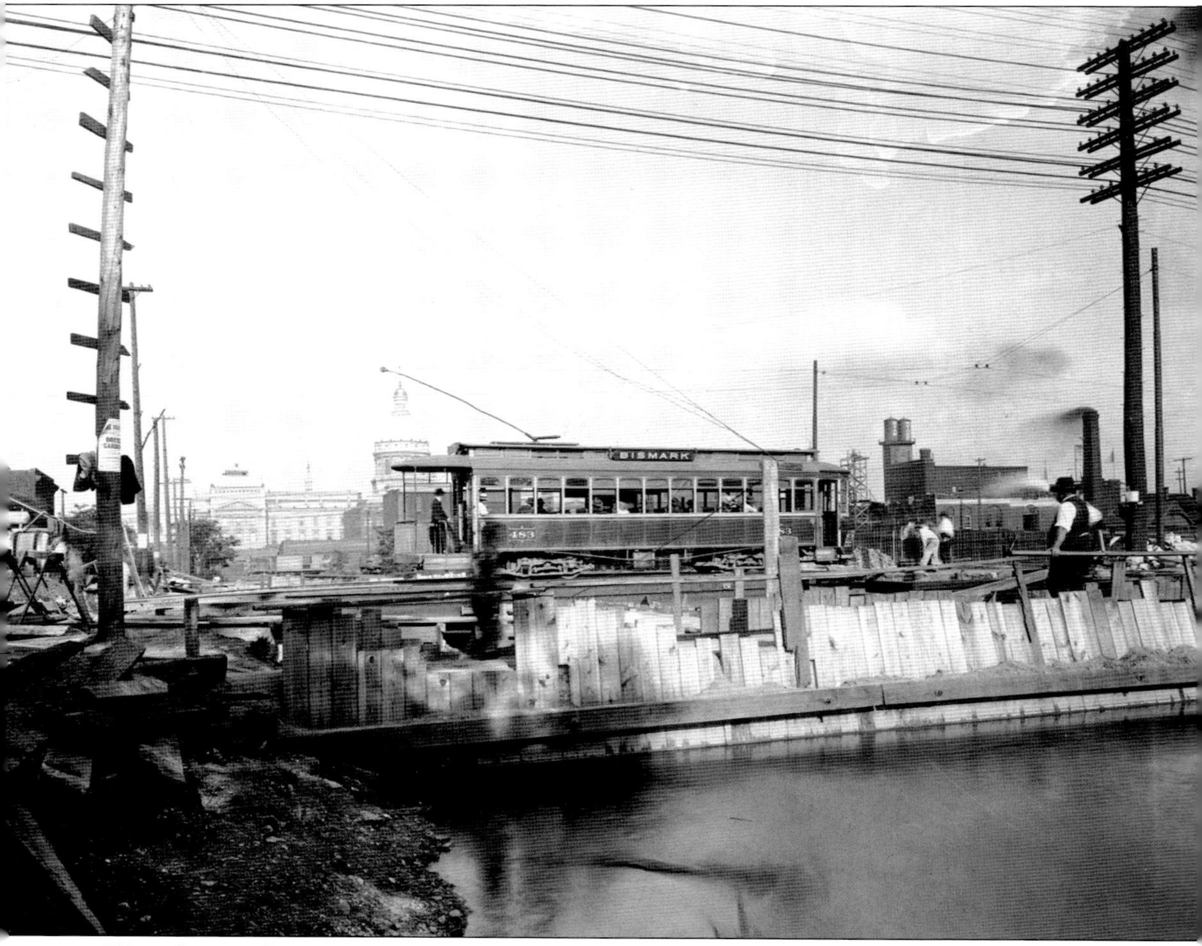

WEST STREET BRIDGE OVER CANAL UNDER CONSTRUCTION—1917. At the advent of decent roads and delivery trucks, the local transportation value of the canal declined, and bridge builders began to span the canal without the need to provide for river-based traffic. Here a streetcar crosses over a new low bridge, still under construction Looking east, the State Capital is visible in the background. (Indiana Historical Society Bass Photo Collection #61054.)

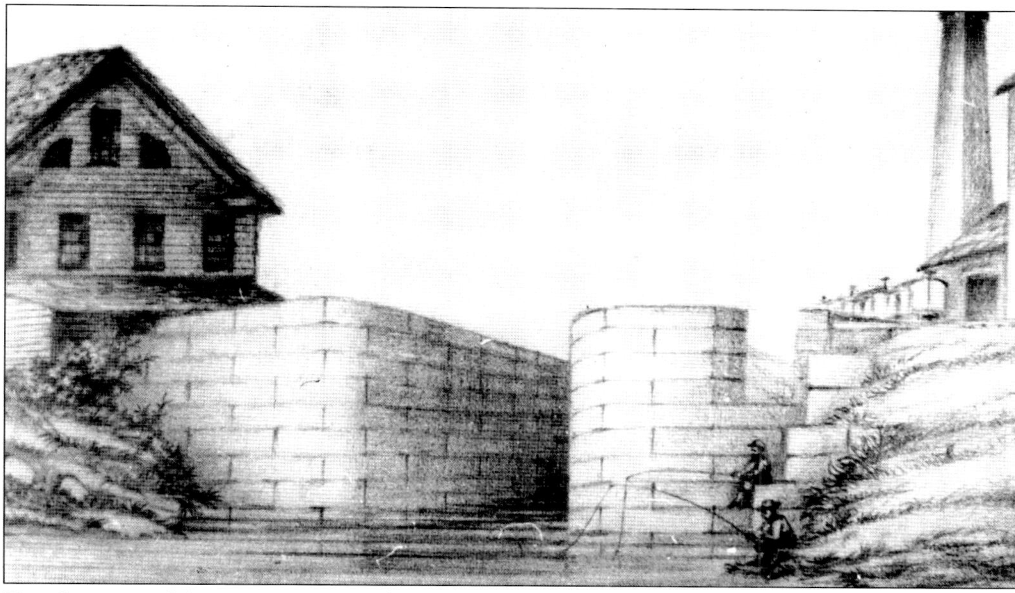

THE LOCK AT MARKET STREET. This is an etching of a stone lock that changed the Central Canal's water level as it passed south of Market Street on the west side of Indianapolis. Parts of this lock were uncovered when workers excavated the Indiana Government Center foundation in the early 1990s. (Courtesy Indiana Historical Society Bass Photo Collection #148694.)

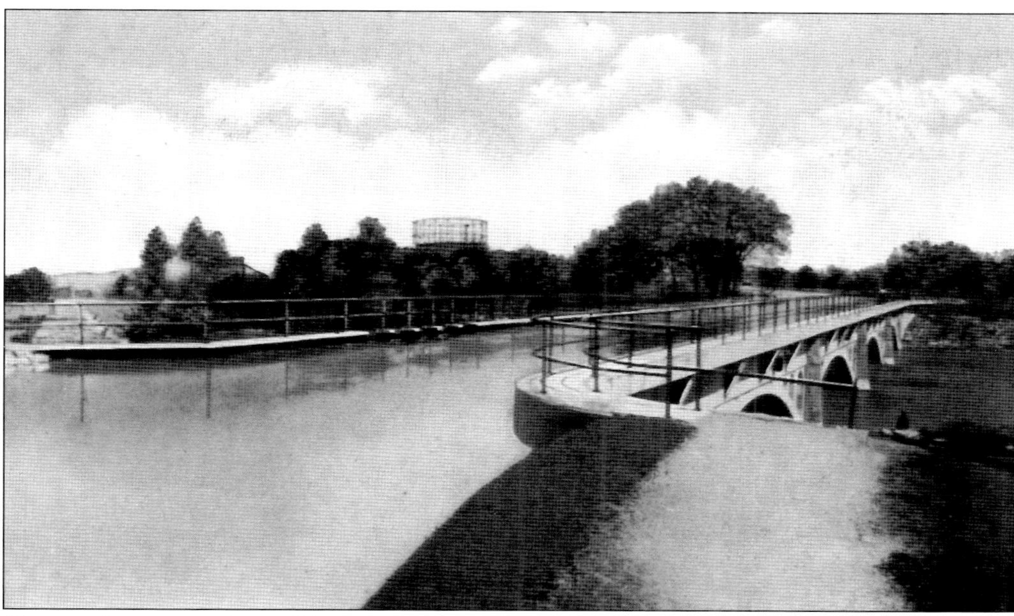

CANAL CROSSING OVER WHITE RIVER. Figuring out how to allow the canal to cross the White River as it turned south presented an interesting problem. As this postcard image shows, engineers constructed an aqueduct over the river itself, maintaining the separation of the waters until they rejoined immediately southwest of downtown.

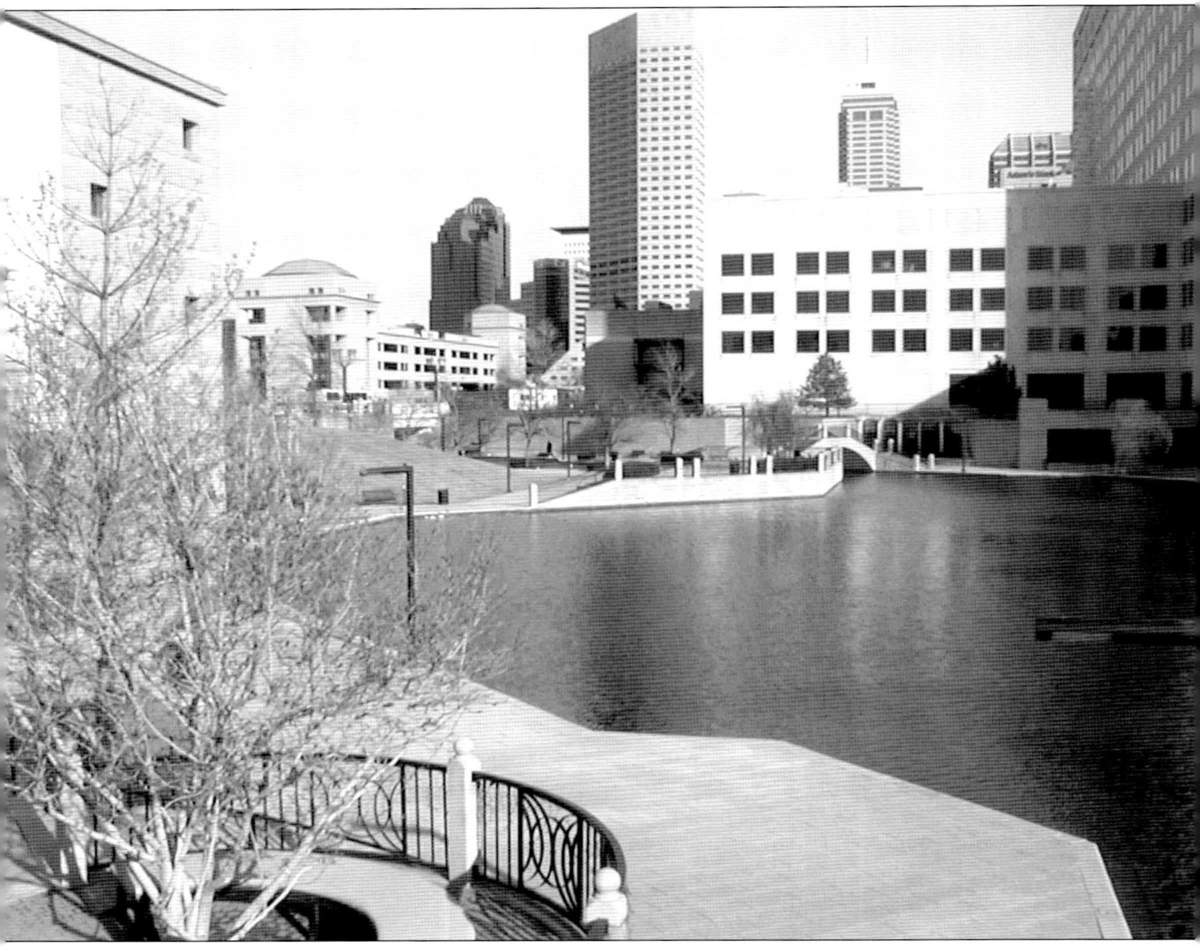

CENTRAL CANAL IMPROVEMENT PROJECT—1987. The City of Indianapolis completed a project to turn a segment of the downtown portion of the old Central Canal into a pedestrian park in 1987. The plan adjusted the path slightly and added bridges, fountains, and extensive landscaping. The city recently extended and expanded the project, including some additional work inside of White River State Park. The visitor's center for the park is inside the old Pump House. Part of the first public water system in Indianapolis, the canal's current powered turbines pumped water to customers in the city.

Two

Union Station

Long before interstate highways converged in Indianapolis, the town was known as the "Crossroads of America" for another reason: the 200 trains a day that came through the city during the height of the railroads.

The very first train into Indianapolis arrived on October 1, 1847. At the time there were many tiny railroad companies throughout the Midwest and East, most existing to serve a single route or two, and all responsible for laying and maintaining their own track. As the railroad companies near Indiana began building lines toward the city, the routing of track to all the various stations for each line became a clear problem.

In 1849, organizers formed the Union Railway Company to lay down a common set of tracks into the city that all competing lines could share. They opened the first station on September 28, 1853, with five tracks and a small brick building. Thus this "Union Station," constructed before the Civil War, got its name from the "union point" of several competing railroad lines, not the Union Army as many believe. This was one of the first such union stations to be built in the country. Passengers transferring between train lines in other cities often rode or walked over to the stations for those competing lines—something that they did not have to endure in Indianapolis, making it a popular transfer point and the rough equivalent to a "hub" in today's airline system.

In 1883, the 15th railroad asked for permission to route trains through the station, which finally proved the original station to be too small. Designed by Thomas Rodd of Pittsburgh, workers laid the cornerstone of a grand, new station in 1886. It would open for business on Monday, September 17, 1888. The station is in the Romanesque Revival style, and is without a doubt one of the city's signature structures. From about 1840 to 1900, this architectural style was popular, especially in churches; indeed, the Grand Hall, with its 1912 stained glass window and the tall clock tower, makes the station seem almost church-like. Other additions also made in 1912 included canopies over the doors.

As an aside, a young Thomas Taggart ran the restaurant in the new depot. Thomas would go on to become Mayor of Indianapolis, building Riverside Park, among other developments, and later serve as chairman of the Democratic Party, a Senator from Indiana, and a developer of the grand French Lick Springs Hotel.

One major drawback of the original station was that the tracks leading in and out were at ground level, which meant trains would block the streets around the station at many hours of the day. In 1915, a project began to elevate most of these tracks, an effort substantially delayed by World War I. It was not until 1920 that the grand concourses connecting the new elevated tracks and shed to the head house were complete.

The station would remain in much the same state from the 1920s until the decline in train travel began in the 1950s. Traffic sagged during the Great Depression, but picked up with wartime travel in the 1940s. However, by 1960, many railroads were abandoning track or going bankrupt, and by the early 1970s, only a couple passenger trains a day came through a station that once saw more than 200 per day at its peak. In October of 1979, the Amtrak National Limited made its final stop in Indianapolis, ending 132 years of passenger service to the city.

Preservation efforts began in 1971, when Mayor Richard Lugar announced that the city would purchase the head house and hold it until a private organization could developed a reuse for it. In 1974, successful effort had the building listed on the National Register of Historic Places. Ironworkers reinforced key parts of the structure, and custodians performed a minimum amount of maintenance. The city explored alternative uses for the building.

Following a successful project in St. Louis in which they converted their train station into a shopping mall, efforts began in the early 1980s to renovate the building and convert it into a "festival marketplace" that would also serve as a tourist attraction. Over $30 million was spent renovating the building, carving out space for stores in the passenger concourses, restaurants in the Grand Hall, and converting the train shed into a giant food court and a unique Holiday Inn Crown Plaza hotel with some guest rooms outfitted in converted train cars. Opened in 1986 with much fanfare, it quickly became one of the top tourist destinations in the city.

By the early 1990s, though, the novelty of the marketplace began to wear off, and local residents, key to its continued success, began to stay away. The marketplace was on life support. The final blow came with the opening of the long awaited Circle Center mall, and most of the the station closed.

The station has recently benefited from yet another rebirth. The Holiday Inn remained open, thanks to its proximity to the expanding Indiana Convention Center. The hotel has turned the Great Hall into a premier banquet facility, perhaps the most unique in the city. A private firm has converted the train shed into a go-cart track, hoping to capitalize on local and visiting racing fans. Today several Amtrak trains between Chicago and Jeffersonville, Indiana, arrive on tracks nine and ten in the station.

Perhaps these new efforts to revive the station will last, but the glory days of passenger train travel are lost. While most of the cargo train lines into the city remain in use today, efforts to build new high-speed trains between Indianapolis and Chicago are moving slowly. One day these new trains may breathe new life into Union Station.

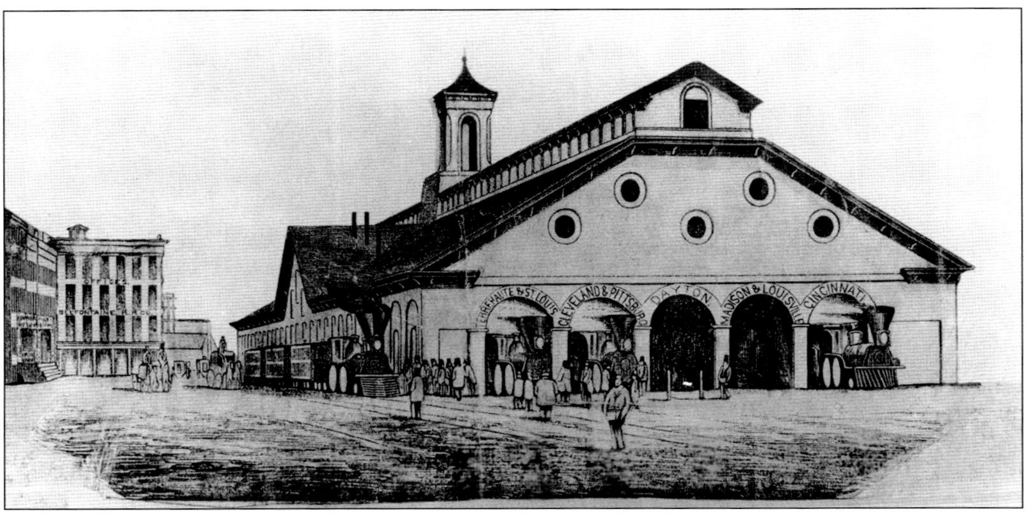

UNION STATION C. 1853. This drawing shows what the original station, constructed from 1852 to 1853, looked like. The city would outgrow the station by the early 1880s. (Indiana Historical Society Bass Photo Collection #5881.)

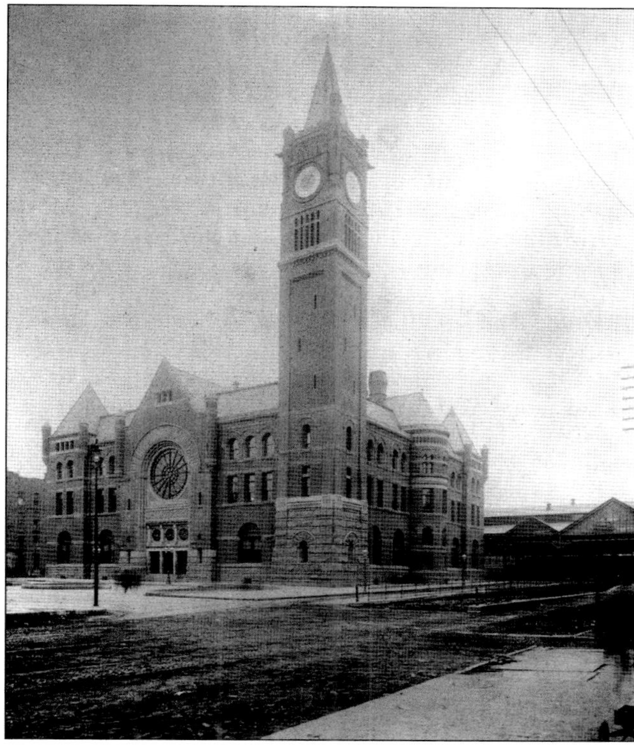

The New Union Station c. 1888. This is a very early photograph of the newly completed Union Station head house. Note that Illinois Street is still unpaved, and the train shed is at ground level, meaning incoming trains might completely block streets while stopped at the station. A narrow tunnel under the tracks allowed mule-drawn trolleys to pass. Rain made this passage slick and dangerous. (Indiana Historical Society Bass Photo Collection.)

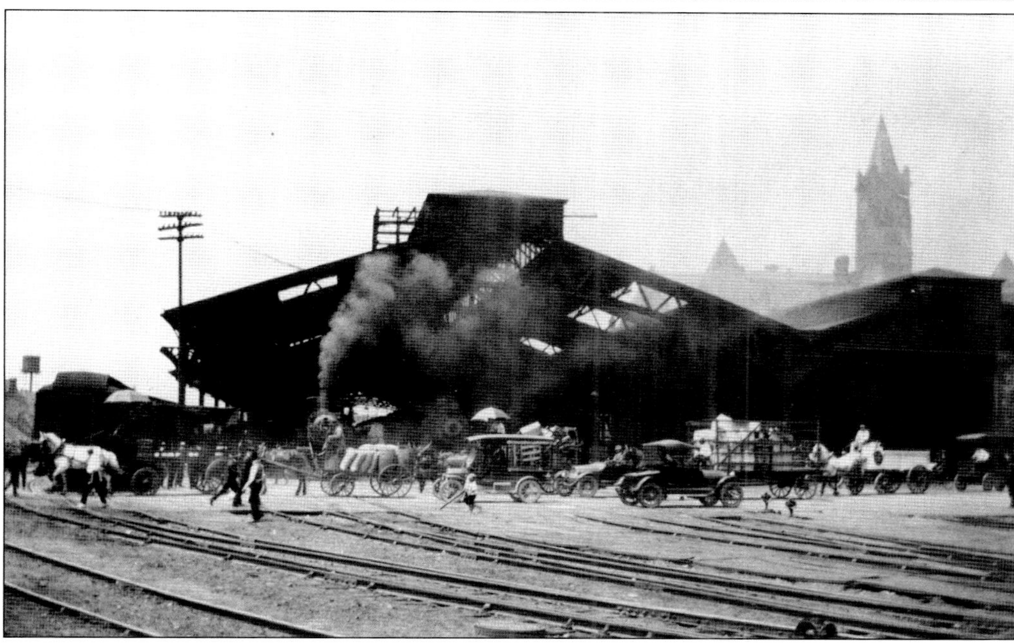

Loading Freight. Horse drawn carts bring freight to be loaded on trains around the turn of the century. The old train shed, located at ground level, looms above. Passengers and couriers often had to cross many tracks to get to their trains—a substantial safety hazard as trains could move in with little warning. (Indiana Historical Society Bass Photo Collection.)

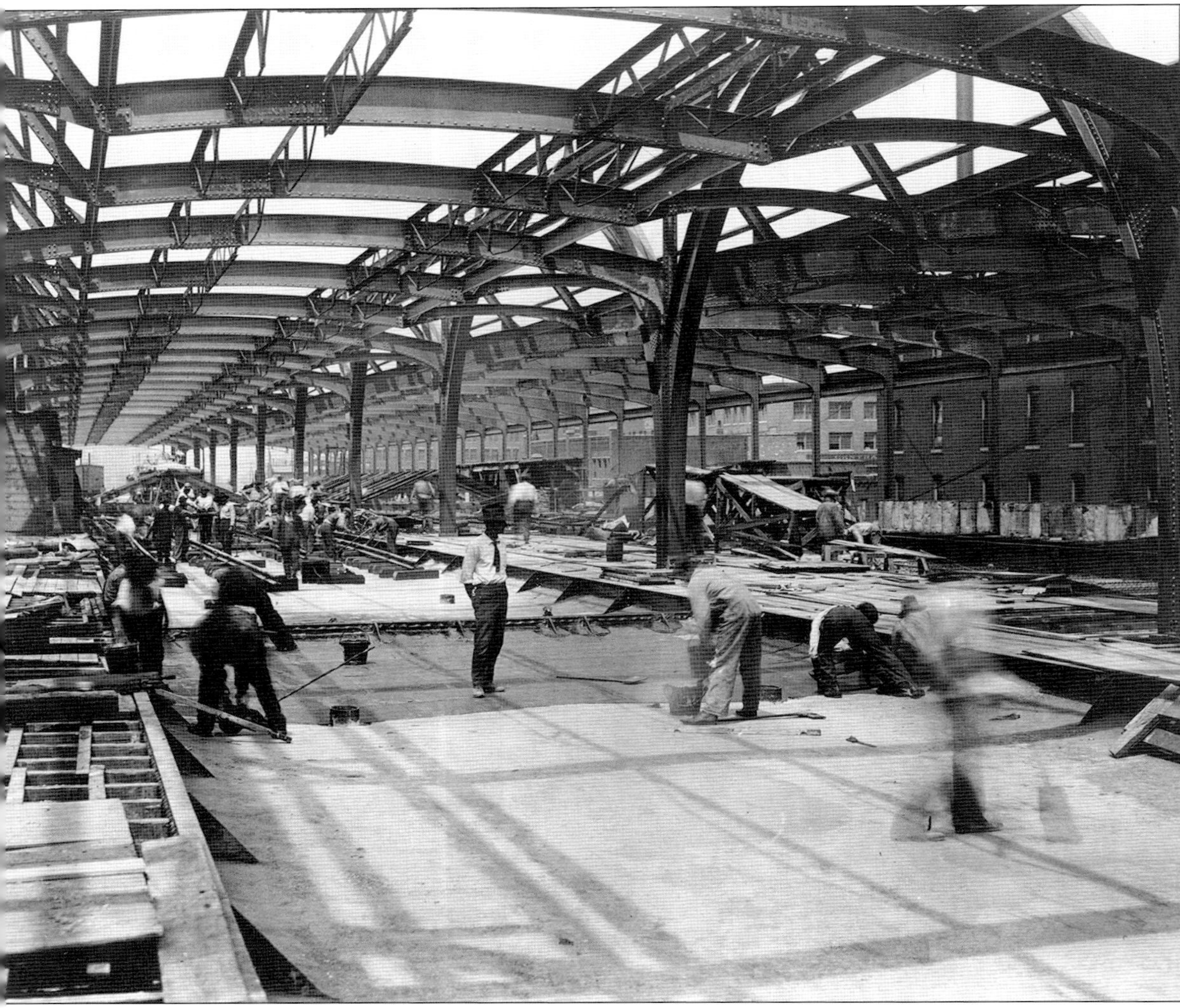

ELEVATED TRAIN SHED UNDER CONSTRUCTION. Taken around 1919, this photo shows rail workers laying the track beds in the new elevated train shed. (Indiana Historical Society Bass Photo Collection #60626.)

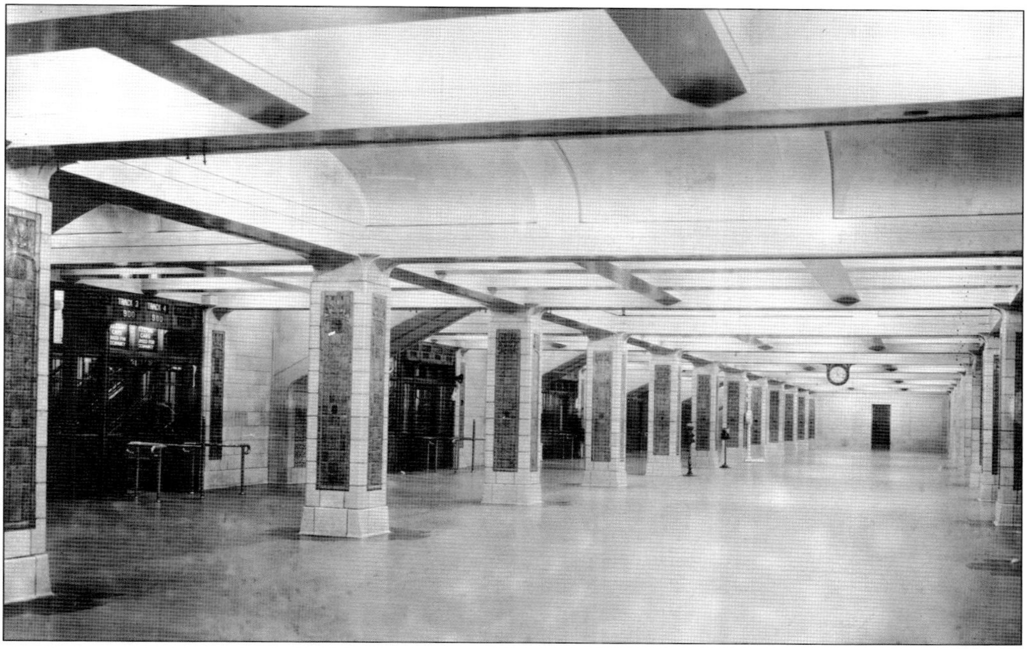

Passenger Gate Concourse—1920. This ground-level concourse allowed passengers to walk under the tracks, through doorways marked with their train numbers, and up staircases to emerge on the correct platform in the covered shed. This substantially improved passenger comfort and safety. (Indiana Historical Society Bass Photo Collection #330101.)

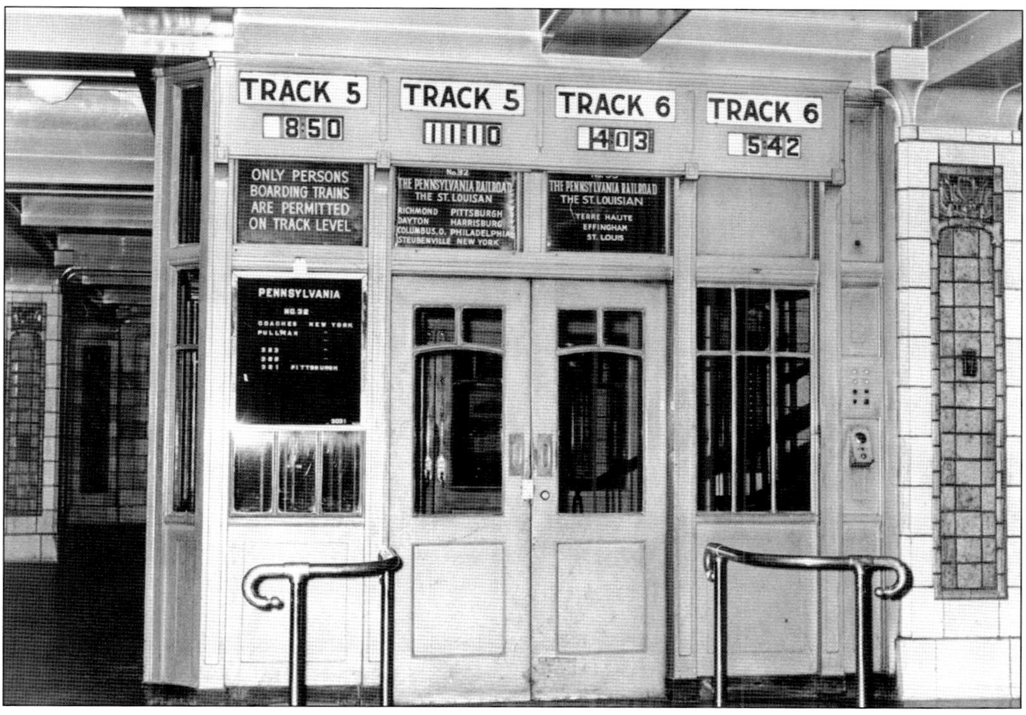

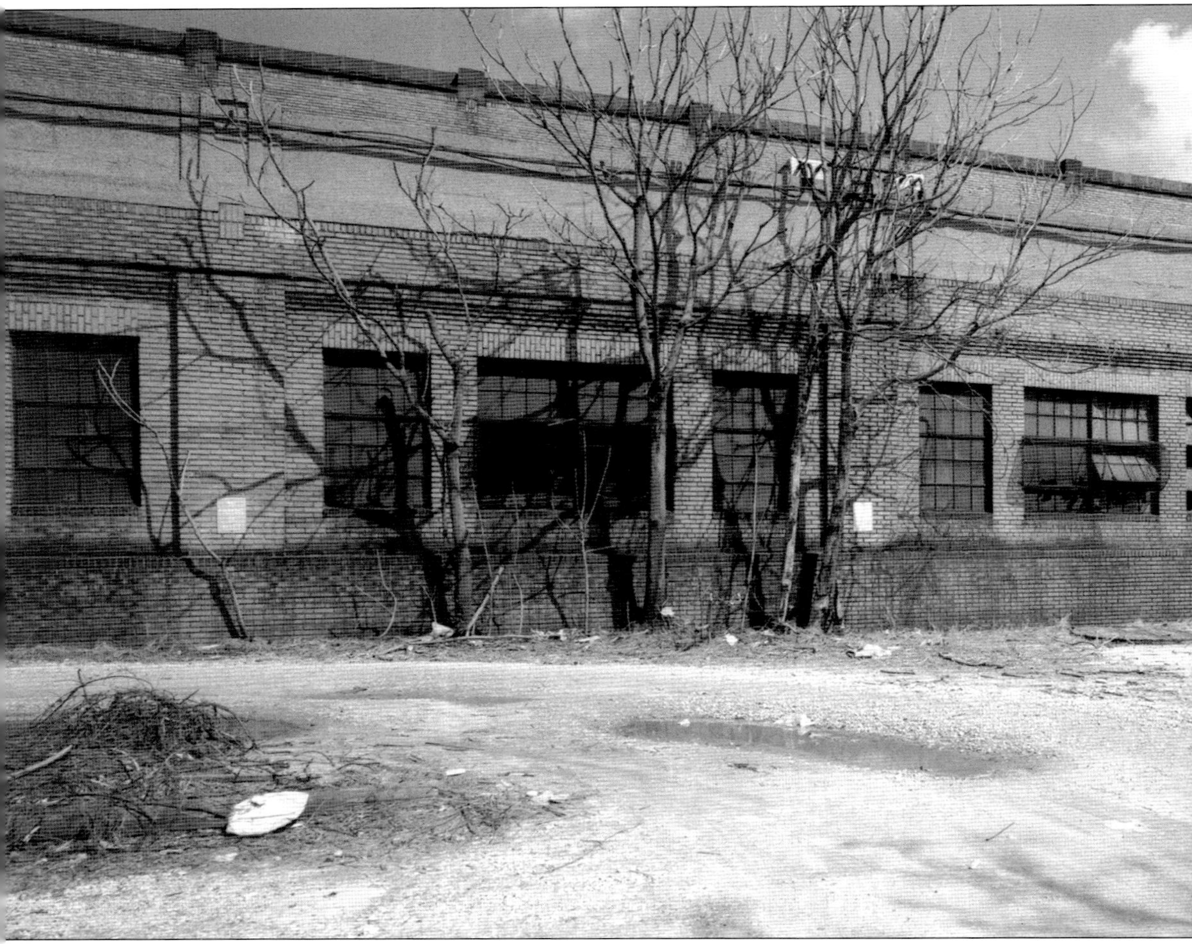

Declining Train Travel. By the 1960s, parts of the station, including the train shed, were in serious disrepair. (Indiana Historical Society Bass Photo Collection.)

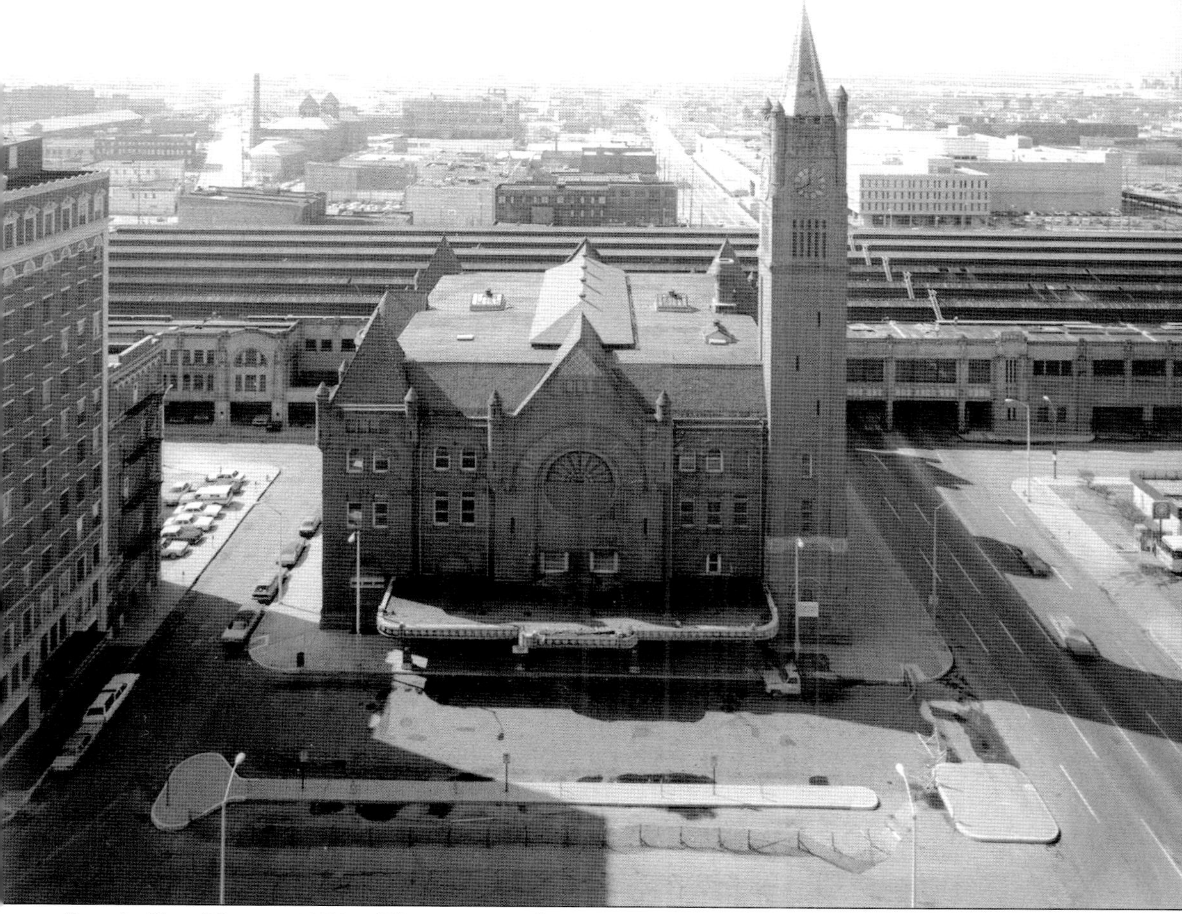

BIRD'S EYE VIEW—1970S. This picture, from a sunny morning the 1970s, shows a nearly abandoned facility. Fifty years earlier the building was bustling with activity at that hour. The long buildings at the rear of the head house are the elevated train sheds. (Indiana Historical Society Bass Photo Collection.)

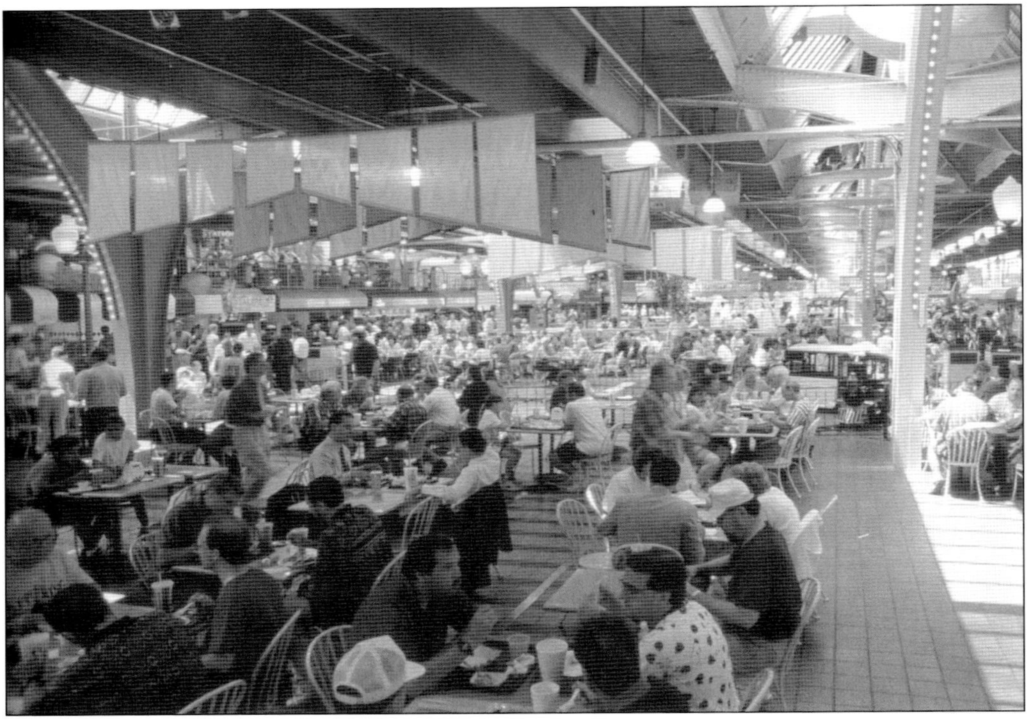

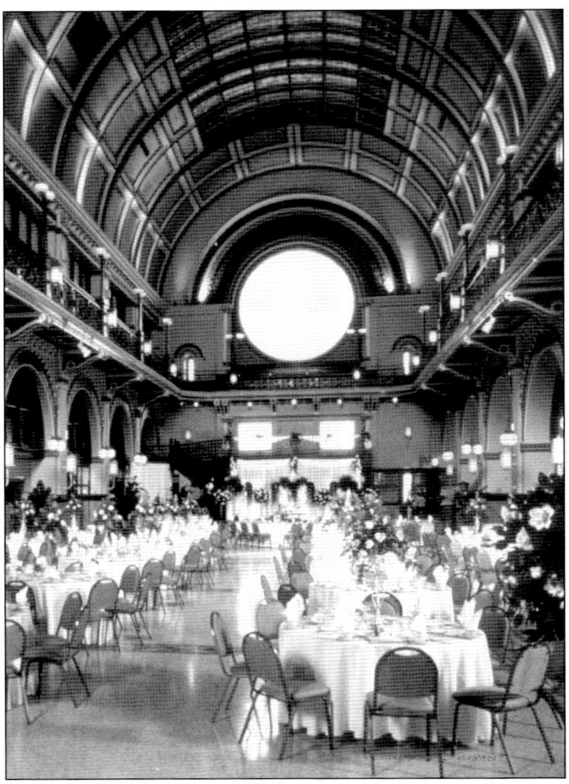

Festival Marketplace—1986. For over a decade, the station welcomed visitors as a tourist attraction and shopping mall. Although the concept failed, substantial renovation probably saved it for the future. (Brad W. Crooks/Hillstrom Stock.)

The Great Hall—2002. Now used as a banquet facility, the Grand Hall is as impressive today as it was when it served as the welcome center for generations of Indianapolis train travelers.

Three

Woodruff Place

Though neighbors often construct fences or plant thick hedges to gain a measure of privacy, rarely do they go as far as the residents of one early Indianapolis neighborhood did. Trying to separate themselves from the growing city that was spreading around them, for a time they actually constructed a concrete wall and dry moat around their community, a structure they referred to as the "spite wall."

James O. Woodruff came to Indianapolis in 1869 to start the Indianapolis Water Company. He was looking for a way to escape the city and invest some of his wealth. In the process, he built what was one of the first suburban subdivisions in the country. Complete with beautiful landscaping and sculpture, Woodruff Place would eventually be home to hundreds of Indy's wealthiest residents. His home would be one of the grandest of them all.

Booth Tarkington lived there for a time and loosely based his Pulitzer Prize-winning masterpiece *The Magnificent Ambersons* around Woodruff Place, represented in the book as the "Amberson Addition." Orson Wells adapted the book into a motion picture of the same name, which the producers mercilessly re-edited in an attempt to make it a popular hit. However, through the film you can still see the social environment that Woodruff Place represented, and the changes brought by the automobile and industrial age.

First platted on June 27, 1872, the original plan had 180 lots and 4 streets: West Drive, Middle Drive, and East Drive, bisected by Cross Drive. Woodruff adorned each street with statuary commissioned by him, and grand fountains at the intersections. Residents quickly petitioned to incorporate into a separate town, which the county granted in 1876. James barely had time to see his vision become a reality, though. He lost his fortune in the Panic of 1873 and sold the grand Woodruff House, a crown of the community. He passed away just six years later, nearly penniless.

By 1890, the growing railroad traffic and industrial boom meant that people of means began to discover the charm of Woodruff Place, and the population grew to 191. Wealthy merchants and business people quickly snapped up the lots that had been slow to fill before 1880. The population peaked in the 1950s, as over 1,500 people called the community home.

As the city of Indianapolis grew, it began to surround the community so that it was not so remote and exclusive anymore. East Tenth Street and East Michigan Street now bordered the property. More wealthy residents began moving to north side neighborhoods. By World War II, many of the residents could no longer afford to make payments on large homes and land that was now aging and becoming difficult to maintain. Investors bought many of the homes and divided them into apartments. By 1970, more than half of the residents were renters, not owners, and had lived in the community for less than two years.

In an attempt to force the residents to become part of the city again, Indianapolis began charging the residents $25,000 each year for police and fire service. In 1962, the town lost a court battle to remain separate, and residents handed the keys to the town hall over to the City of Indianapolis.

Crime increased and the community further deteriorated, so that by the mid-1970s one of the stately homes actually served as the headquarters of the Outlaws Motorcycle Club. By this time, even James Woodruff's original home at 735 West Drive had been razed.

A series of efforts to revitalize the community began on July 31, 1972 with its listing on the National Register of Historic Places. By 1982, the city began to grant funds to improve paving and curbs, largely due to the efforts of the Near East Side Community Organization, founded in 1970, and the East Side Community Investments organization, founded by NESCO in 1976 to address the financial aspects of redevelopment and improvement.

In 2001, the Indianapolis Historic Preservation Commission adopted a plan for the neighborhood that was part of the overall plan for the City of Indianapolis. In it, the commission detailed the challenges facing the community and they recommended continuing and enhancing its preservation.

While the exclusive, cloistered community that Woodruff Place once was will never return, today the Woodruff Place Civic League continues to fight for issues affecting the residents of the community. The charm of these older residences is attracting a new set of buyers who are renovating many of the properties and returning them to single-family homes. A new wave of concerned residents donates time and resources to restore the fountains, statuary, and fences neglected over the years. Slowly, Woodruff Place is bringing itself back from lost Indianapolis.

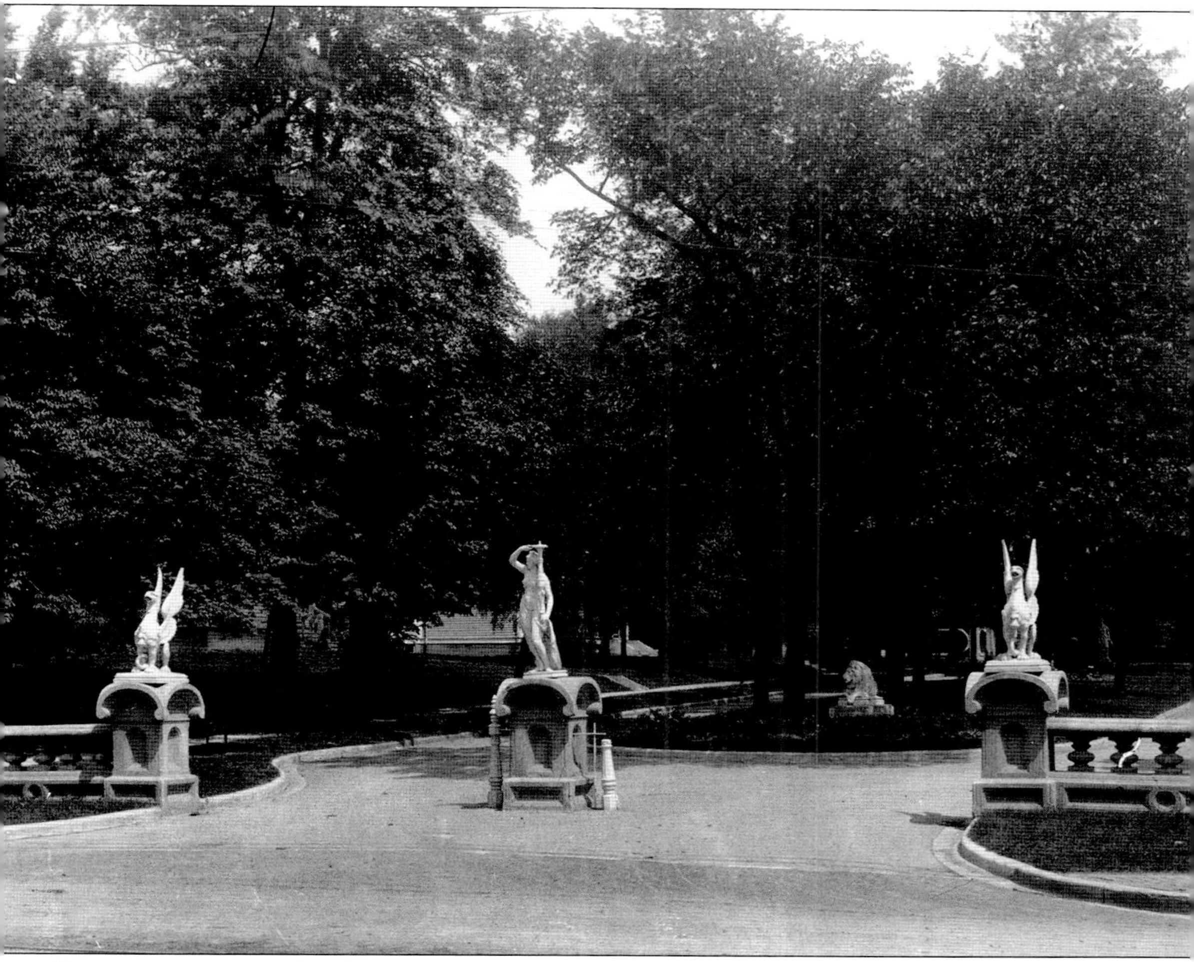

ENTRANCE—1905. This elegant statuary once graced the entrance to the community. Vandals have stolen or damaged many pieces. (Indiana Historical Society Bass Photo Collection #204209-F.)

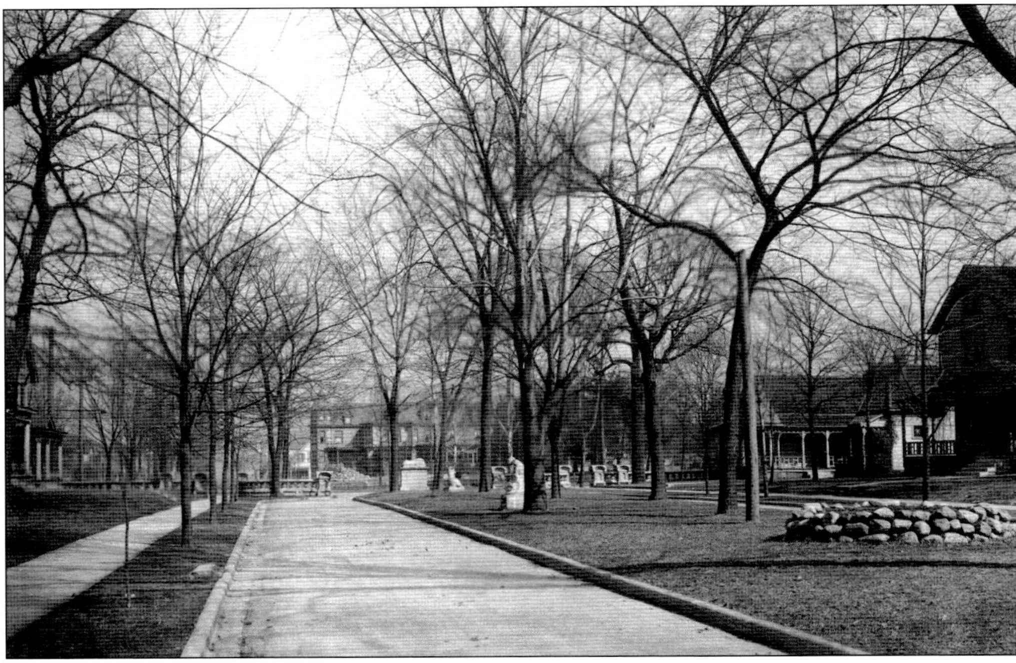

WOODRUFF PLACE MIDDLE DRIVE—1906. Beautiful homes, tree-lined streets, and statuary explain why Woodruff Place was popular with the wealthy during its peak. (Indiana Historical Society Bass Photo Collection #8731)

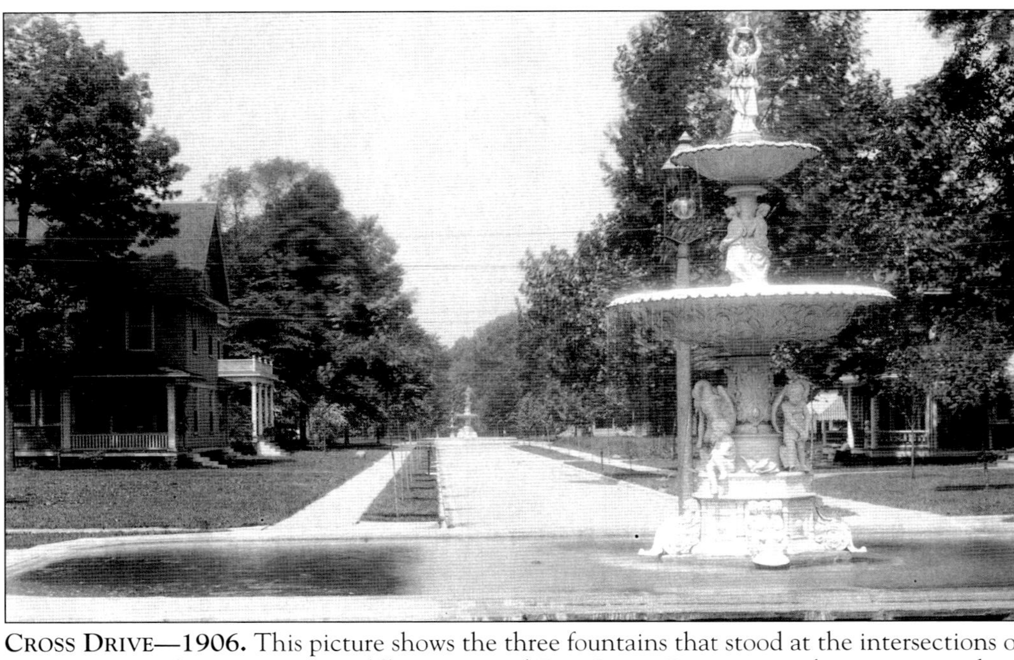

CROSS DRIVE—1906. This picture shows the three fountains that stood at the intersections of Cross Drive and West Drive, Middle Drive, and East Drive. Restoring and maintaining these fountains is now the work of the Woodruff Place Civic League. (Indiana Historical Society Bass Photo Collection Bass #4600)

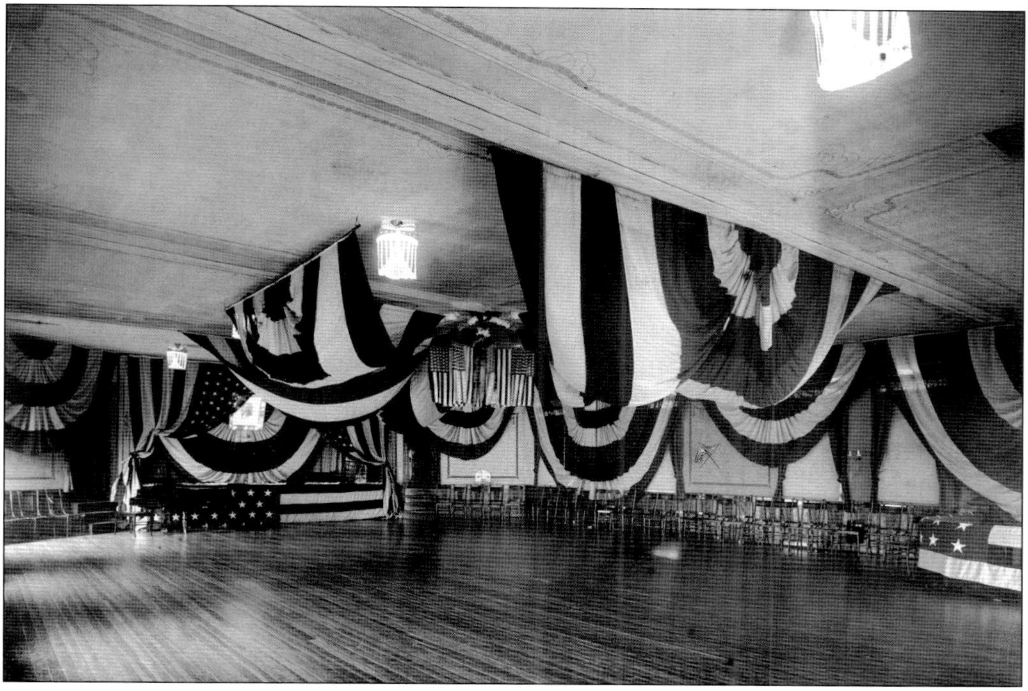

Woodruff Place Club—1910. The club was the center of an active social scene. The lower photo shows the stage set for what might have been a holiday play. (Indiana Historical Society Bass Photo Collection Bass #24489 and #24029.)

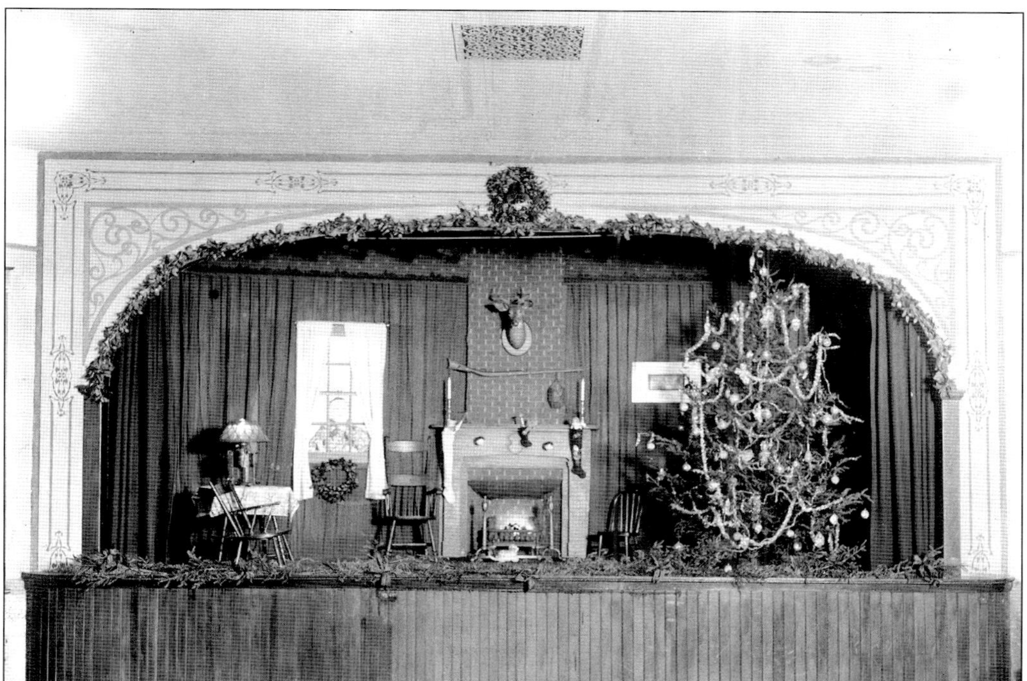

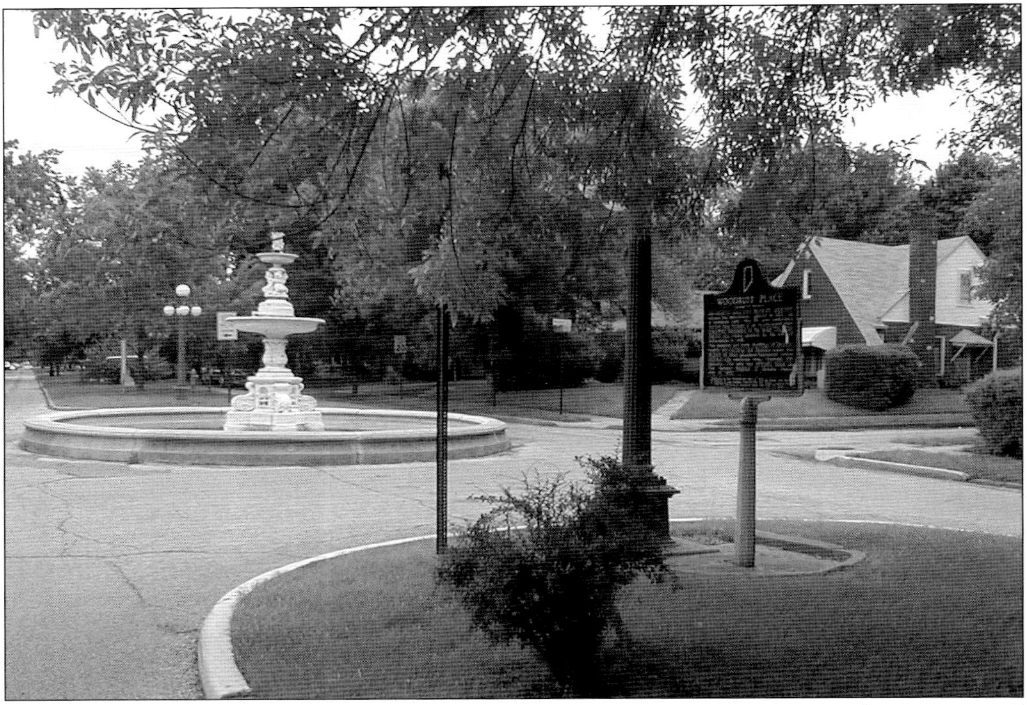

CROSS DRIVE FOUNTAIN—2002. Residents continue to raise money to restore the statuary and fountains that grace the esplanades down the middle of each of Woodruff Place's four streets.

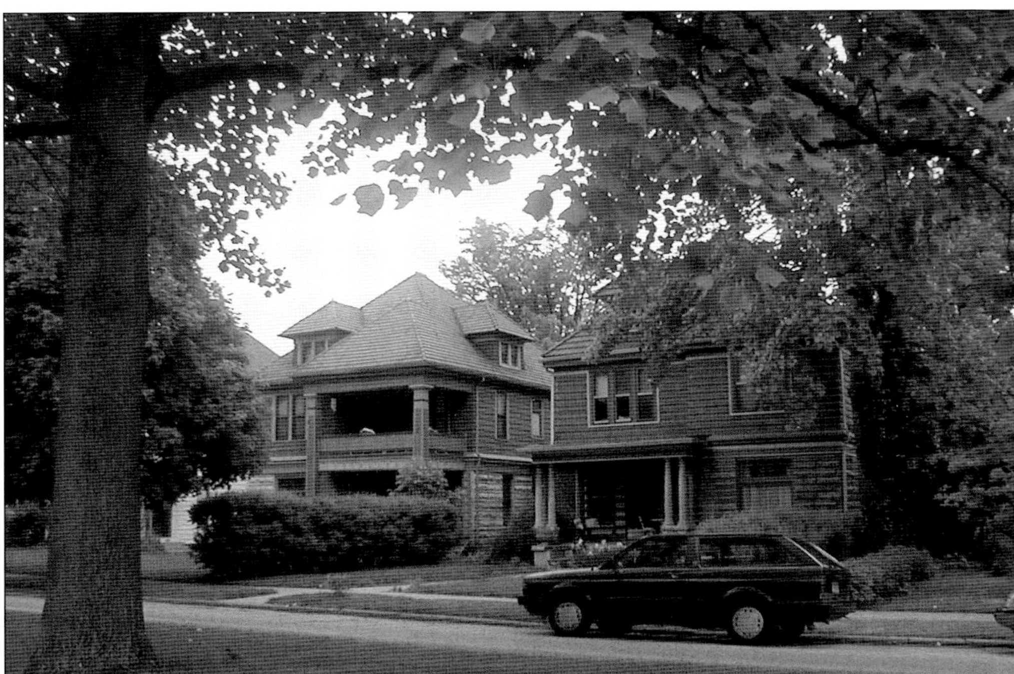

RESTORED HOMES—2002.

Four

INTERURBANS AND STREETCARS

With the exception of walking, there were only a few ways to get around in the days before automobiles. Perfect for long journeys, the steam railroad was the way to travel between major cities. For running around town, the family horse and buggy would do.

However, what if you wanted to travel to a city or town far enough to make the buggy treacherous, but too close for scheduled rail service? What if, for instance, you wanted to travel from downtown Indianapolis to towns like Broad Ripple, or even to outlying "suburban" communities like Woodruff Place? Even if your stops could support a steam train, the timetables were often not frequent enough. In bad weather, you certainly could not rely on the new "horseless carriage" to get you to work or your goods to market.

The answer was the interurban, the forerunner to the modern light rail or subway system. Time was when hundreds of miles of track covered central Indiana and downtown Indianapolis, making it one of the largest systems in the country. Indeed, even the name Interurban, which literally means "between cities," was coined by Indiana congressional representative Charles Henry.

Charles wanted make sure his town of Anderson was a center for commerce in the surrounding area, so he created the Union Traction Company (UTC) of Indiana to build short run rail lines connecting towns and cities. By the early 1900s, there were some 165 miles of track to places like Muncie, Pendleton, McCordsville, Oaklandon, and Marion. Cars reached as far south as Broad Ripple, where summertime crowds took the line to spend the day at the White City Amusement Park. The park was such a traffic draw that after much of it burned down in 1908, the UTC actually purchased and rebuilt it.

Connections to Indianapolis were vital, as it was the center for long-distance rail traffic through the giant Union Station. The Broad Ripple Transit Company, developer of the White City Park, built the first interurban line to Broad Ripple in September of 1894 via Illinois Street, later Central Avenue and finally College Avenue. On January 4, 1901, the Union Traction Company would open a direct line from Anderson to downtown Indianapolis.

Mules pulled cars through local Indianapolis streets starting in the mid-1860s, but with investment money from Chicago, the Citizens Street Railroad Company, owner of those lines, electrified the system from 1890 to 1894. This caused quite an issue among the mule drivers themselves, culminating in a strike in 1892 that would weaken the company. Hugh J. McGowan, who actually started as a mule driver for the car system in Kansas City, took advantage of the company's financial trouble by founding his own company—the Indianapolis Street Railway—and by purchasing the system in 1899.

On December 6, 1903, the Anderson-based Union Traction Company renamed itself "Indiana Union Traction Company" and added service from Indianapolis to Kokomo. Lines to

Fort Wayne and other cities soon followed. It became clear that a new, central station for both the local and interurban lines was needed in downtown Indianapolis. McGowan responded by forming a separate operation in 1903, the Indianapolis Traction and Terminal Company, to build and finance the new station. The nine-track Indianapolis Traction Terminal opened on September 12, 1904, located on the north side of Market Street between Illinois and Capitol Avenue, on the site currently occupied by the Adam's Mark Hotel.

Traffic peaked in 1916, when almost 700 cars per day serviced over 7 million passengers. However, the automobile was now becoming an item that many could afford. Indianapolis itself was a center of the new industry, and with improved roadways, and the inability of a train to provide "door-to-door" service the way a delivery truck could, the need for rail transportation declined. In 1919, McGowan's two companies merged to stay afloat, but by 1920, the Terre Haute, Indianapolis and Eastern Railroad purchased the firm. On December 31, 1924, the Union Traction Railroad itself was placed into receivership.

The lines had built large electric power plants to run their cars, and had sold extra electricity to the local town. As the rail business faded, these power plants became the core business, and in order to protect them, the companies were eager to unload their rail systems.

Samuel Insull, an entrepreneur who had co-founded General Electric with Thomas Edison, moved to Chicago in 1892 and began building an empire around electric utilities and electric railroad transportation. Seeking to create a single interurban system in the Midwest, he purchased the Union Traction Company of Indiana and combined it with the Northern Indiana Power and Service Company (NIPSCO, now NiSource) and Interstate Public Service Company (now Cinergy, formerly Public Service of Indiana, or PSI Energy) to form an operating group called the Indiana Railroad System. Containing almost 800 miles of rail, it linked cities in Indiana with Louisville, Ohio, and Detroit.

The combined system promptly slimmed down to about 600 miles of track, and the company operated it through most of the Great Depression. By 1938, though, the Indiana Railroad had already begun converting some of its lines to bus service, seeking to maintain employment for some of its hundreds of workers.

The final blow came from the Securities Exchange Act, which made holding companies like Insull's illegal. The courts tried Insull three times for securities fraud in the 1930s, largely as a scapegoat for the country's financial ills, and he died penniless of a heart attack in a Paris subway in 1938. The Act forced the separation of power and railroad companies, and being unable to make a profit on their own, they started to close. By January 19, 1941, the company abandoned the Fort Wayne to Indianapolis line, leaving only a single running train between Indianapolis and Seymour because of a right-of-way lease, which tied the ability to run power lines to continued rail service on the line. On September 8, 1941, this lone remaining passenger car almost impossibly crashed into the line service car near Columbus. Unable to carry traffic, the lease was broken, and interurban service in Indiana faded into history.

Meanwhile, traffic inside the city limits would continue, despite the fact that the city streetcars, now run by the Terre Haute, Indianapolis and Eastern Railroad went into receivership itself in 1930. Charles W. Chase led a group of investors in the creation of the Indianapolis Railways Corporation in 1932, and promptly dared to revitalize the system. He began by purchasing new cars from depressed manufacturers, who were eager to sell to anyone. These new cars debuted a few years later, along with the "trackless trolley"—a car that ran via overhead wires but had tires to run on city streets.

Unfortunately, this only delayed the streetcar's demise. Though mass transit was attractive to depression-era commuters, the postwar boom brought an onslaught of automobiles and substantial investment in interstate highways. By January of 1953, the streetcars were silent, and a driver made the final trackless trolley run on the historic route up College Avenue to Broad Ripple in 1957.

Today there is much talk of building new high-speed rail service lines between Indianapolis and Chicago, but with the prevalence of automobiles and commuter airlines, we are unlikely to see this piece of "Lost Indianapolis" again.

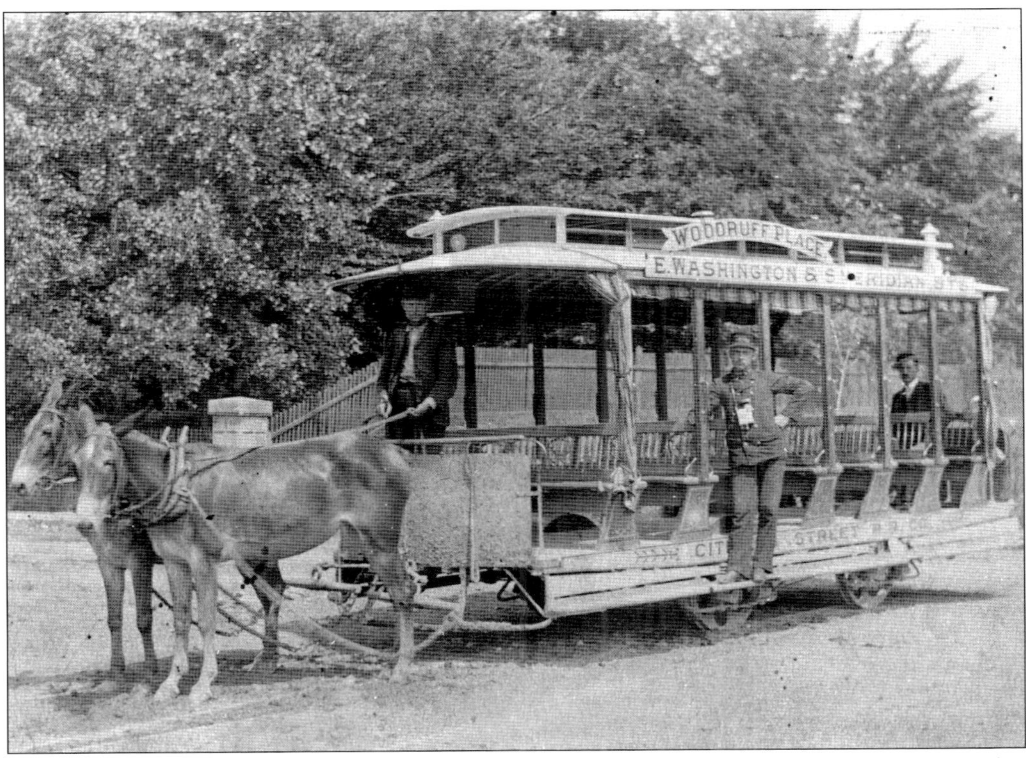

MULE PULLED STREET CAR. An early example of commuter railroads in Indianapolis, this car made trips up and down Washington Street from downtown to Woodruff Place. (Indiana Historical Society Bass Photo Collection Bass #130766.)

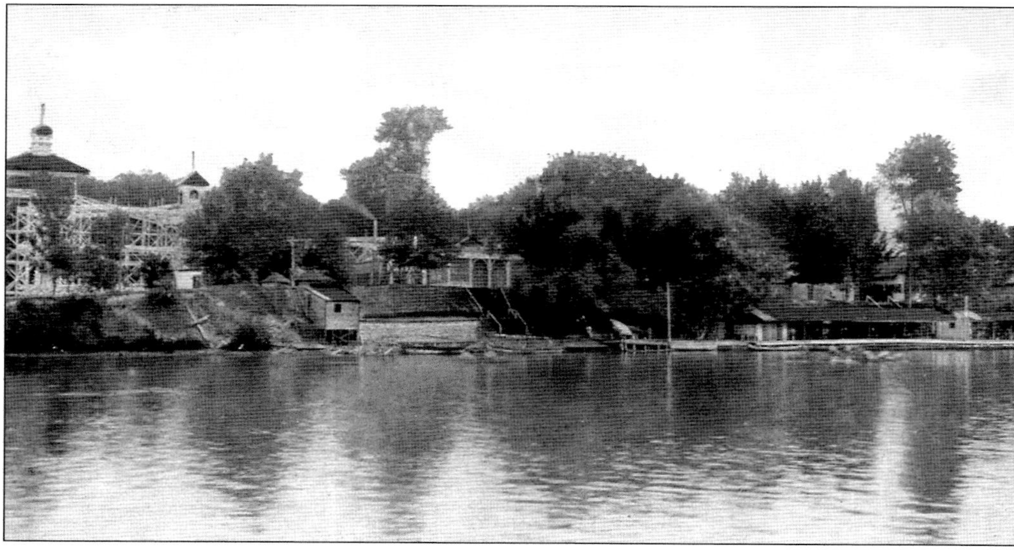

POSTCARDS FROM BROAD RIPPLE AMUSEMENT PARK. The south shore of the White River had been a bathing beach for the sleepy town of Broad Ripple, miles from the north edge of Indianapolis. The owners of the Broad Ripple Transit Company opened the White City Amusement Park here on May 26, 1906, to draw traffic on their interurban line from Indianapolis. After burning to the ground on June 26, 1908, the Union Traction Company purchased the land and rebuilt the park, seeking to continue the traffic on their interurban. They added a 250- by 500-foot swimming pool, then the largest in the world. The owners sold the park in May of 1922, and the new group renamed it the "Broad Ripple Amusement Park." The City of Indianapolis purchased the land in 1945 as a city park, selling the rides and eventually filling in the original swimming pool. Only one ride remains—the carousel—now at the Children's Museum of Indianapolis.

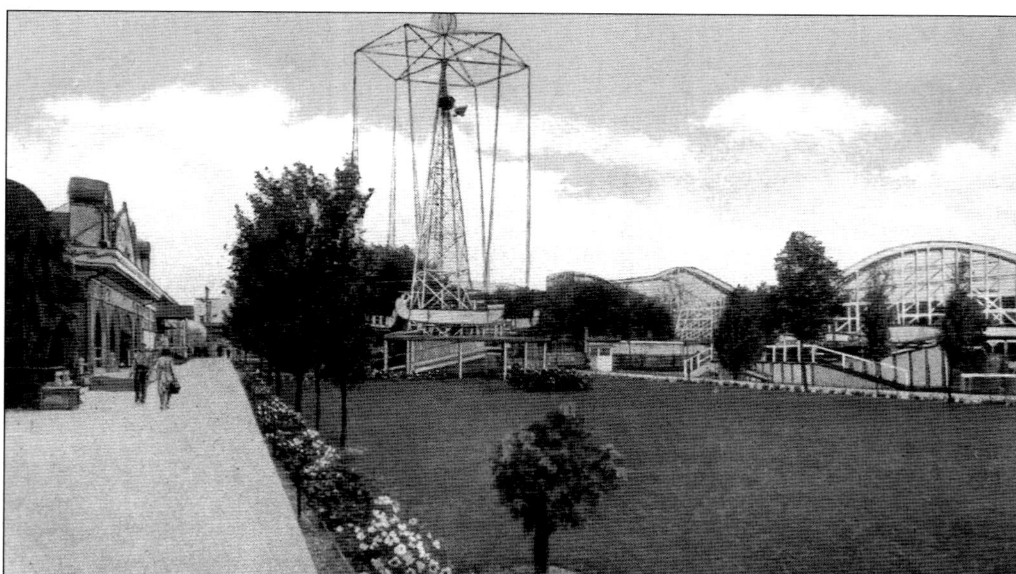

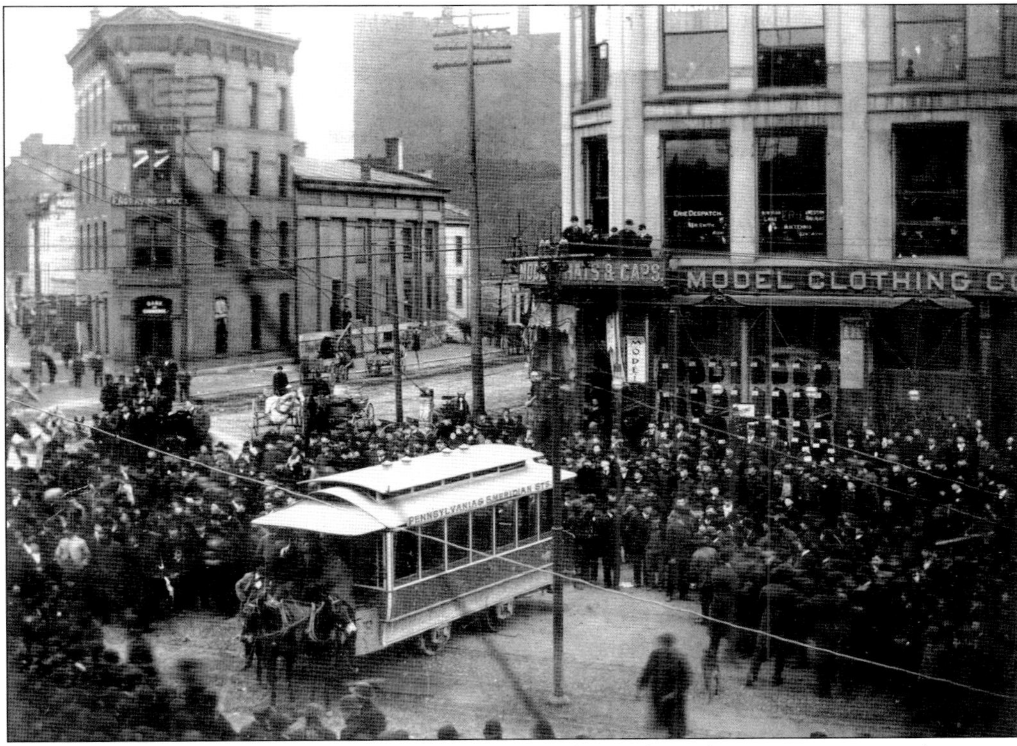

STREETCAR STRIKE—1892. This scene shows crowds watching demonstrators near the corner of Pennsylvania and Virginia Avenue. This strike helped provide the instability that allowed Hugh McGowan to gain control of the system in 1899. (Indiana Historical Society Bass Photo Collection Bass #15314.)

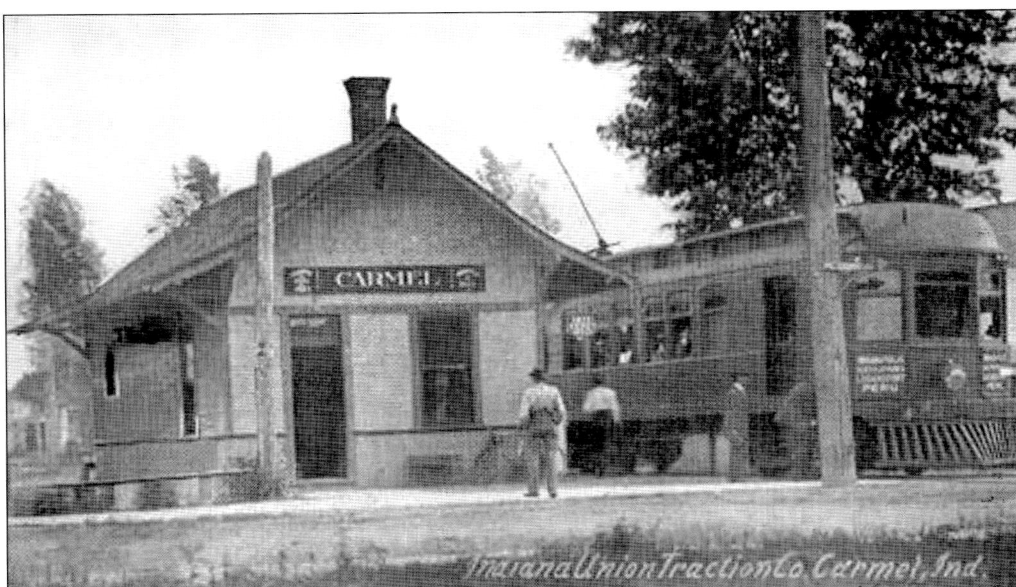

POSTCARD SHOWING CARMEL UNION TRACTION COMPANY INTERURBAN STATION.

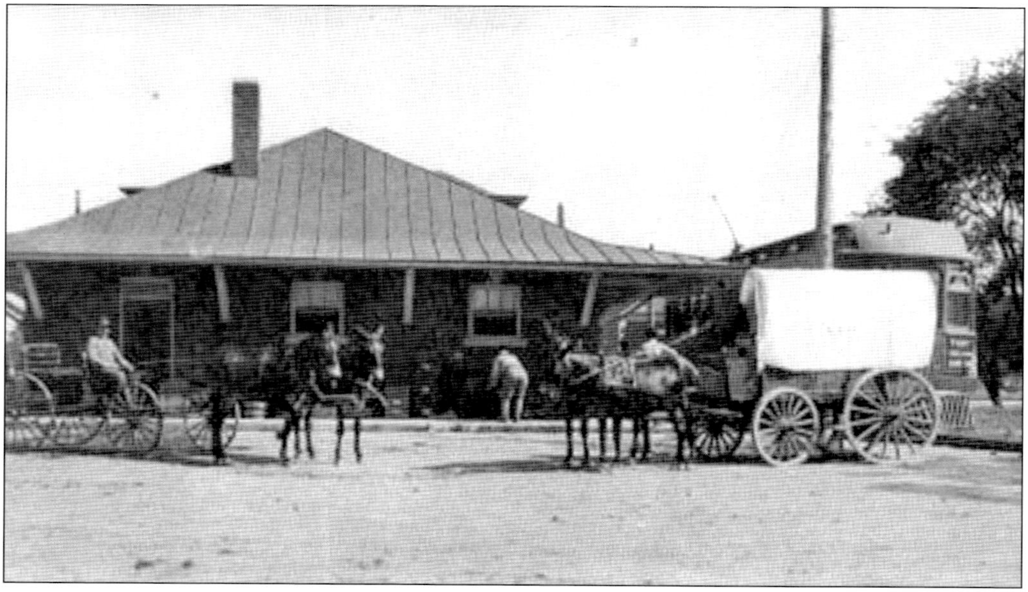

Fort Benjamin Harrison Interurban Station. The Army used the building as the fort's post office for many years after the interurban closed.

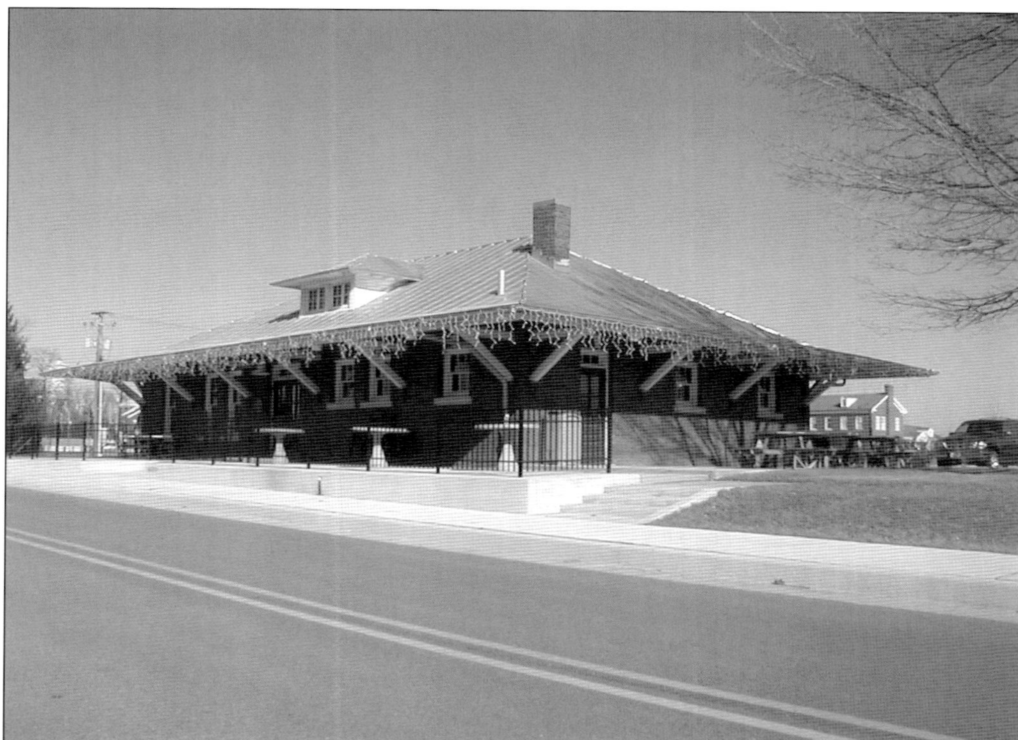

Fort Benjamin Harrison Interurban Station Today. The same station building is still in use today as a cafe.

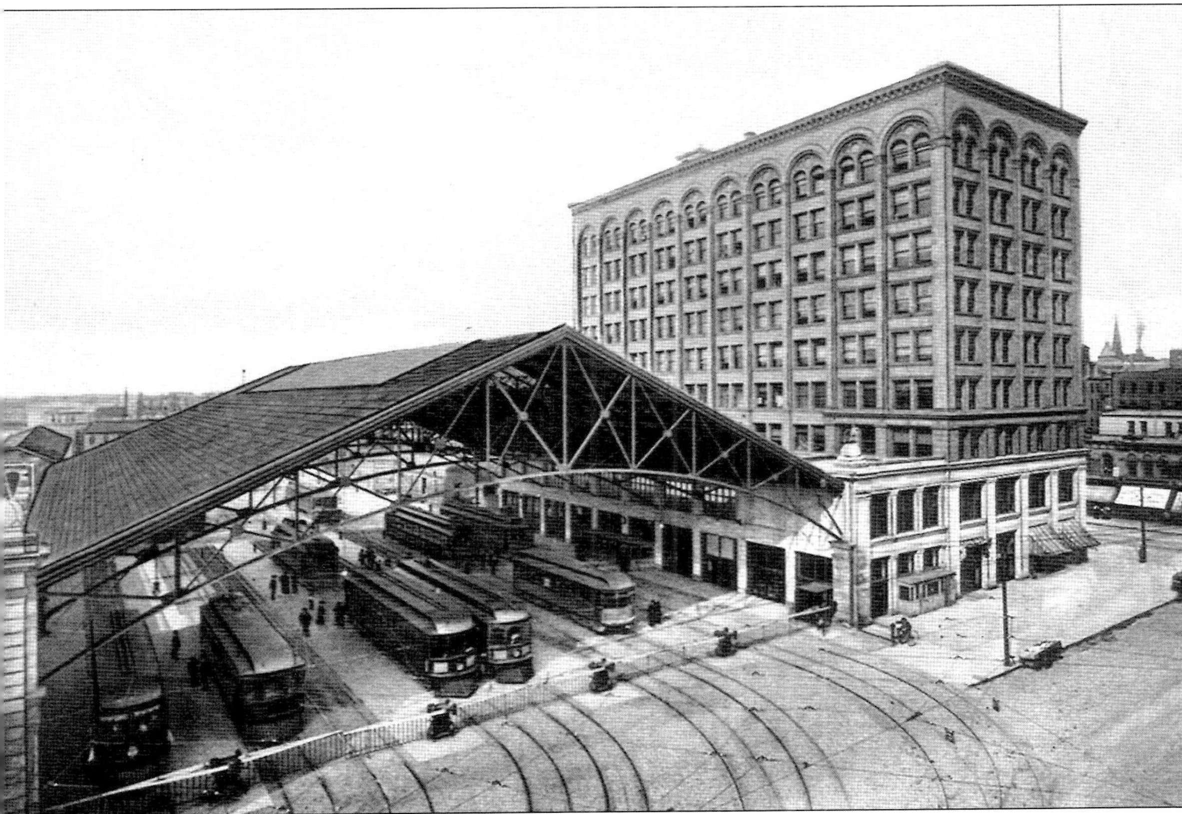

INDIANAPOLIS TRACTION TERMINAL. Opened in 1904, this grand facility once served as the hub for regional and local train service. Large freight barns stood behind, helping to transport goods and farm products from outlying areas to the long distance trains at nearby Union Station.

CONDENSED SCHEDULES

FAST LIMITED TRAIN SERVICE

De Luxe All Steel Equipment

6 Fast Through Trains Daily Each Way Between

INDIANAPOLIS and FORT WAYNE

Read down — VIA MUNCIE AND BLUFFTON — Read up

PD PM	PM	AM		PD AM	PM	PM
5 00	1 00	7 00	Lv. Indianapolis Ar.	10 20	2 10	8 10
6 20	2 20	8 22	Anderson	9 00	12 55	6 55
6 50	2 50	8 50	Muncie	8 25	12 20	6 20
7 22	3 22	9 22	Hartford City	7 49	11 44	5 37
7 38	3 38	9 38	Montpelier	7 33	11 27	5 21
8 00	4 00	10 00	Bluffton	7 15	11 08	5 03
8 45	4 45	10 45	Ar. Ft. Wayne Lv.	6 30	10 20	4 15
PM	PM	AM		AM	AM	PM

Read down — VIA KOKOMO AND PERU — Read up

PM	PM	PD AM		AM	PM	PD PM
7 00	1 00	7 00	Lv. Indianapolis Ar.	11 15	5 05	9 25
7 55	1 55	7 55	Noblesville	.0 20	4 10	8 31
8 25	2 20	8 20	Tipton	9 54	3 45	8 05
8 55	2 47	8 50	Kokomo	9 25	3 15	7 37
9 30	3 25	9 25	Peru	8 50	2 40	7 00
9 53	3 46	9 46	Wabash	8 23	2 13	6 35
10 24	4 19	10 19	Huntington	7 48	1 42	6 02
11 10	5 05	11 05	Ar. Ft. Wayne Lv.	7 00	1 00	5 20
PM	PM	AM		AM	PM	PM

PD-Carries Parlor-Dining Car.

8 Trains Daily Each Way between

INDIANAPOLIS and LOUISVILLE

SOUTH BOUND

	PD AM	AM	PD AM	PM	PM	PD PM	PM	S PM
Indianapolis	7 00	9 00	11 00	1 00	3 00	5 00	7 00	11 30
Franklin	7 51	9 51	11 51	1 51	3 51	5 51	7 51	12 28
Columbus	8 31	10 29	12 31	2 29	4 31	6 31	8 29	1 10
Seymour	9 05	11 00	1 05	3 00	5 05	7 05	9 00	1 50
Jeffersonville	10 28	12 19	2 28	4 19	6 28	8 28	10 18	6 32
Louisville	10 45	12 35	2 45	4 35	6 45	8 45	10 35	6 50
	AM	PM	PM	PM	PM	PM	PM	AM

NORTH BOUND

	AM	AM	PD AM	PM	PD PM	PD PM	PM	PM
Louisville	7 15	9 45	11 45	1 15	3 45	5 45	8 15	11 30
Jeffersonville	7 30	10 01	12 01	1 30	4 01	6 01	8 30	11 48
Seymour	8 50	11 25	1 25	2 50	5 25	7 25	10 05	1 35
Columbus	9 20	11 55	1 55	3 20	5 55	7 55	10 36	2 13
Franklin	9 59	12 35	2 35	3 59	6 35	8 35	11 12	2 56
Indianapolis	10 50	1 25	3 30	4 50	7 30	9 25	11 59	6 30
	AM	PM	PM	PM	PM	PM	PM	AM

PD-Carries Parlor-Dining Car. S-Sleeper.

Parlor-Dining Car Service

Parlor-dining cars operated in Indiana Railroad System trains between Indianapolis and Fort Wayne and Indianapolis and Louisville are equipped with every facility for the traveler's comfort and pleasure. Luxurious, deep-cushioned arm chairs, wide vision rear observation windows and other comforts invite complete relaxation. Excellent foods, cooked enroute, are served by skilled attendants at extremely moderate cost. The menu ranges from light refreshments to a full course steak dinner.

Sleeping Car Service

Nightly sleeping car service between Indianapolis and Louisville, Ky., offers the added luxury of new coil spring mattresses, extra long berths and upper berth windows. You can board these fine all-steel sleepers in Indianapolis or Louisville at 9.00 P. M. Train leaves at 11:30 P. M., arriving Indianapolis or Louisville just before seven in the morning. Passengers may occupy berths until 9:00 A. M.

STEAM, ELECTRIC RAILWAY AND MOTOR COACH CONNECTIONS

ALEXANDRIA–Big Four Route. Nickle Plate Road.
ANDERSON–Big Four Route. Newcastle Bus Lines. Pennsylvania Lines.
BLUFFTON–Nickle Plate Road.
COLUMBUS–Pennsylvania Lines. Big Four Route. Leppert Bus Line. White Star Bus Line. Columbus, Shelbyville, Rushville Bus Line.
DELPHI–Monon Route. Wabash.
ELWOOD–Nickle Plate Road. Pennsylvania Lines.
FORT WAYNE–Fort Wayne-Lima Railroad. Nickle Plate Road. Pennsylvania Lines. Wabash Railroad. New York Central. Greyhound Lines, Inc.
FRANKFORT–T. H. I. & E. Traction Co. Monon Route. Nickle Plate Road. Pennsylvania Lines.
FRANKLIN–Big Four Route.
GARRETT–Baltimore and Ohio.
HARTFORD CITY–Nickle Plate Road. Pennsylvania Lines.
HUNTINGTON–Erie Railroad.
INDIANAPOLIS–T. H. I. & E. Traction Company. Indianapolis and Southeastern Railroad. Monon Route. Nickle Plate Road. Baltimore and Ohio Railroad. Illinois Central. Pennsylvania Lines. Big Four Route.
KENDALLVILLE–New York Central. Pennsylvania Lines. Frurip Bus Line.
KOKOMO–Nickle Plate Road. Pennsylvania Lines.
LAFAYETTE–T. H. I. & E. Traction Company. Monon Route. Nickle Plate Road. Wabash. Big Four Route. Crawfordsville-Lafayette Bus Line.
LOGANSPORT–Pennsylvania Lines.
LOUISVILLE–Southern Railway. Louisville and Nashville. Chesapeake and Ohio. Illinois Central. Monon Route. Baltimore and Ohio. Big Four Route. Louisville and Interurban Railway.
MARION–Chesapeake and Ohio. Pennsylvania Lines. Big Four Route.
MUNCIE–Nickle Plate Road. Chesapeake and Ohio. Big Four Route. Pennsylvania Lines. A. B. C. Coach Line (Winchester, Richmond and Cincinnati). Lake Shore Coach Line (Portland).
NEW ALBANY–Monon Route. Southern Railway.
NEW CASTLE–T. H. I. & E. Traction Company. Nickle Plate Road. Pennsylvania Lines. Big Four Route.
PERU–Winona Railroad. Nickle Plate Road. Chesapeake and Ohio. Indiana Motor Bus Co. (Rochester and Plymouth).
SEYMOUR–Baltimore and Ohio. Chicago, Milwaukee, St. Paul and Pacific. Studebaker Bus Lines. Seymour-Bedford Bus Line. Leppert Bus Line.
SCOTTSBURG–Greyhound Bus Lines.
TIPTON–Nickle Plate Road.
WABASH–Big Four Route.
WATERLOO–New York Central.

INTERURBAN TIMETABLE—1930. This is page 11 of the September 28, 1930 timetable for the Indiana Railroad. In addition to regularly scheduled passenger service between cities, the company operated these limited-stop express trains at popular times of day between Indianapolis and Fort Wayne and Louisville, Kentucky. More closely resembling their steam railroad service competition, they provided dining cars during the day and sleeping cars at night. Rural residents, who were used to being able to flag down a passing interurban along the line, became frustrated with these limited-service trains, as they would not stop to pick them up. Management adjusted the timetables to allow some slack for these unscheduled stops, but eventually they eliminated these expensive lines.

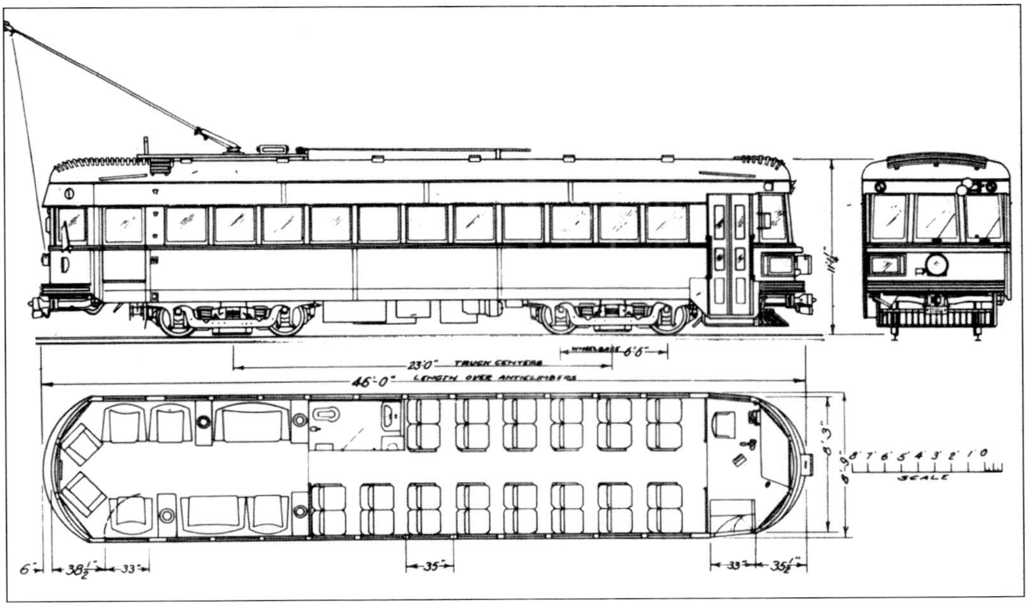

INSIDE AN INTERURBAN CAR. The company placed these "high speed" cars into service during the summer of 1931. They provided an "observation lounge" in the rear of the car as well as regular seats; passengers could use the lounge without extra charge. Intended to compete with motorcar travel, the Pullman Company built them at a cost of $28,000 each. They averaged about 45 miles per hour on a typical run, slowing to 15 miles per hour within a town and back up to 60 in the open countryside. They allowed the retirement of older wooden cars from the Union Traction era, and represented the final advancement in interurban travel in Indianapolis.

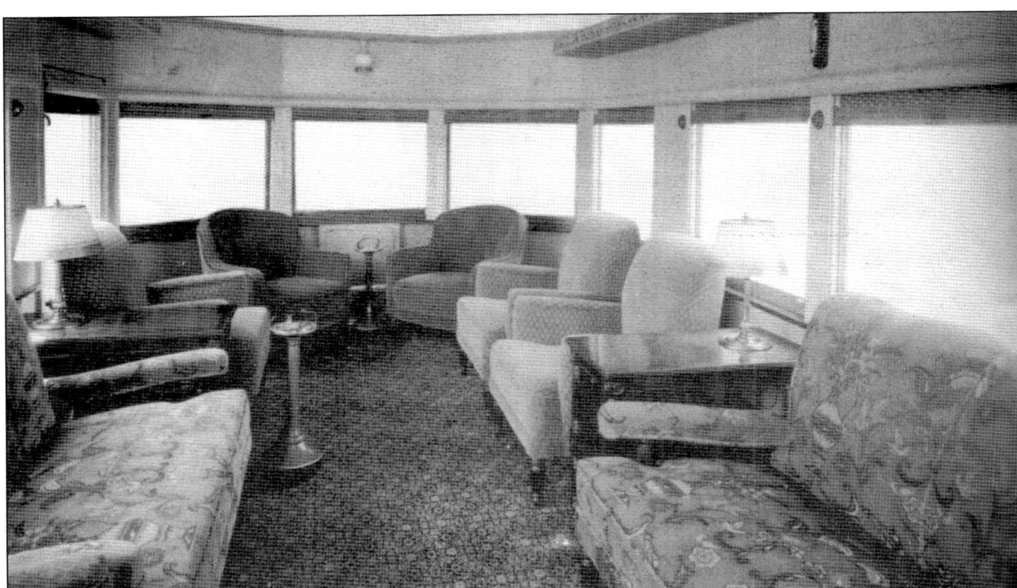

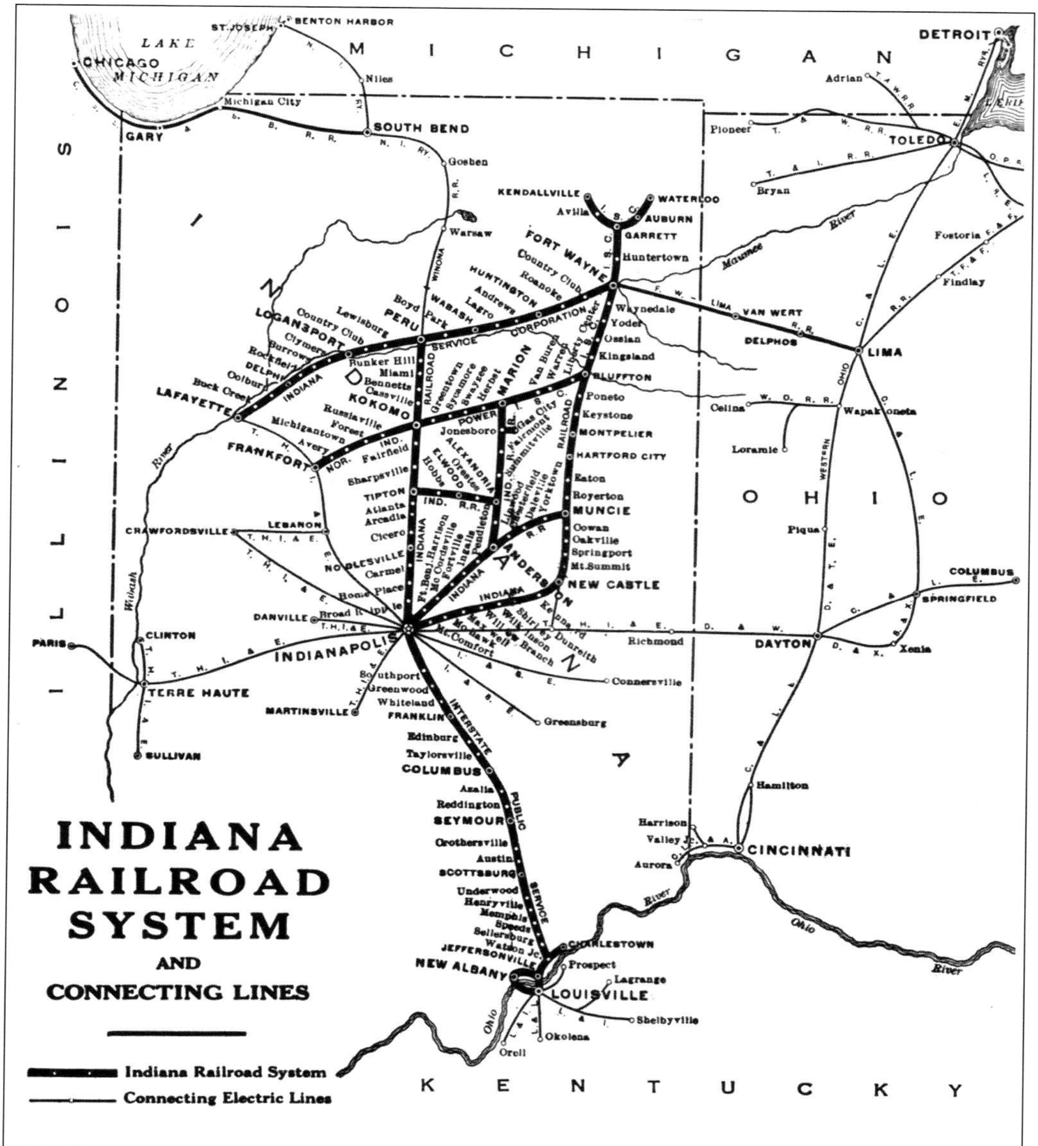

Indiana Railroad Route Map—September 9, 1930. At its peak, the newly combined Indiana Railroad connected hundreds of small towns in Indiana to major cities within the state and beyond. The job of powering and maintaining such a vast network was substantial, and as the equipment aged, it became more difficult to provide reliable service. Lines supplemented their income by offering freight services, providing free pickup and delivery truck service to businesses and farms surrounding a station. Indiana was slower to adopt paved highways and interstates than its Midwestern neighbors, mainly due to its expansive, high quality interurban system.

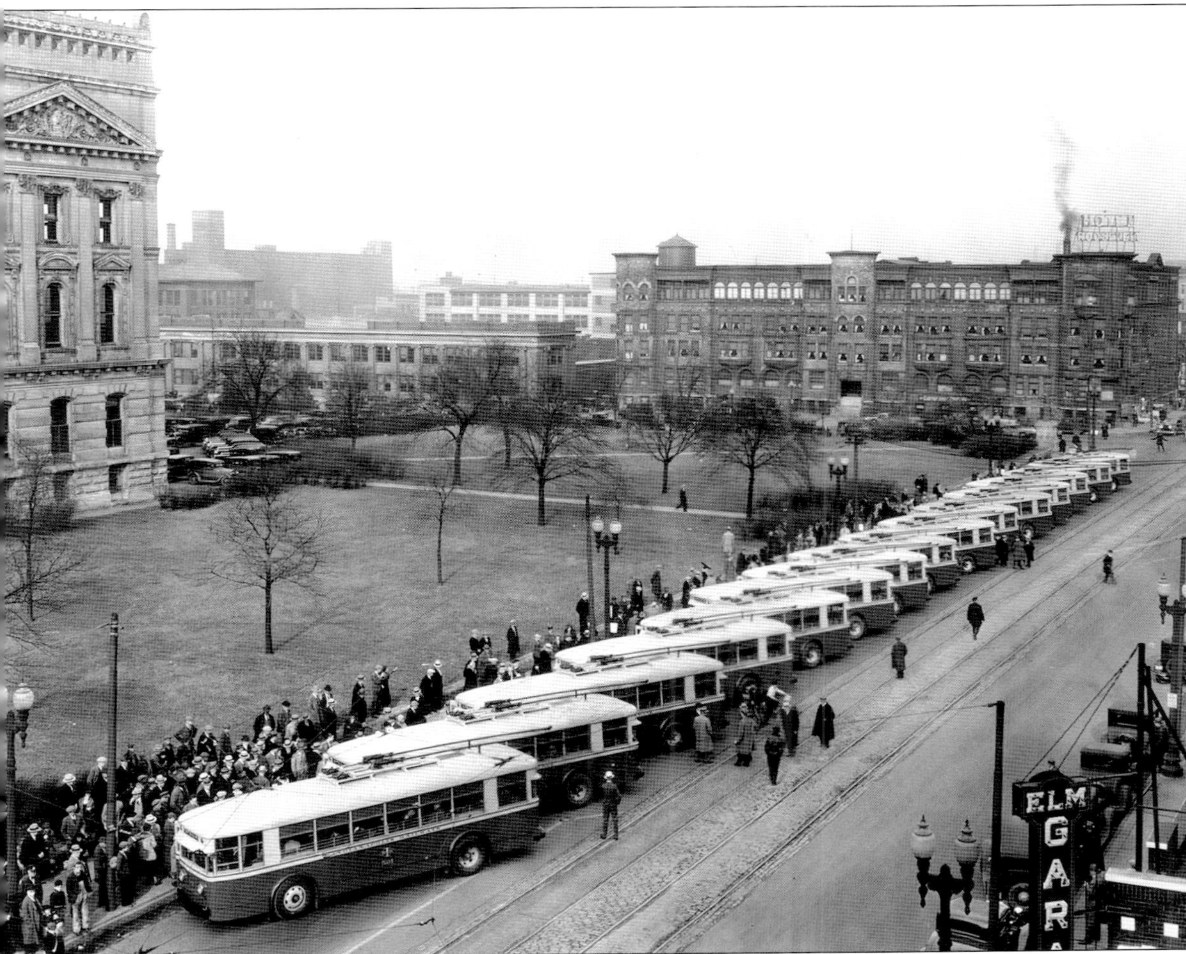

ELECTRIC BUSSES—1939. Crowds turned out to view the new electric busses, parked for display along the front of the Indiana State House. (Indiana Historical Society Bass Photo Collection #245744.)

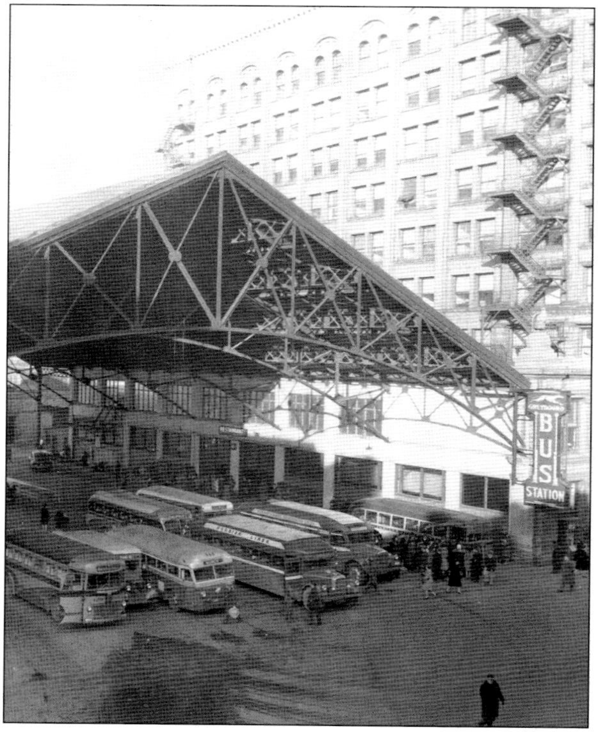

BUS STATION—1945. The Greyhound Bus Company used the old Traction Terminal as a bus station until they constructed a new terminal in 1965. Today this block contains the Adam's Mark Hotel, the Indiana State Teachers Association Building, and a parking garage. (Indiana Historical Society Bass Photo Collection.)

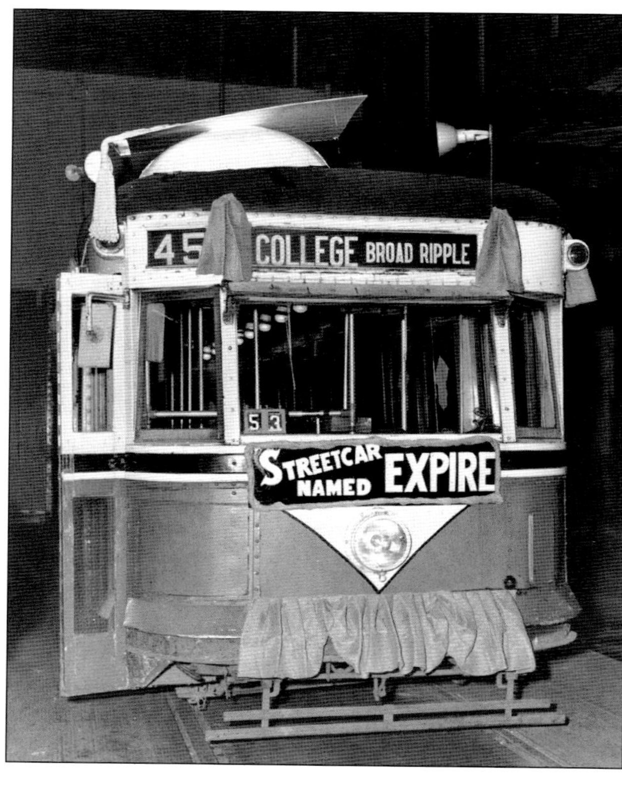

FINAL STREETCAR—1953. Symbolically, the last streetcar to be retired was the College Avenue car between downtown and Broad Ripple. For the final few days, workers decorated the car with signs like "Bus-s Me Goodbye" and "Don't Kick Me—I'm Full of Scrap". By 1957, the company discontinued the trackless trolley bus as well, and the overhead lines came down. (Indiana Historical Society Bass Photo Collection #114579-3.)

Five

L.S. Ayres Downtown

A woman searches her open closet for the perfect hat to match her dress. Stacks of round boxes greet her, adorned with a cursive "L.S. Ayres and Company." She is about to meet some friends for lunch at the Tea Room at that very store downtown, perhaps later selecting some shoes or a new gown, again to be wrapped in those familiar boxes.

This is how it was for women of Indianapolis for decades, as the great L.S. Ayres and Company was the queen of the department stores. Before suburban shopping malls, indeed, before automobiles, the Ayres family store anchored the retail center, which included the William H. Block Company as well as Wasson's, and several other smaller operations.

Lyman S. Ayres was born in Oswego, New York on September 4, 1824. In 1843, he followed the population movement westward, opening a series of stores in Ohio, bringing goods from New York into the Midwest. Expanding his empire, he purchased the Trade Palace store in Indianapolis, which stood at 26 West Washington Street. For several years, he stayed in New York as the buyer for the store, moving to Indianapolis in 1874.

Lyman continued to grow his company, expanding to 33 West Washington a few years later. By the mid-1890s the company had outgrown this location, and Lyman purchased the land at the southwest corner of Washington and Meridian streets for a grand new facility.

Unfortunately, Lyman did not see his dream come to reality, as he died on May 7, 1896. His son, Frederic M. Ayres, took over the company and built the new store in 1905.

The original building was eight-stories tall, with the administrative staff occupying the top floor. In these early days, goods purchased and shipped in from outside of town were expensive and slow to arrive. Like many large department stores of the time, Ayres actually built or constructed many of the items it sold. Complete floors were devoted to the construction of picture frames and cabinets and another to hundreds of dressmakers who assembled both custom creations and the racks of ready-to-wear dresses on sale below. Most of the rest of the store was dedicated to sales, with the basement reserved for economy items, markdowns, and a large soda fountain.

The jewel of the store, however, was the Tea Room, originally located on the fifth floor of the first building. Since its opening in 1929, generations of Indianapolis residents can recall childhood memories of trips to the restaurant and recipes like Chicken Velvet Soup.

In 1936, the company introduced an ad campaign, simply titled "That Ayres Look". Using the company's script logo, these were frequently the only words on the page. Elegant and colorful sketches and drawings of the latest clothing for the upcoming season filled the balance of the page. Scanning old magazines and newspapers for these ads will give one a comprehensive tour of fashion though the century.

Starting the Christmas of 1947, Ayres began the season by mounting a 1,200-pound bronze cherub atop the Arthur Bohn five-ton electric clock on the corner of Meridian and Washington

Streets. Children raced past window displays filled with moving figurines to line up for seats on the Santa Claus Express electric train that would take them to Santa Claus himself.

As the city expanded into the suburbs, so too did Ayres, becoming an anchor of the new Glendale Center in 1958. Under the leadership of Lyman S. Ayres II, who took over the company in 1954, there were eventually ten stores open around the city and state.

Ayres diversified in 1961 with the creation of Ayr-Way Stores, a discount operation designed to compete with K-Mart. In the mid-1970s the CEO of Ayr-Way was John Geisse, who had been a cofounder of Target Stores in 1962 and of Venture Stores, a unit of the May Company of St. Louis, in 1968. Later he formed Wholesale Club, a members-only warehouse that he sold to Wal-Mart in 1991.

By the early 1970s, the department store landscape in Indianapolis was crowded, and downtown shopping in serious decline. The Associated Dry Goods Company acquired L.S. Ayres and Ayr-Way in 1972, operating both as separate divisions. In the early 1980s, Ayr-Way sold out to Dayton-Hudson, parent company of Target Stores, and the May Company of St. Louis purchased L.S. Ayres and Company in 1986.

Despite loosing over $2 million on the downtown store in 1988, the May Company signed up to become an anchor for the proposed Circle Center Mall. After years of delays, they closed the facility in January of 1992. Workers stored many of the historical items, including the cherub and the Santa Claus Express train, and 120 years of L.S. Ayres downtown ended.

However, not all has been lost to memory. The Circle Center Mall opened in August of 1995, anchored by a Parisian Department Store that occupied the first three floors of the former L.S. Ayres downtown store. The Indiana State Museum recreated the Tea Room in their newly completed facility in 2002, and continued a popular Christmas-time exhibit, including that same electric train which once again delivers children to a waiting Santa Claus.

The cherub has returned, too, reappearing each Christmas in its rightful place over that historic corner at Meridian and Washington as a part of Circle Center's Christmas decorations. Today you can still shop on the very floor that generations of Indianapolis residents visited, and imagine what it would have been like one hundred years before.

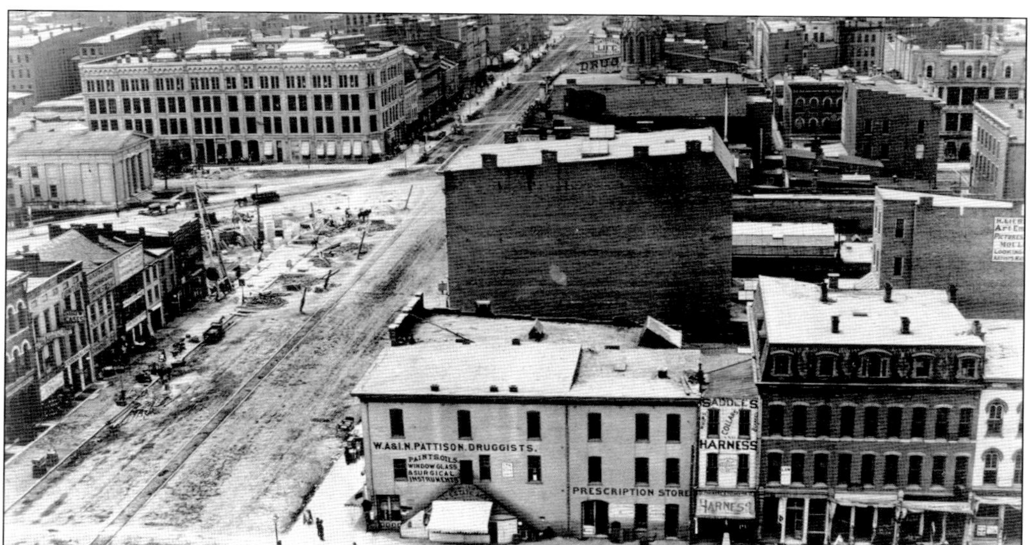

WASHINGTON STREET FROM DELAWARE STREET—1875. Indianapolis was still a rough town with dirt streets when Lyman Ayres moved to town. (Indiana Historical Society Bass Photo Collection #92094.)

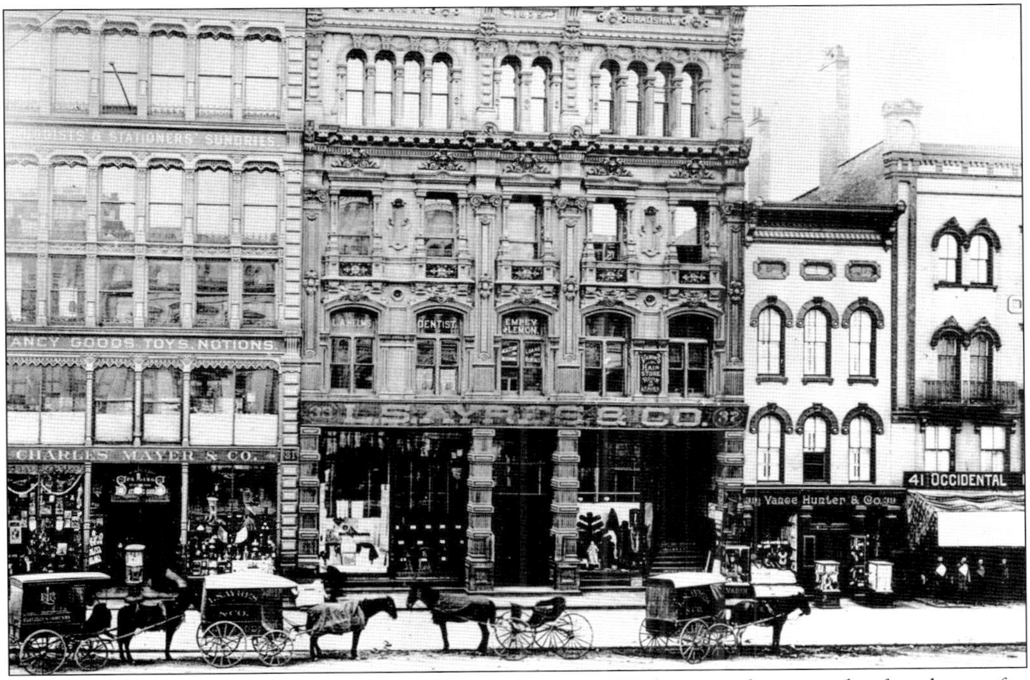

L.S. AYRES—1875. This new building at 33–37 West Washington became the first home for the company after they outgrew the former Trade Palace facility across the street at 26–28 West Washington. (Indiana Historical Society Bass Photo Collection.)

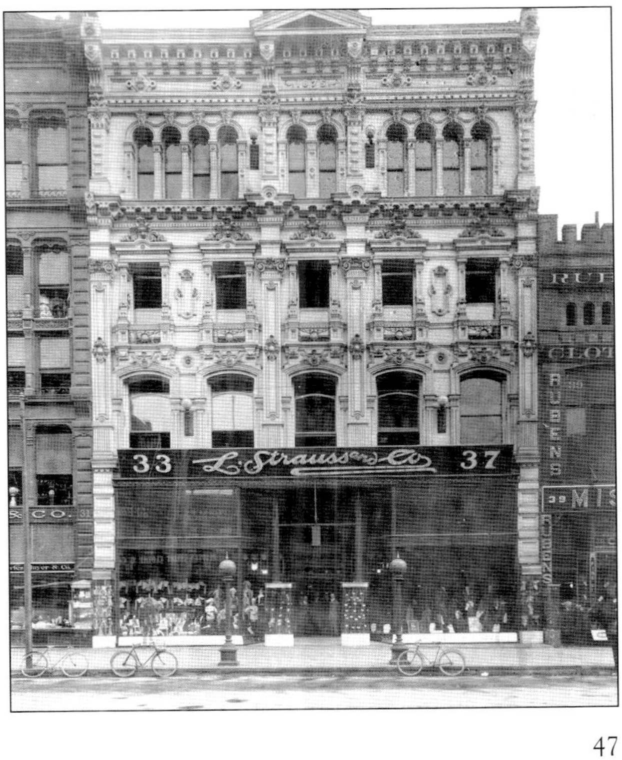

33–37 WEST WASHINGTON STREET—1905. After Ayres moved into the new building in 1905, their former store became the home of L. Strauss & Company, another leading retailer. The script on the sign closely copied L.S. Ayres' own logo, no doubt in the hopes of confusing a few shoppers. Named for Leopold Strauss, a young tailor who started as a clerk and eventually bought the company, they would move again in 1946 to the corner of Washington and Illinois street, in 1985 to Claypool Court, and in 1991 to Monument Circle. They declared bankruptcy in 1993, after over 140 years of business in Indianapolis. (Indiana Historical Society Bass Photo Collection #6518.)

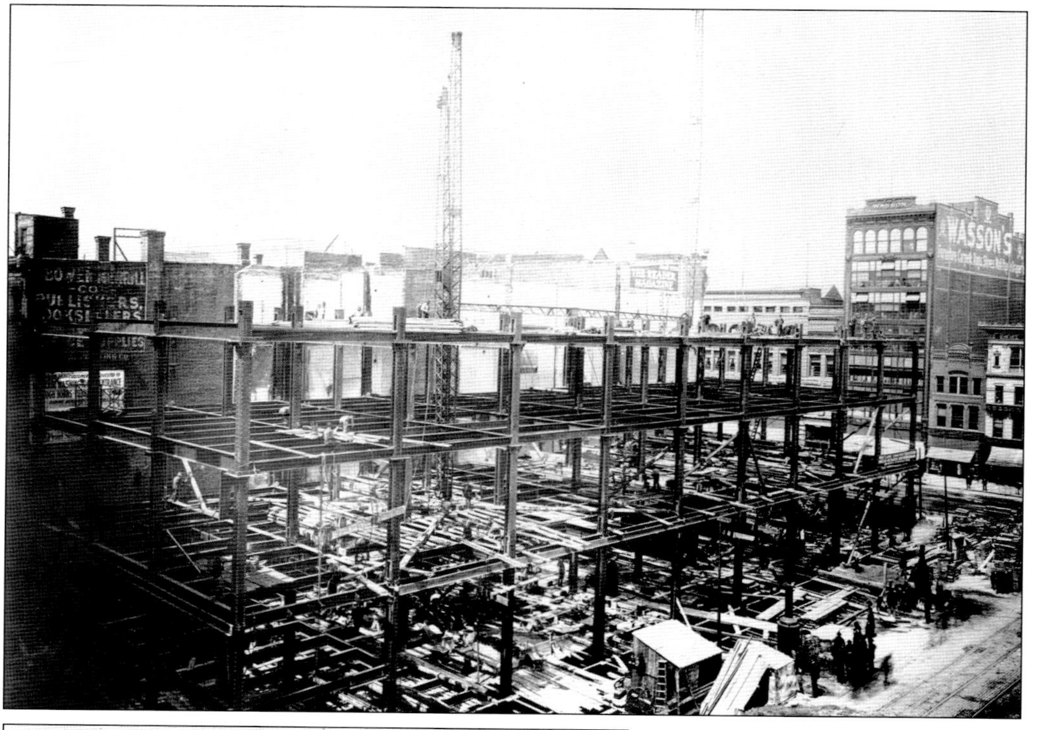

UNDER CONSTRUCTION—1905. Along with the Merchant's Bank building east on Washington Street, Ayres was one of the first steel-framed structures in the city. (Indiana Historical Society Bass Photo Collection #4314.)

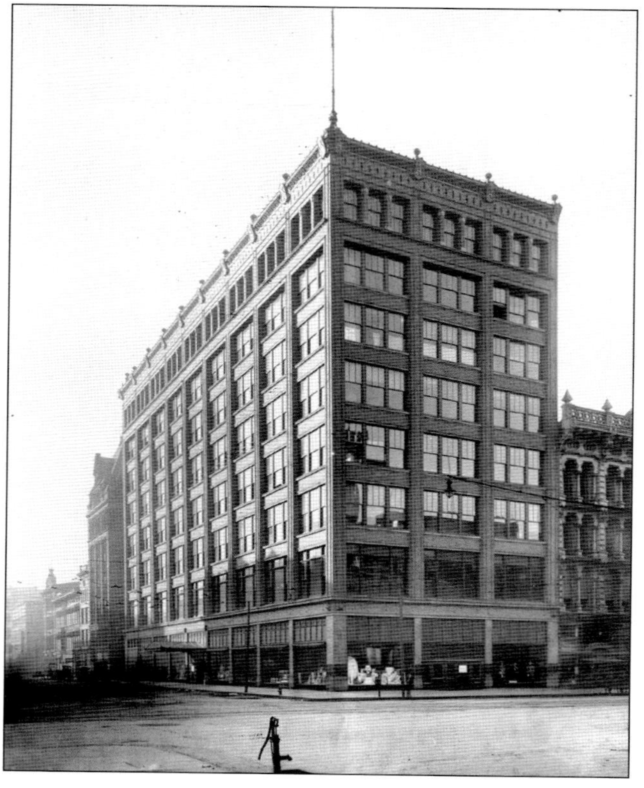

NEW L.S. AYRES STORE—1905. The eight-story building at the southwest corner of Washington and Meridian Streets opened on October 2, 1905. It was the largest store in the state at the time. Note the water pump for horses in the foreground. (Indiana Historical Society Bass Photo Collection #5772.)

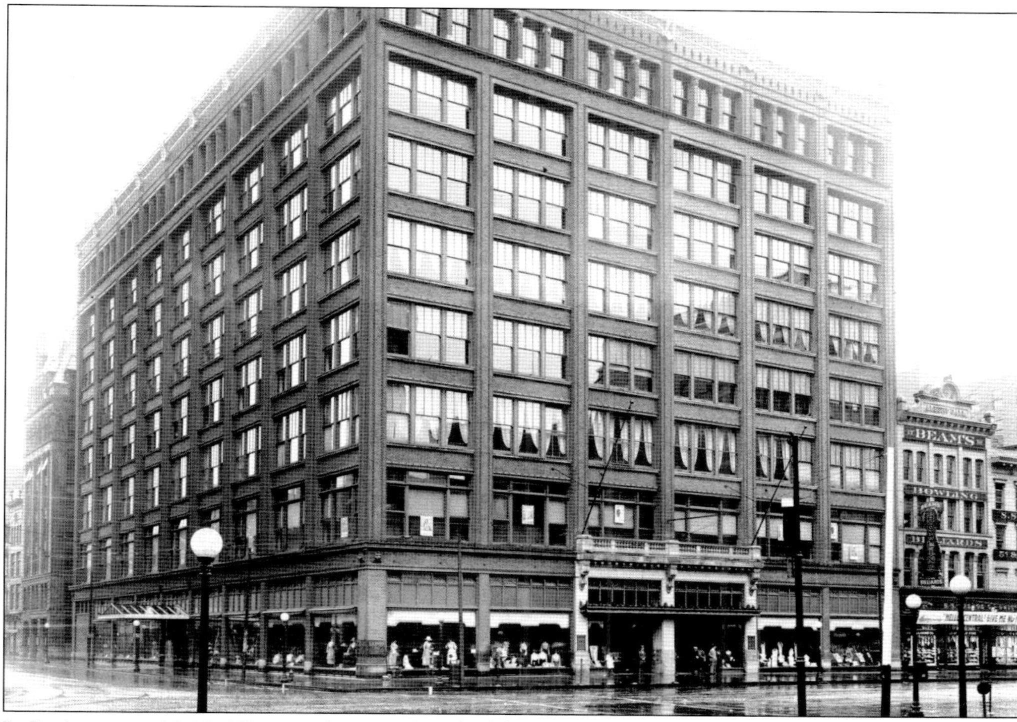

L.S. AYRES—1918. The newly completed addition doubled the store's size. Expansions would continue for decades. (Indiana Historical Society Bass Photo Collection 63688-F.)

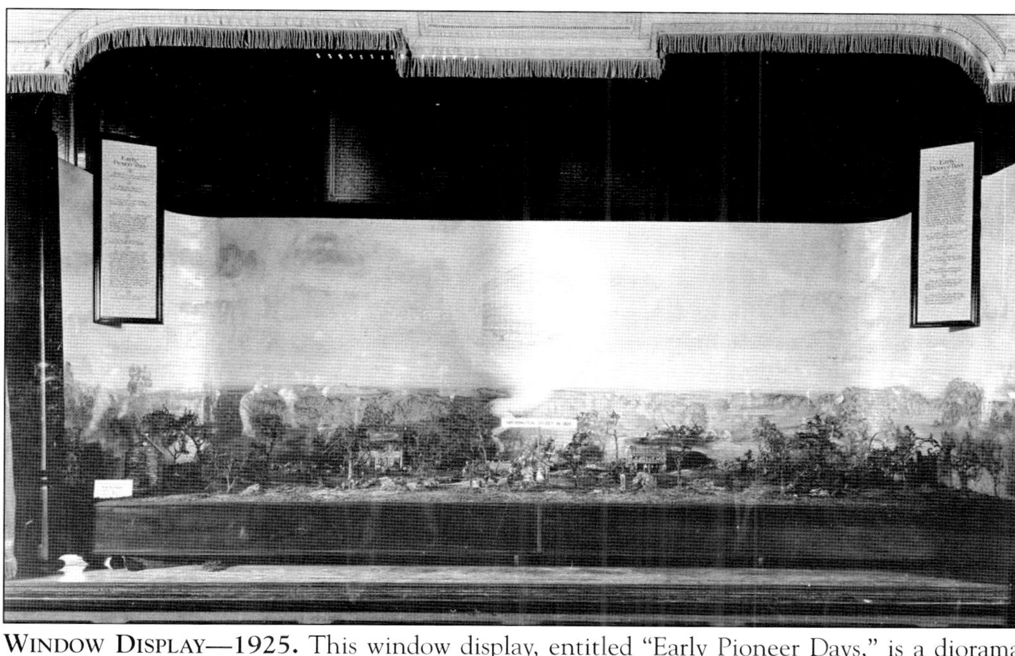

WINDOW DISPLAY—1925. This window display, entitled "Early Pioneer Days," is a diorama depicting Washington Street 100 years earlier in 1825. (Indiana Historical Society Bass Photo Collection 70720-F.)

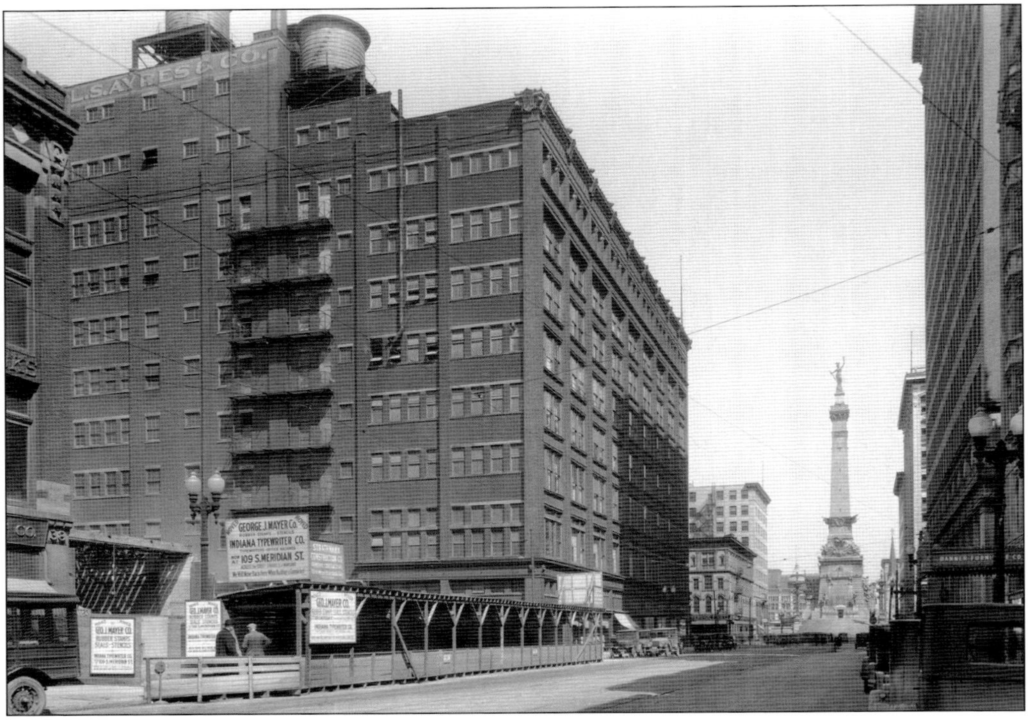

NEW EXPANSION—1928. Construction begins on yet another addition to the L.S. Ayres store. (Indiana Historical Society Bass Photo Collection 206848-F.)

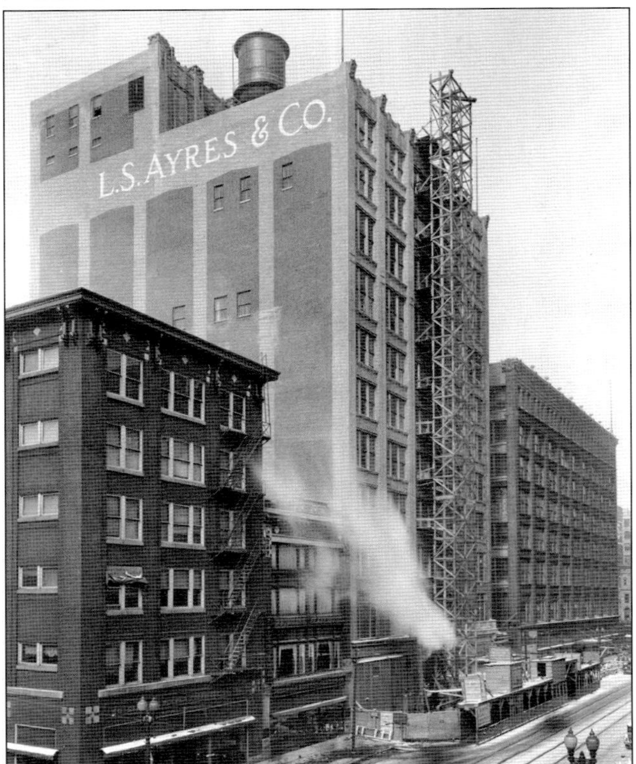

FINALIZING NEW EXPANSION—1929. Work on the last major expansion of the store nears completion. It allowed the expansion of the home and men's departments. (Indiana Historical Society Bass Photo Collection 210302-F.)

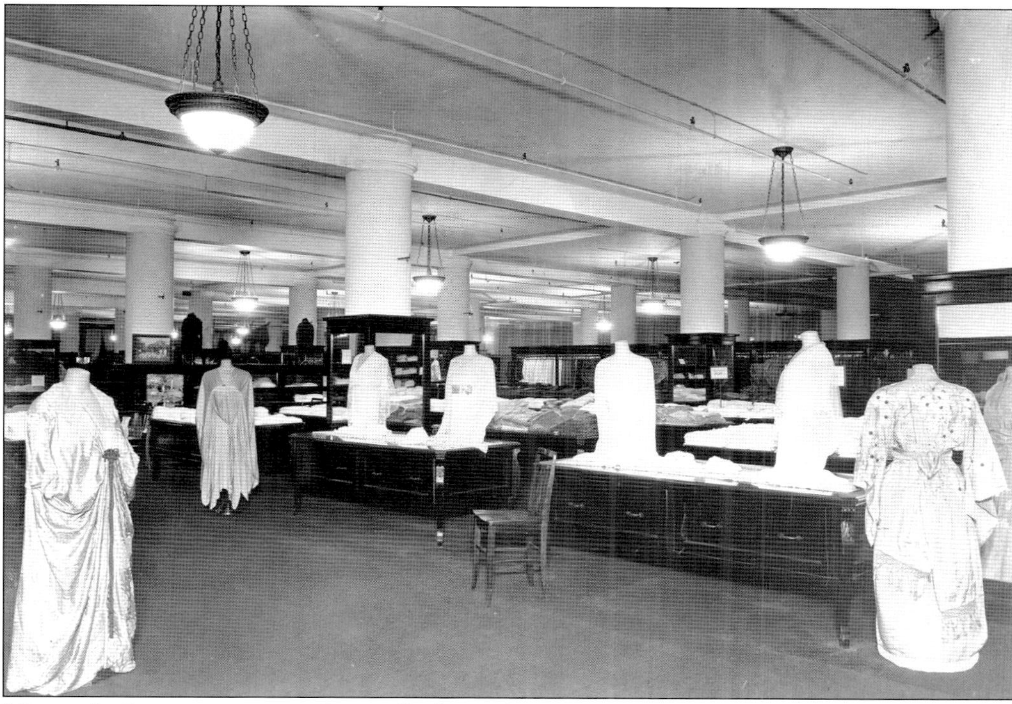

WOMEN'S DRESSES—1919. Originally housed on the third floor, Ayres carried an extensive line of ready-to-wear dresses and custom designs, built by over 180 on-site dressmakers working in another part of the building. (Indiana Historical Society Bass Photo Collection 68061-F.)

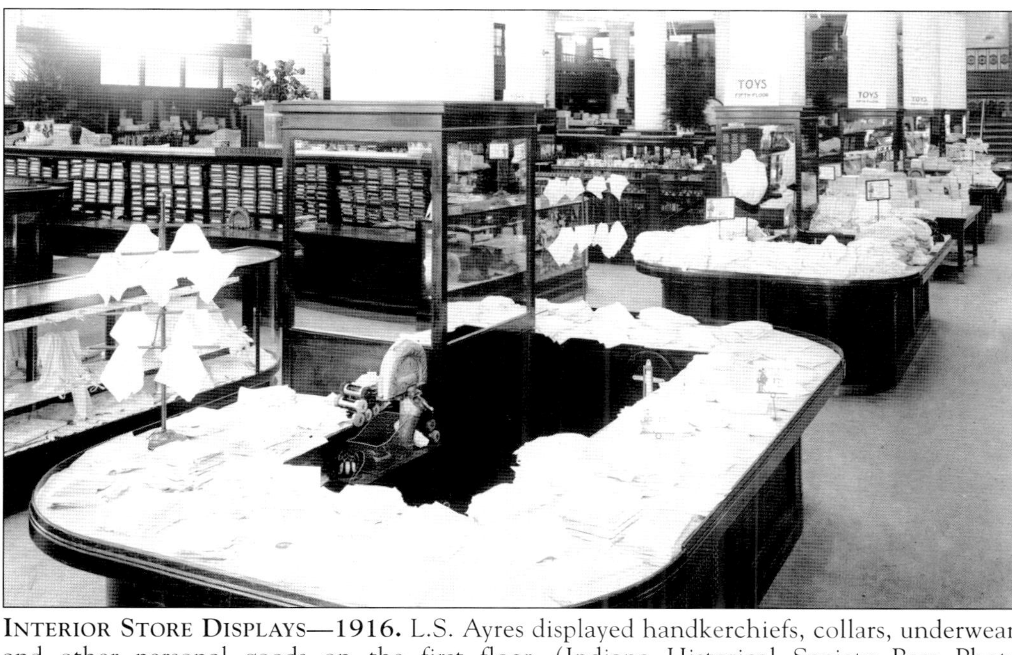

INTERIOR STORE DISPLAYS—1916. L.S. Ayres displayed handkerchiefs, collars, underwear, and other personal goods on the first floor. (Indiana Historical Society Bass Photo Collection 49570-F.)

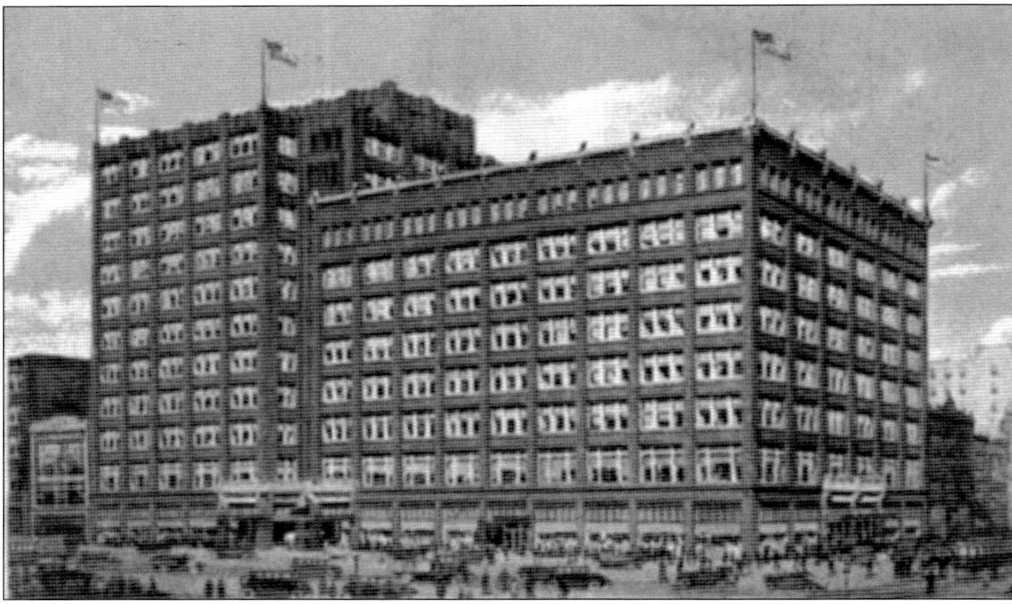

L.S. AYRES AND COMPANY—1930. This postcard image shows L.S. Ayres at its peak. This building was, and in many ways still is, an anchor of the downtown shopping district.

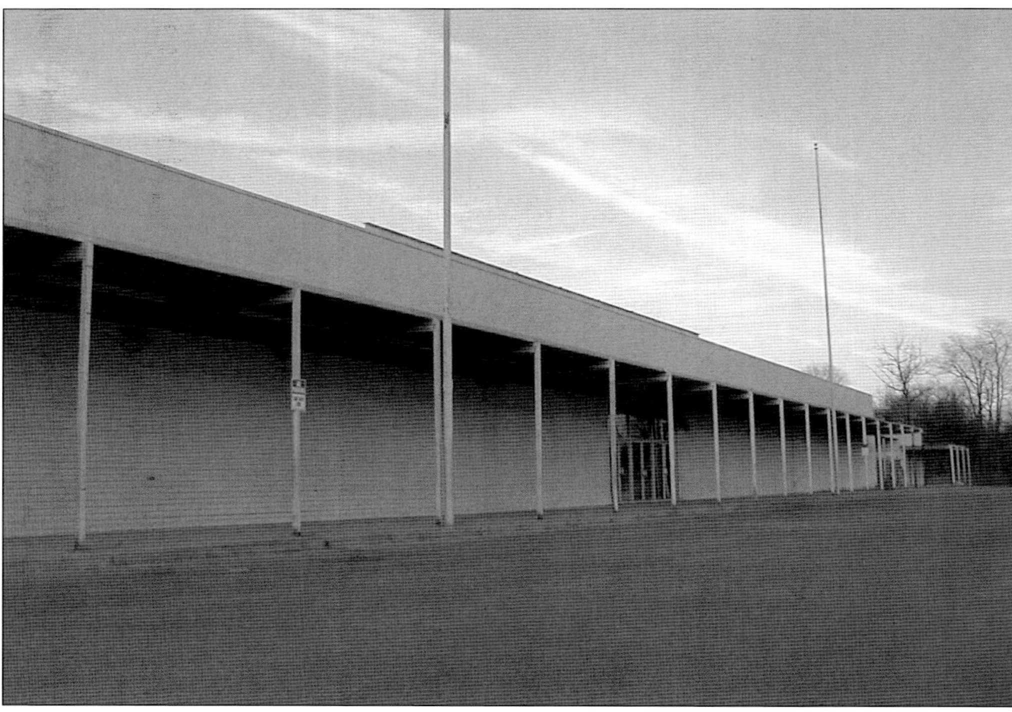

AYR-WAY. The company launched the cavernous Ayr-Way East and West discount stores in 1961. They contained complete grocery stores inside the buildings, though a separate company operated them and they had their own entrances. The former Ayr-Way West building sat vacant and decaying until the Harvest Prayer Center converted it into a school and church.

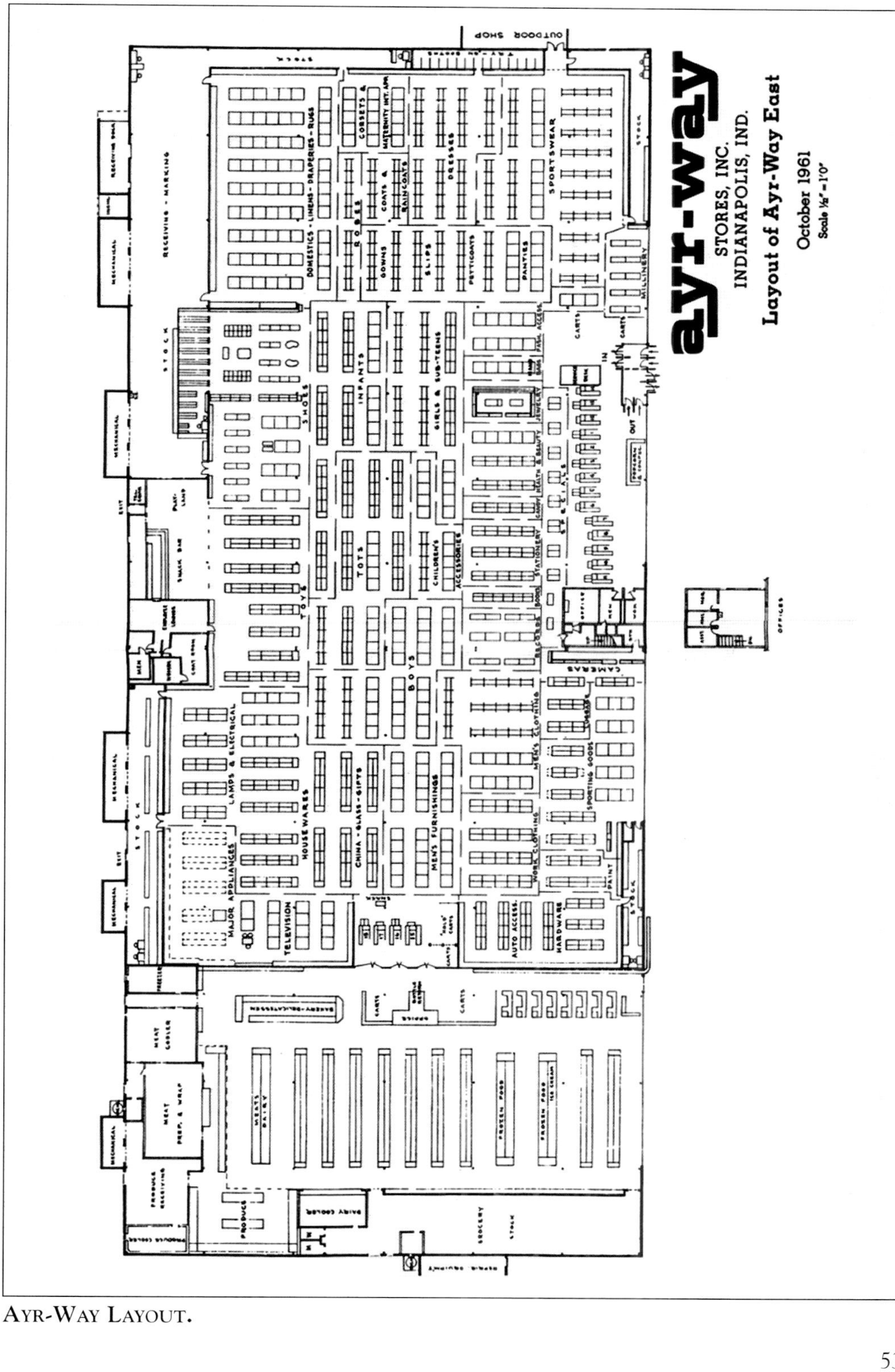

AYR-WAY LAYOUT.

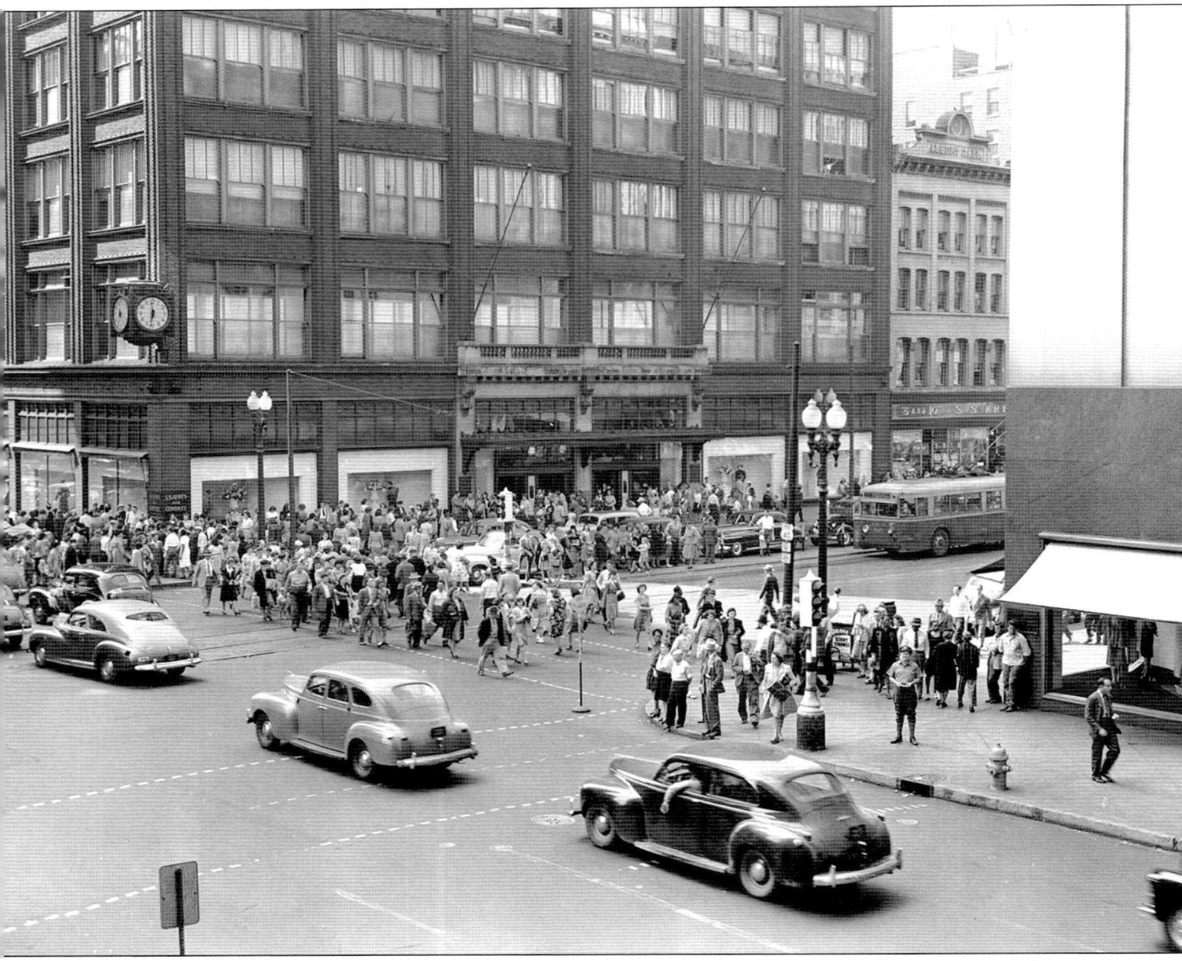

WASHINGTON AND MERIDIAN—1940S. A typical scene at the peak of downtown shopping, crowds cross Washington Street between Wasson's and L.S. Ayres. (Indiana Historical Society Bass Photo Collection #331352.)

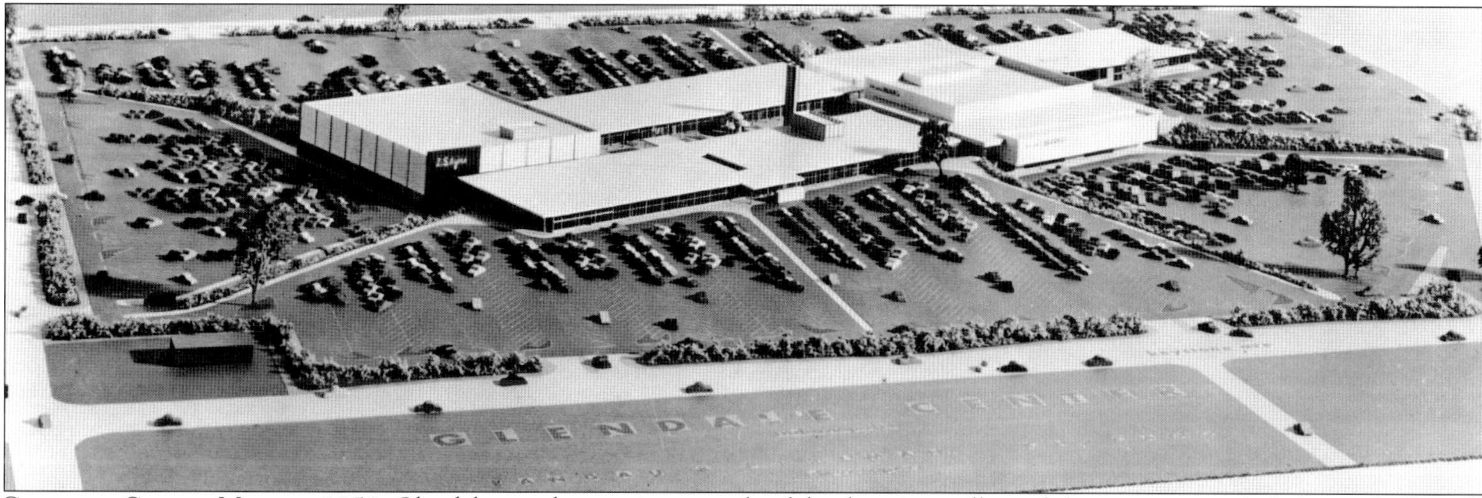

Glendale Center Model—1958. Glendale was the premier example of the shopping mall trend that swept not only Indianapolis, but also the nation at large. Previously, suburban shopping centers were usually L-shaped with a parking lot sandwiched between the building and the street. These new malls were different, with strips of stores facing inward around an open courtyard and expansive parking lots surrounding the building. Usually several large anchor stores were built as well. Around 1969, the mall began covering the open courtyards. Over 20 of these types of malls opened in Indianapolis over the next 15 years, driving the percentage of department store sales by the downtown stores from 90 percent in the early 1950s to less than 20 percent by the early 1970s. (Indiana Historical Society Bass Photo Collection #298460.)

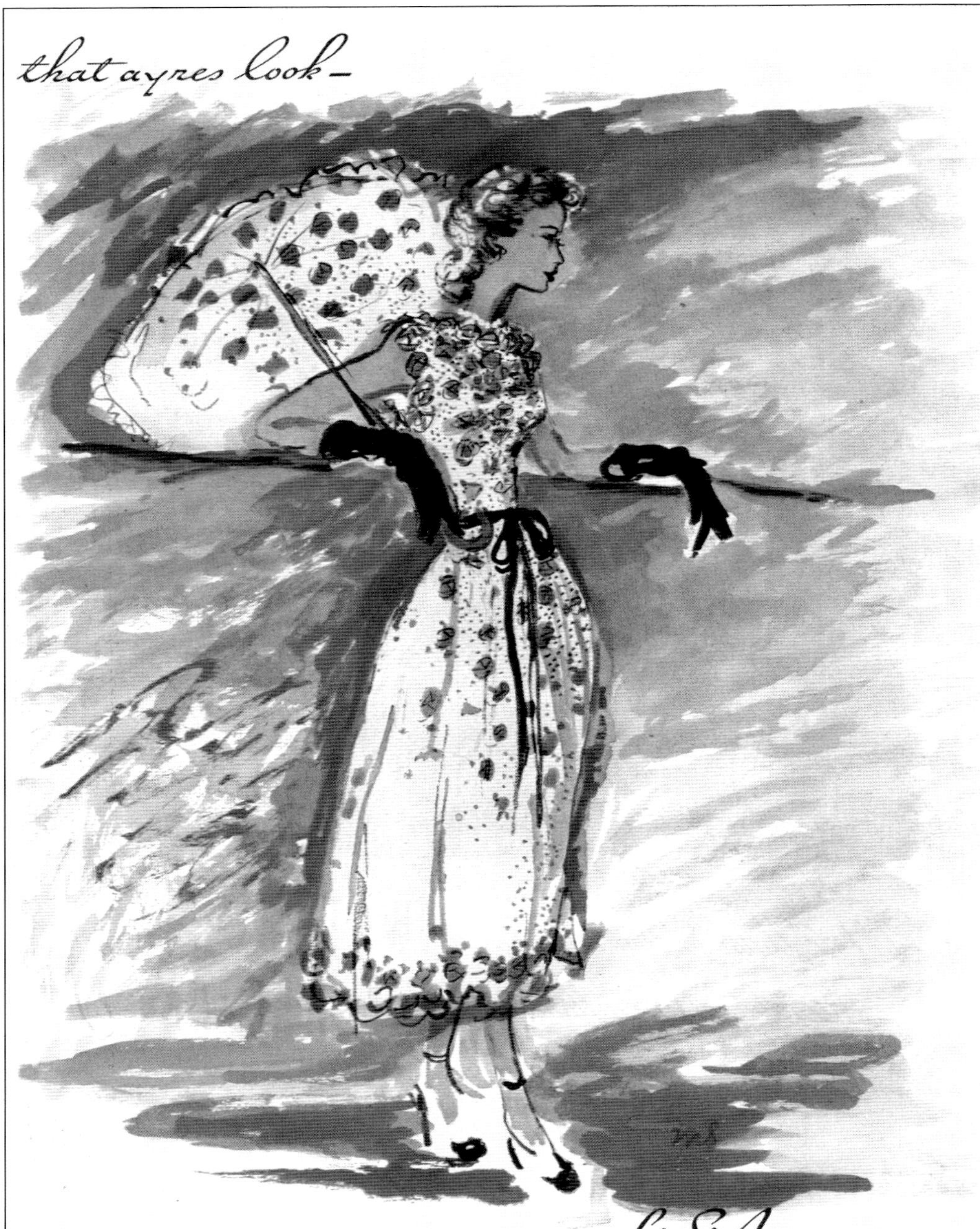

L.S. AYRES AND COMPANY MAGAZINE AD—1947. Through the decades, Indianapolis women of all ages could see next year's styles simply by reviewing Ayres' striking ads.

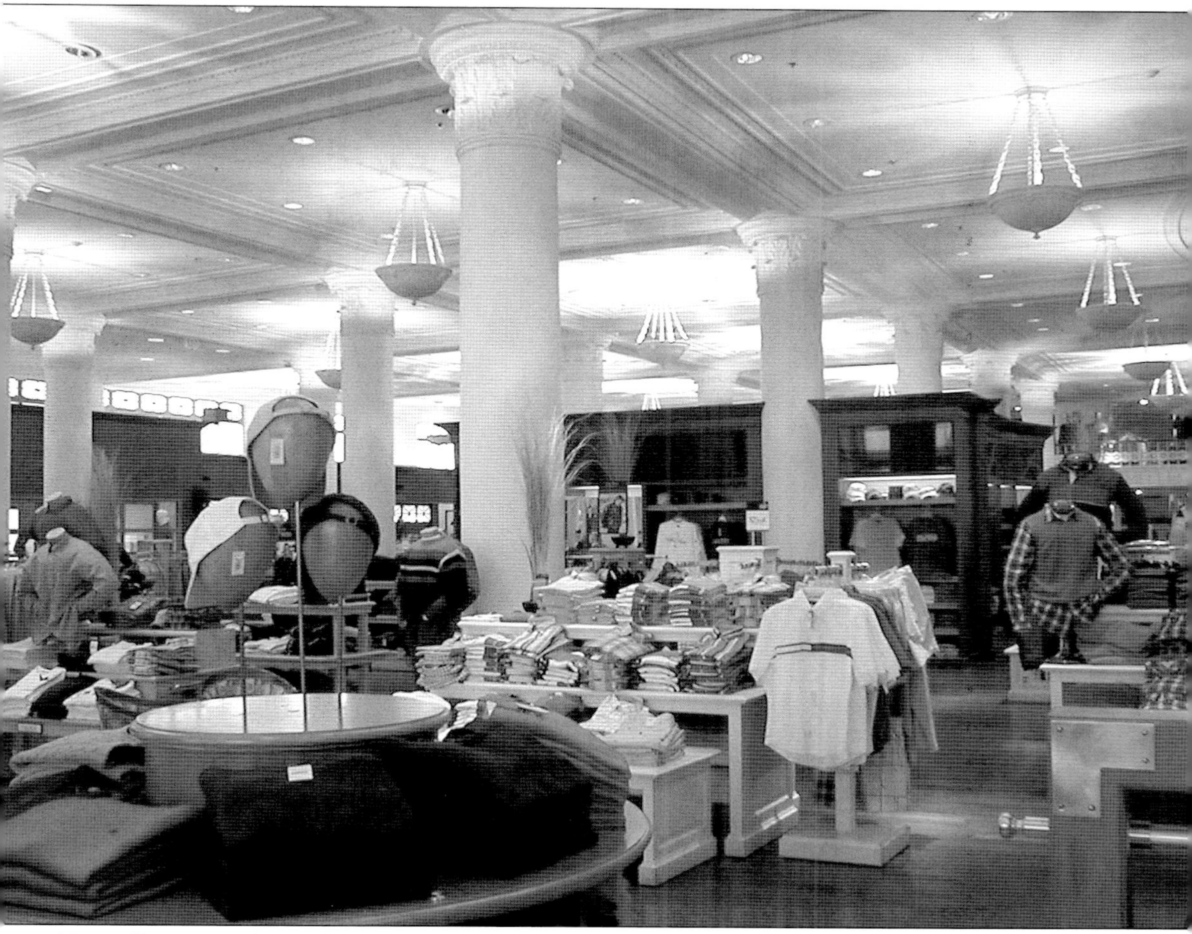

First Floor of Parisian Department Store—Circle Center. The first floors of the old L.S. Ayres Department Store now contain the Parisian downtown location. An anchor store for Circle Center, the mall undertook extensive restoration to return at least part of the building to its former grandeur.

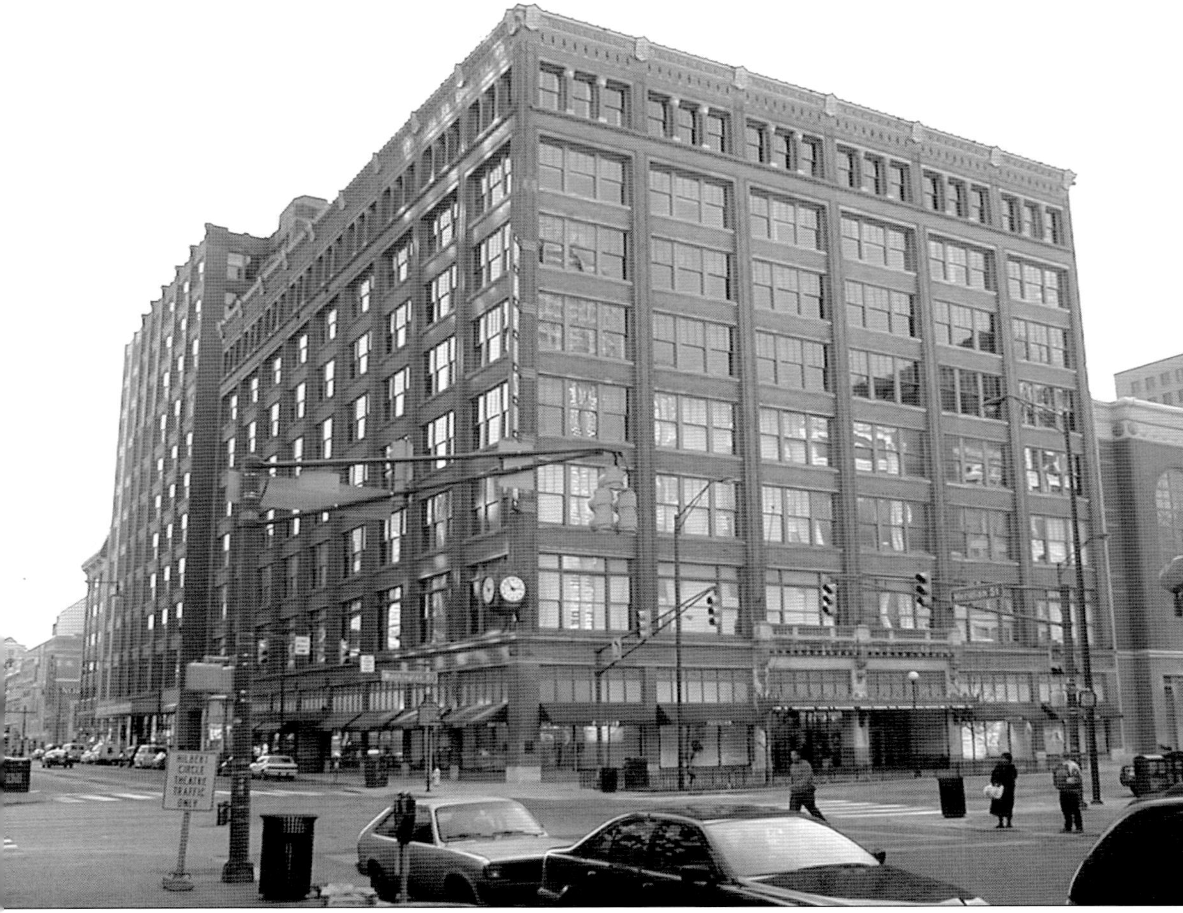

FORMER L.S. AYRES AND COMPANY—2002. Now an anchor for the rest of Circle Center, the former headquarters and flagship store for L.S. Ayres enters the new century as a working retail store.

Six

The Claypool Hotel

Even before the state capital officially moved to Indianapolis in 1824, the corner of Illinois and Washington Streets was known as a place to stop when visiting. Thomas Carter opened what was probably the first business on the corner, a tavern, in 1822, and there it stayed until after the city began to emerge as a rail hub in the mid 1850s.

Looking to capitalize on the influx of railroad travelers, Hervey Bates began construction in 1852 on a boarding house that bore his name. Completed in 1853, the Bates House was one of the finest hotels in the city for 50 years. Bates also had a distinguished career outside of the hotel business—in 1822, he won the very first election ever held in Marion County and became its first sheriff. Later he went on to help organize a bank and a predecessor of the Citizen's Gas and Coke Utility of today. One notable event occurred at the hotel - on February 11, 1861, President Elect Abraham Lincoln would stay at the Bates House and address a crowd on the streets below from his balcony.

By the turn of the century, though, the Bates House was aging and was a bit too small to stay competitive. Edward Fay Claypool, the son of one of the first settlers in Connersville, Indiana and a local entrepreneur, met with Henry Lawrence, and together they decided to purchase the Bates House and build a new, grand hotel befitting the stature Indianapolis had risen to by 1903.

Lawrence contracted Frank M. Andrews, a noted architect from Dayton, Ohio. Andrews went on to build the Battle Creek Sanitarium, a six-story Italian Renaissance Revival-style building in Battle Creek, Michigan that replaced a facility that burned down in 1902. Dr. John Harvey Kellogg operated the sanitarium. Beyond pioneering the use of radiation therapy for cancer patients; he also invented flaked cereal.

Andrews was instructed to "think big," and that he did. He started by planning a grand lobby, which, at the time, was believed to be the largest in the country. He created a series of large meeting and dining rooms, including the Florentine room with elaborate woodcarvings and painted ceilings and the Riley Room, named after Hoosier poet James Witcomb Riley. The guest rooms were large by the day's standards, and included a unique idea promoted by the Statler chain of hotels: a private bath in each room.

Construction began in 1903, and soon the structure rising above the street was unlike anything residents had seen before. Eight-stories high with 450 guest rooms, Henry completed the decorations with furniture made of the best mahogany, brass, and textiles available. From the first night, the Claypool had no trouble filling its guest list with the most powerful and influential.

Sitting only steps away from the State Capital, the Claypool would play an important role in state politics for over a half a century. Most political conventions occurred in the grand ballrooms of the hotel, and many a state and national candidate would call the hotel home as election night arrived.

Many Indianapolis businesses started in the Claypool, as well. Optometrist Dr. David Tavel, builder of a large chain of optical stores in the state, opened his first office in the Claypool in 1946. Ross and Babcock, a local travel agency, began in a small office under a stairwell in the hotel in 1949. Even the Alpha Gamma Rho fraternity was formed there on April 4, 1908.

Two notable murders occurred at the Claypool as well, the most sensational of which was that of Dorothy Poore. The 18 year old was found stuffed in a dresser drawer in 1954—a suspect was later found and charged with the murder. Actress Carole Lombard, wife of Clark Gable, spent the last night of her life at a suite in the Claypool as well. After speaking at a war-bond rally on January 15, 1942, where she helped raise a record $2.5 million, she boarded a TWA DC-3 at 4:00 a.m. the next morning that crashed into a mountain outside of Las Vegas later that day.

Shortly after the war, suburban sprawl began to affect travel patterns in the city. Overnight guests now arrived by automobile or airplane as often as by train, and frequently wished to stay nearer to business and friends living outside of downtown. At the same time, the grand hotel was aging, and was not able to compete with the shiny new motels springing up along the highways leading in and out of town. Suffering from reduced occupancy, the owners struggled to maintain the property.

The final blow came on June 23, 1967, when a fire caused one quarter of a million dollars in damage to the building. The hotel closed and sat vacant and decaying for almost two years. Seeking to rid a prime lot of what had become an eyesore in an age where rehabilitation of older structures was not as popular as it is now, the city granted a permit to demolish the building in 1969. The site served as a parking lot for state workers and other downtown employees for almost 15 years.

In the early 1980s, Simon and Property Group, an Indianapolis-based shopping mall developer, proposed a plan to build a new hotel and a small shopping court on the site. Very little downtown shopping remained at the time, but the city was undergoing a downtown revitalization that made the opportunity to support retail more positive than in the past. Construction began on Claypool Court in 1985, which included an Embassy Suites hotel above a multilevel food court and shopping mall.

With the opening of Circle Center Mall in August of 1995, the site changed once again. The $12 million Indianapolis Arts Garden, a glass-domed rotunda suspended over the intersection of Washington and Illinois, now connected the Claypool Court with Circle Center itself. While the hotel remains, the owners reconfigured the retail area to support new retail stores and an off-track betting facility.

The Claypool played a central role in the transformation of a small Midwestern town into a major city, and along the way played host to visitors large and small. Throughout the century, the northwest corner of Illinois and Washington has served as the city's welcome mat, and today you can still walk the streets around its current occupant and imagine a time fading from memory.

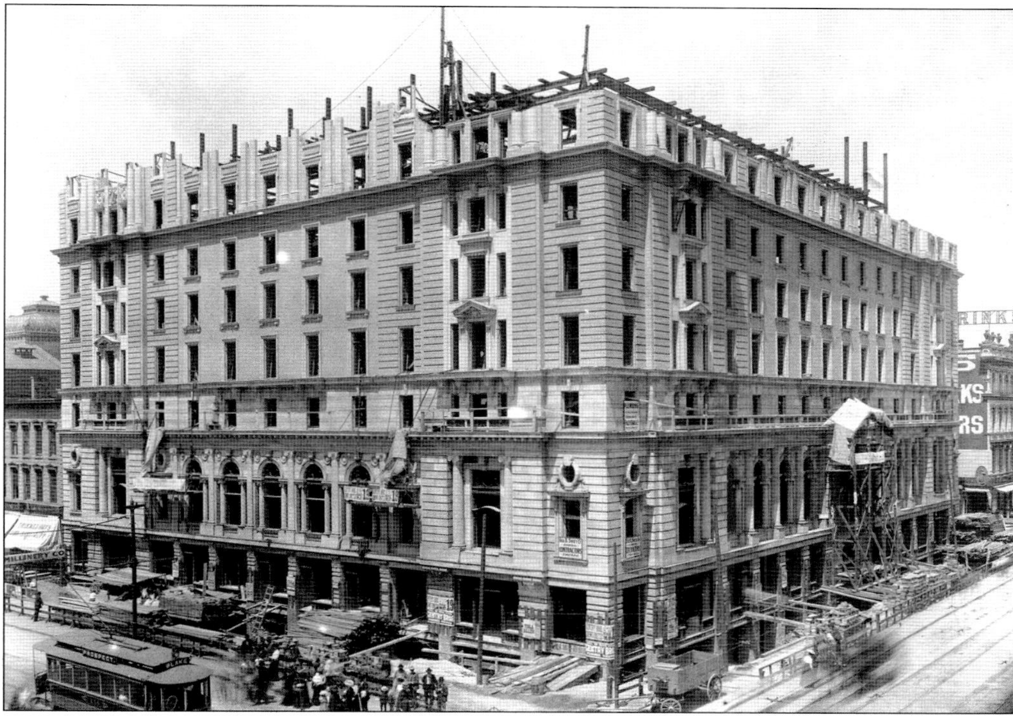

Claypool Hotel Under Construction—1903. (Indiana Historical Society Bass Photo Collection #67290-F.)

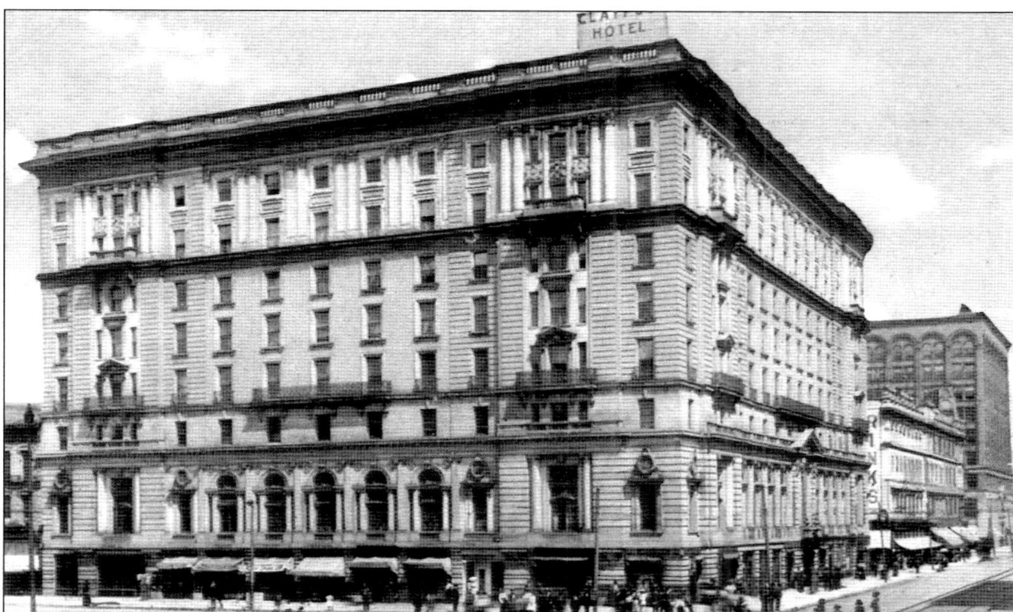

Postcard Image of Newly Completed Claypool Hotel—1905. There were still very few automobiles on city streets—most visitors arrived by train.

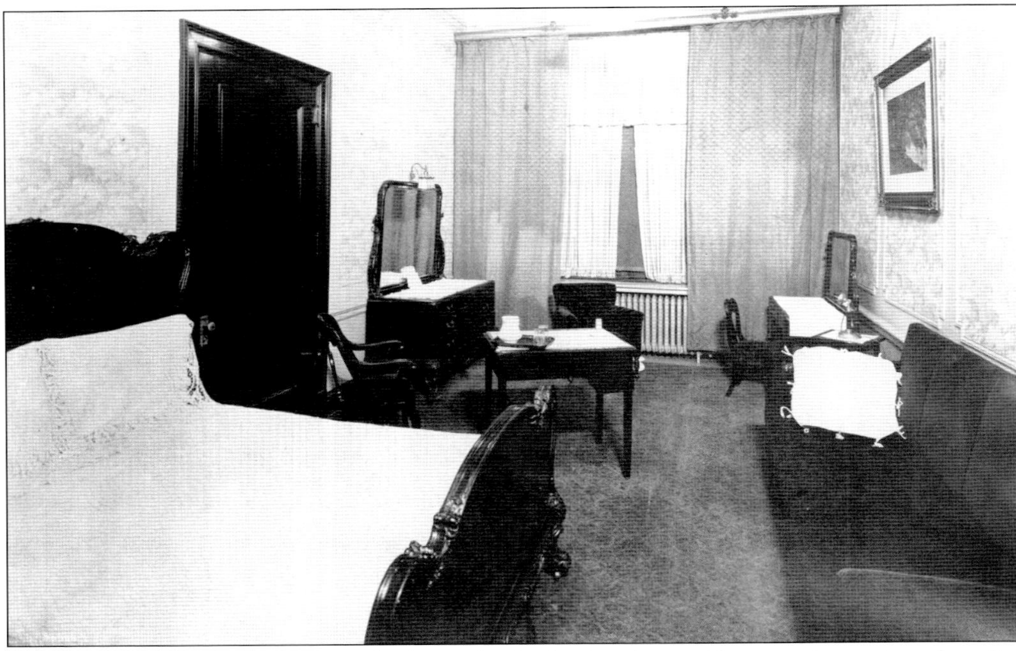

GUEST ROOM—1921. Tiny by today's standards, the hotel was able to wedge no less than five pieces of furniture and three chairs into this typical guest room. (Indiana Historical Society Bass Photo Collection #55566-F.)

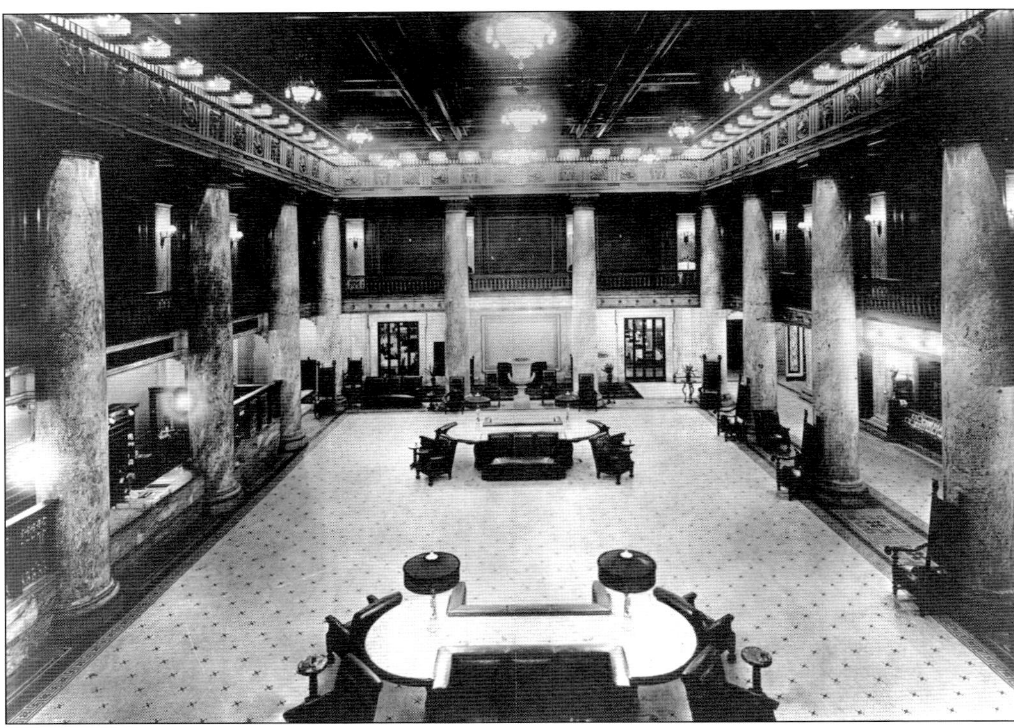

MAIN LOBBY—1924. (Indiana Historical Society Bass Photo Collection #94007-F.)

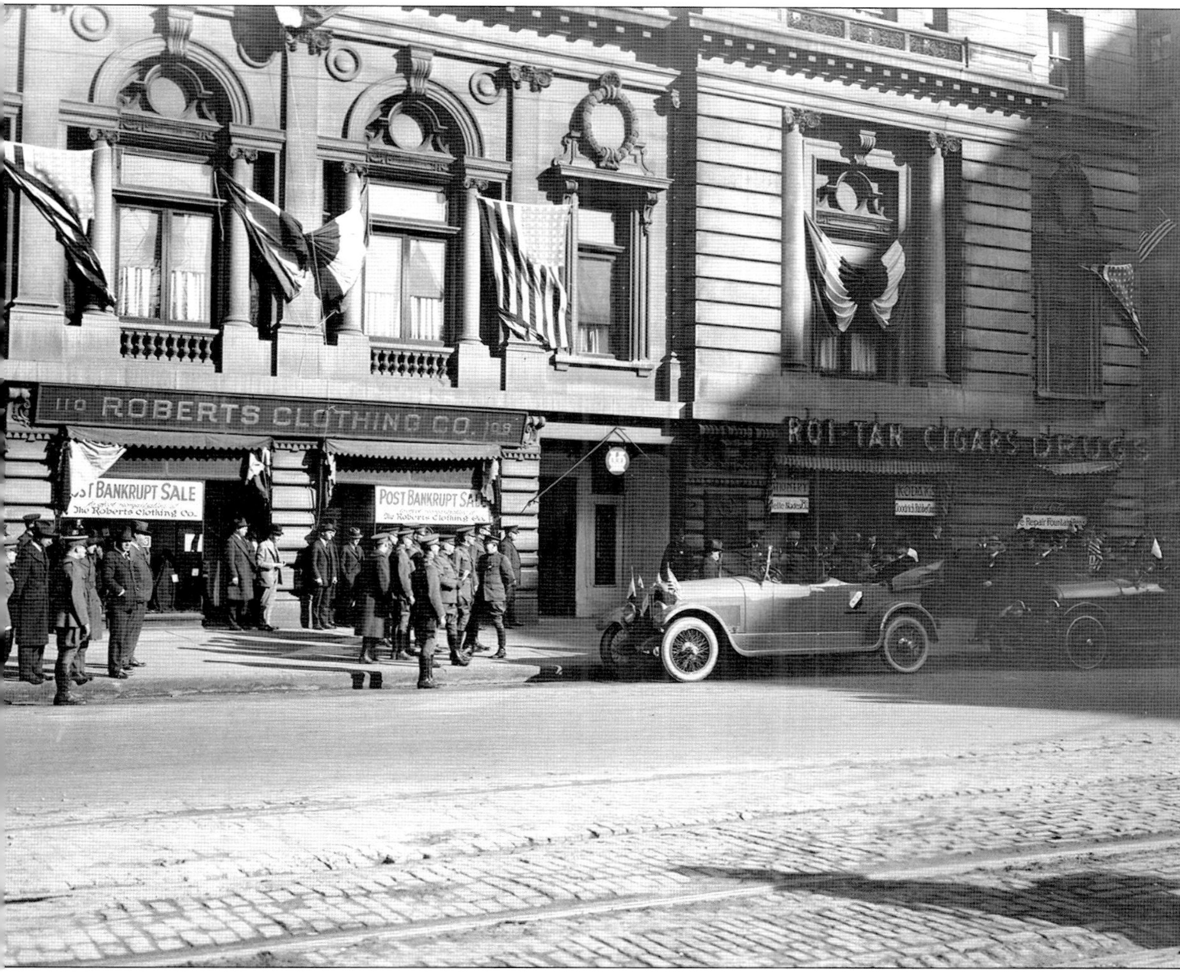

MARSHAL FOCH DAY—NOVEMBER 4, 1921. Ferdinand Foch was commander of the western front in World War I, and the American Legion organized a tour of the U.S. for him with a stop in Indianapolis. Foch arrived at Union Station in the morning, and was driven to the Claypool Hotel for a reception where this picture was taken. Later he had lunch with the governor, watched a specially-organized 25-mile race at the Indianapolis Motor Speedway, helped dedicate the Indiana World War Memorial, and capped off his busy day with a dinner back at the Claypool. After attending a rally at the Cadle Tabernacle where over 14,000 guests joined him, he left again that evening. (Indiana Historical Society Bass Photo Collection #76455-F.)

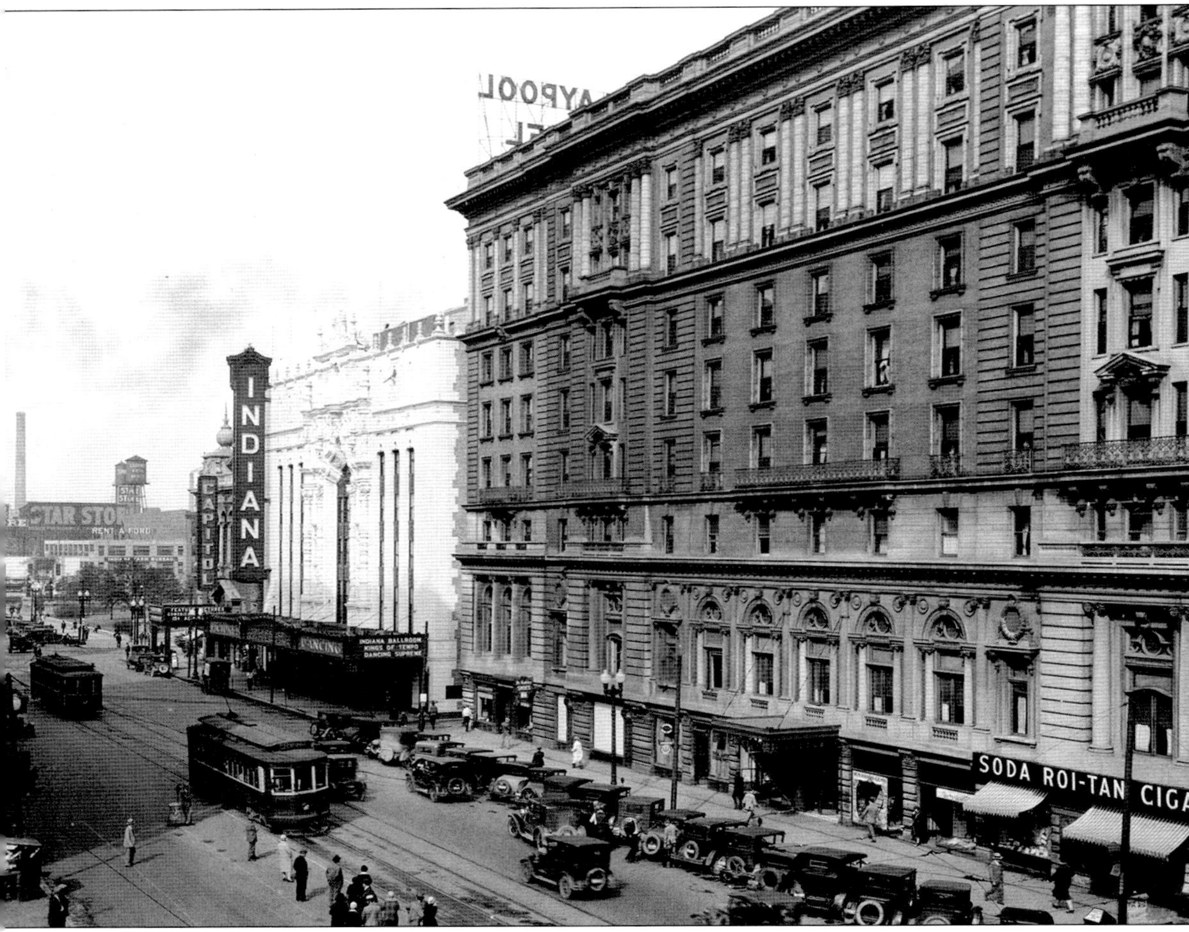

Claypool Hotel and Indiana Theater—1927. The massive Indiana Theater was built in 1927 immediately to the West of the Claypool Hotel on Washington Street. Originally housing a 3,200-seat theater, the largest ever built in Indianapolis; it also featured a bowling alley, a soda fountain, a billiard room, and a barbershop. It was a working cinema until 1975, when the Indiana Repertory Theater purchased and remodeled it in 1980. (Indiana Historical Society Bass Photo Collection #204197-F.)

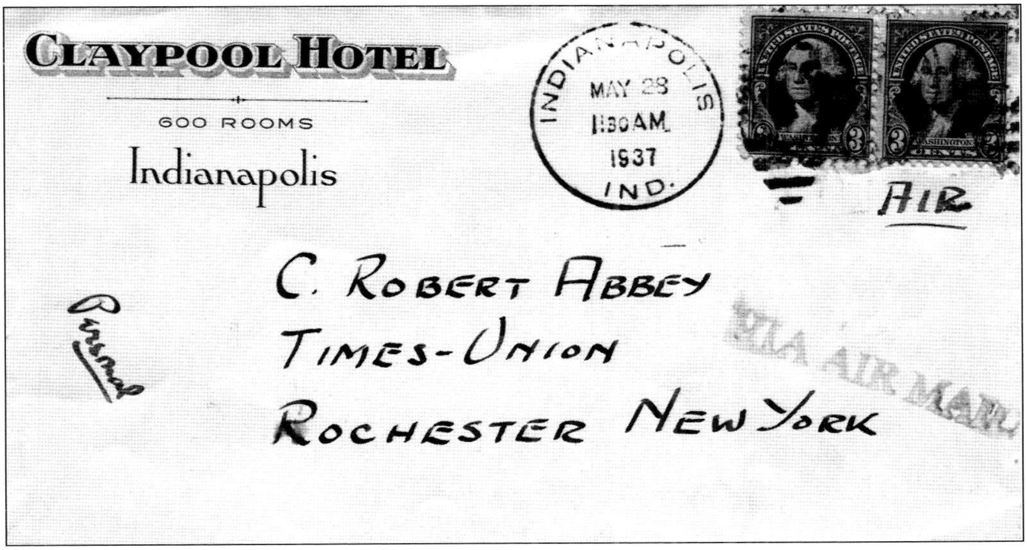

HOTEL GUEST ENVELOPE—1937. Sent from the hotel during the peak of its popularity, this envelope is proud to describe why Indianapolis was such a rail and transportation hub at the time. The Claypool existed at a time when the primary method of travel was rail, and, being situated only a few blocks from Union Station, it served as a home away from home for business travelers and tourists alike. Owing to the date of the postmark and the destination address, the sender might have been a newspaper correspondent in town for the Indianapolis 500-Mile Race. In the early days of automobile travel, roads between cities were mostly rut-filled dirt paths. The last thing that these mud-covered adventurers wanted to do was trudge through the lobby of an ornate downtown hotel, and so auto parks and motor courts sprang up on the outskirts of town. Eventually these would develop into the motels and suburban hotels of today, rendering facilities like the Claypool obsolete.

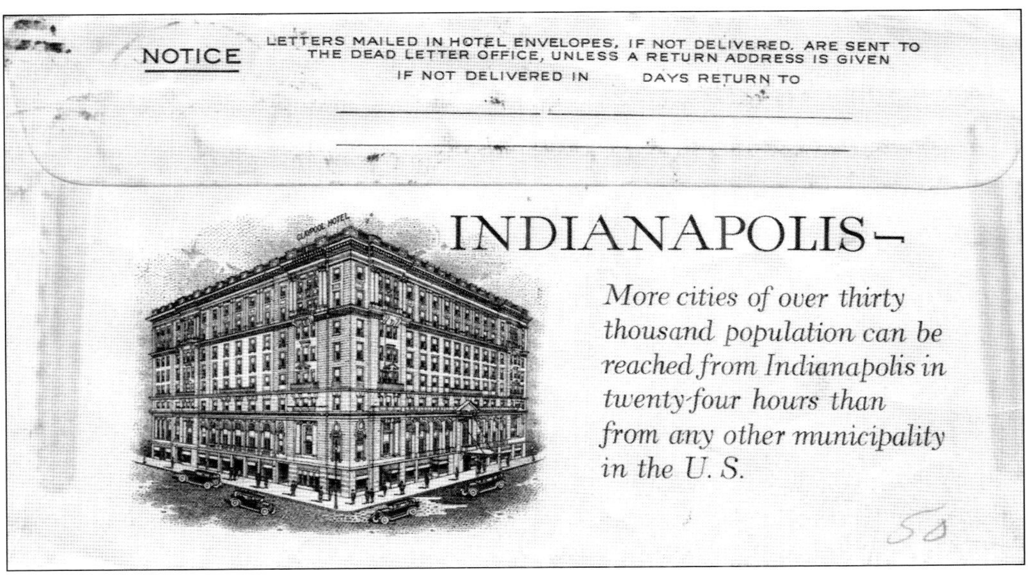

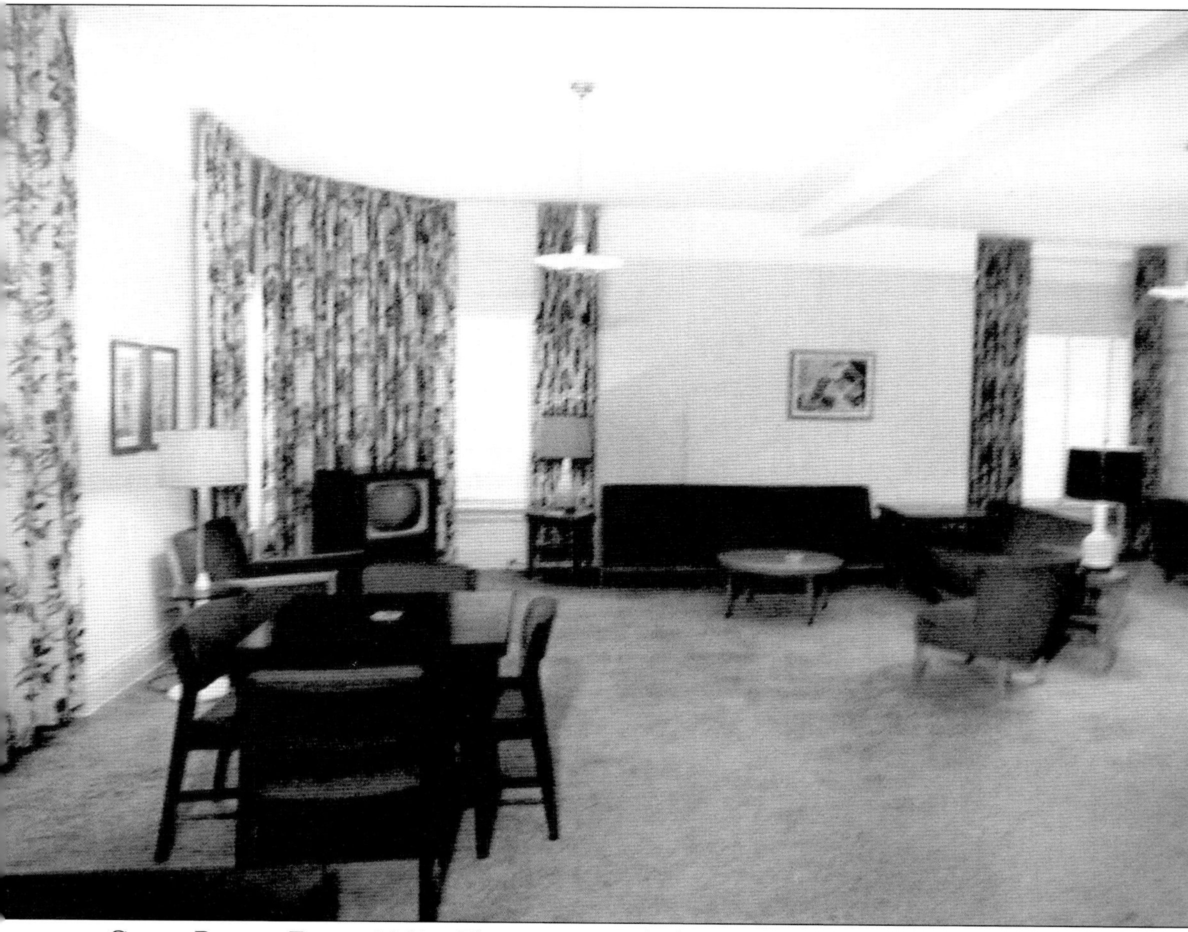

GUEST ROOM—EARLY 1960S. This promotional photograph of a corner room at the hotel tried to show how spacious the guest accommodations were. In reality, there were many different sized rooms. Some, built for business travelers in the 1920s, were likely large enough only for a bed and small dressing table. This room was likely originally two rooms, with the wall removed where the beam appears across the ceiling.

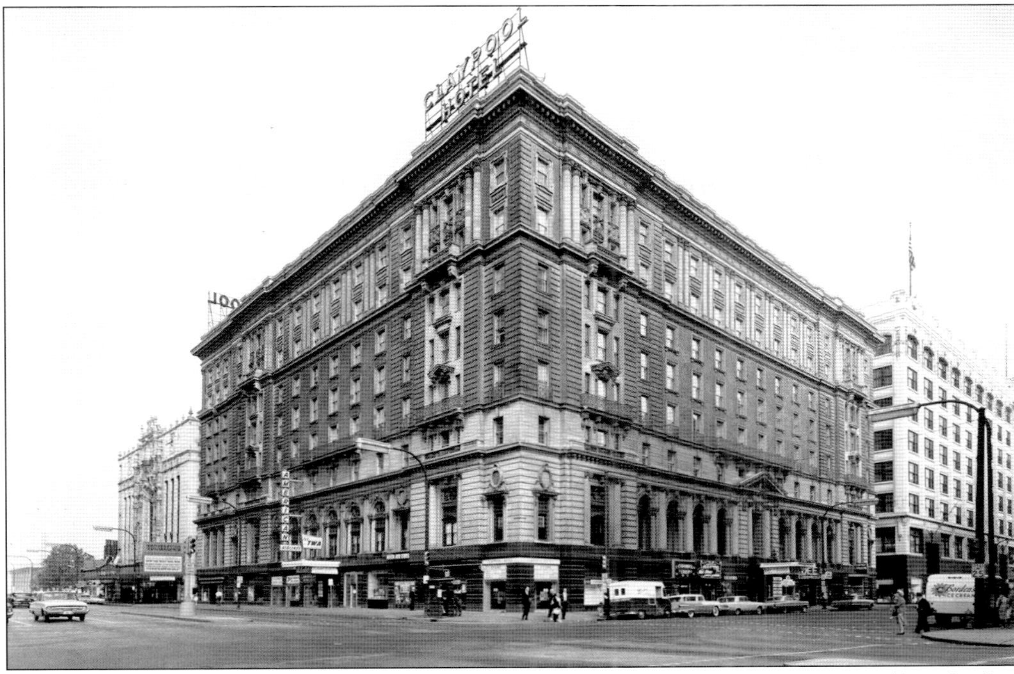

Claypool Hotel—1963. By this time competition from newer hotels, especially suburban ones, meant hard times for the once-great hotel. (Indiana Historical Society Bass Photo Collection #312516.)

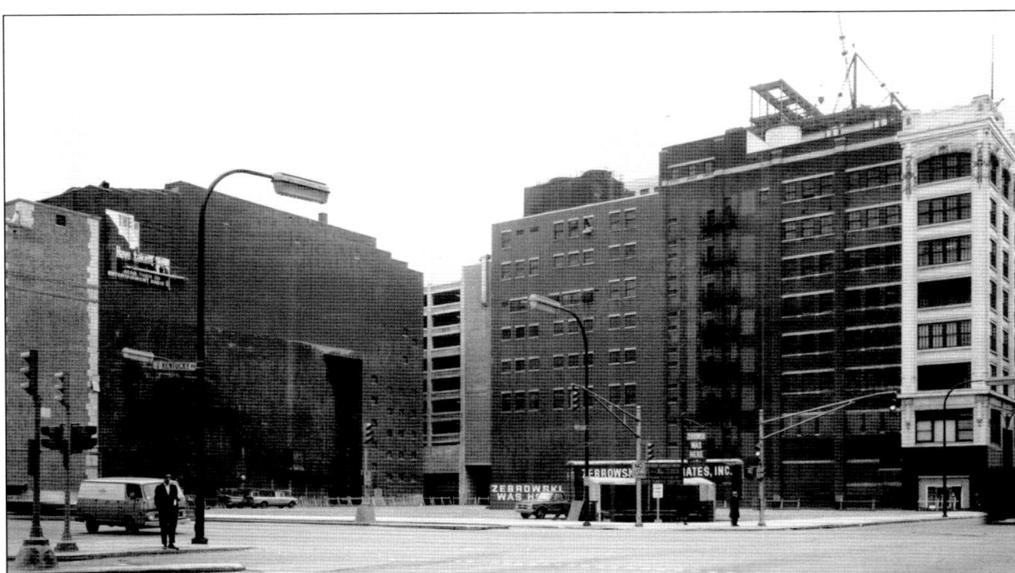

Claypool Hotel Site—1969. After a devastating fire in June of 1967 that closed the hotel, the giant sign "Zebrowski Was Here" proclaims the name of the company that demolished the building in 1969. The space served as a parking lot until Simon Property Group built Claypool Court and the Embassy Suites Hotel on the site in 1985. (Indiana Historical Society Bass Photo Collection #325661.)

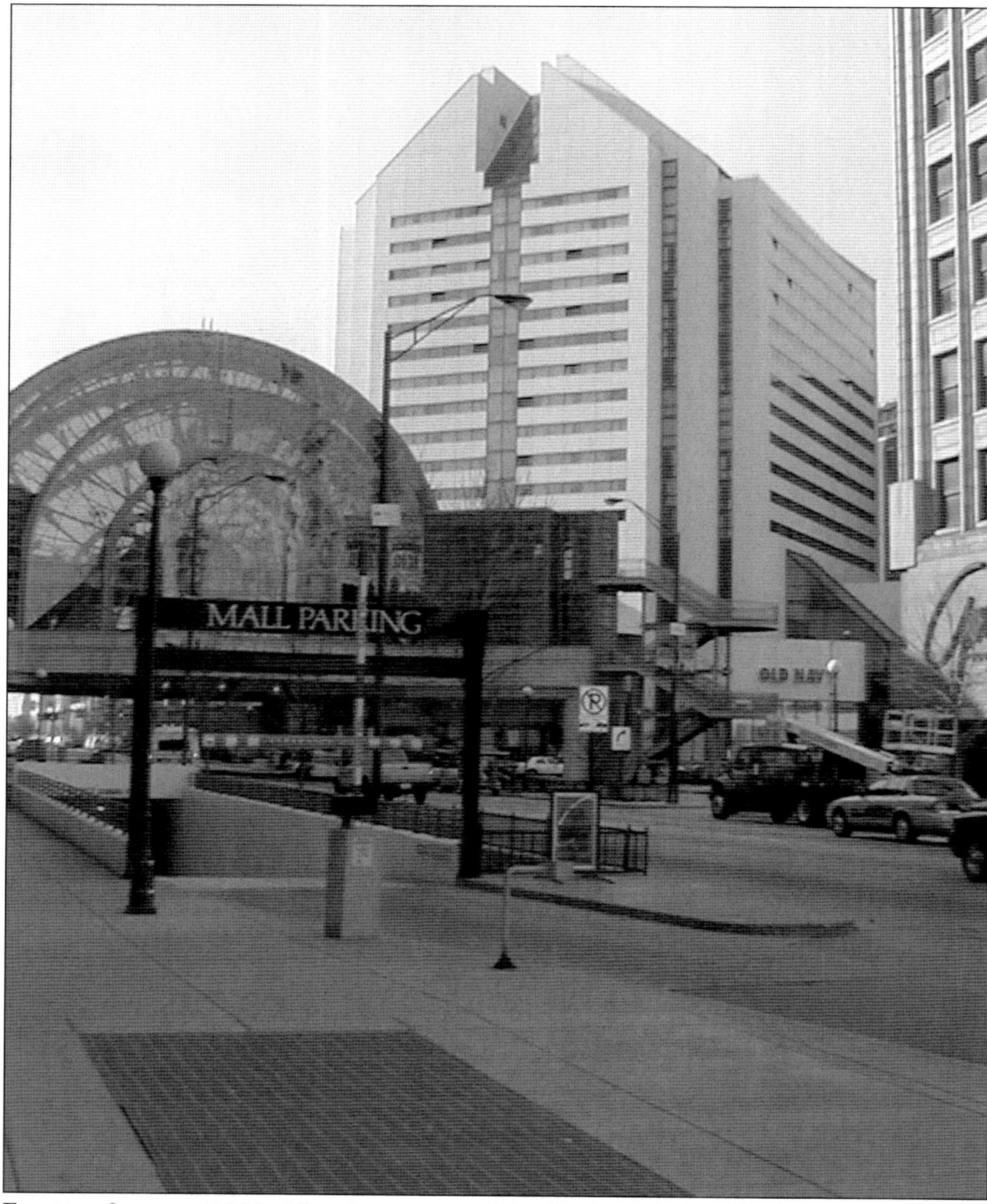

EMBASSY SUITES—2002. After the opening of the Circle Center Mall, owners renovated and connected Claypool Court to the mall structure through the Arts Garden, a glass and steel structure suspended over the street corner. Several retail stores occupy the first two floors, and the Embassy Suites hotel occupies the rest. This photograph looks west down Washington Street near the entrance to the old L.S. Ayres downtown store.

Seven

THE STUTZ COMPANY

After slaving away at a series of auto parts companies for years, Harry Clayton Stutz decided that it was time to make his own automobile.

Born on September 12, 1876, in Dayton, Ohio, he had only a grade school education. He went to work for a time at National Cash Register while taking classes in mechanical engineering at night. Upon graduation, he moved to Indianapolis to be close to what was then the headquarters of the automotive industry. Taking a series of jobs, first at an axle company, then a tire firm, and finally a carburetor concern, he learned how to build the critical parts of autos—which he applied on his first design job for the now-defunct American Motors Company: the Underslung.

The name came from the unique way Stutz "hung" the body from the chassis instead of mounting it on top of springs. It gave the car a unique look and a smoother ride—but there were other innovations too. He created a ball-bearing gearbox that allowed him lay the drive shaft almost vertical, which greatly reduced the loss of power experienced by the angled drive shafts of competitors. The car was a genuine success—but Harry did not stay around for long.

He moved to the Marion Motor Car Company and designed a combination transmission and differential gearbox. Calling it a "transaxle," it is a key technology used in front-wheel drive cars to this day. He formed the Stutz Auto Parts Company to sell this device.

That was when Harry heard about a 500-mile race some of the other automotive leaders in Indianapolis were organizing at a new track west of town. Knowing that he needed a "big splash" to launch his own company into a crowded market, he hastily constructed a car at night in only five weeks and entered the race, hoping for a top ten finish.

On May 30, 1911, he came in 11th, which itself was a major victory considering that nearly half of the field dropped out before the end of the seven-hour race. He created the slogan, "The Car That Made Good in a Day" and announced the new Ideal Car Company in partnership with Henry F. Campbell. The company built their first factory at 221 West Tenth Street.

In the beginning, the company produced passenger car versions of this successful racecar as a four-passenger coupe, a five-passenger touring car and an open-top roadster. By 1912, the roadster version of this "Stutz Model A" evolved into the "Bearcat." Produced for a decade, it became not only the company's signature car, but also a classic sought after by collectors to this day. With a top speed of over 80 miles per hour, it became a legend on the racetrack as well, winning races all over the country and feeding the marketing engine of the young company.

In 1913, Harry merged Ideal Car Company with his other enterprise, the Stutz Auto Parts Company, to form the new Stutz Motor Company. Increasing demand necessitated a new factory, so they purchased most of the 1000 block of North Capital Avenue. The first building on the site, building "A", was completed in 1914. By 1917, the company's output was 2,207 cars, and the factory expanded again.

In 1915, Stutz organized a campaign to demonstrate the reliability of their cars. They hired Erwin G. "Cannonball" Baker to drive a Stutz from San Diego to New York. He completed the task in 11 days, 7 hours, and 15 minutes. This story inspired the *Cannonball Run* movies of the 1980s. Erwin went on to become the first commissioner of NASCAR.

Like many visionaries, Harry was not quite as good of an executive as he was an engineer. A group of Wall Street investors, led by financier Alan Ryan, bought controlling interest in the company in 1916. Harry agreed to stay on as president for three years, but began selling off his interest slowly over that time.

In 1919, Harry left the company he founded, but he did not leave the car business. He formed the HCS Motor Car Company (named after his initials) and the Stutz Fire Apparatus Company just a few blocks away at 1402 North Capital. The fire engine company proved to be the more successful of the two ventures, and Harry became a major producer of fire equipment in the early 1920s. Many larger city fire departments, including Indianapolis, were anxious to get rid of their old horse-drawn manual pump trucks, and Harry was there to serve the need.

The HCS car company struggled, however. A post-World War I recession hit the country in 1920, and many smaller automobile companies were finding business conditions difficult. In 1924, Harry left the Fire Engine company to focus on HCS, but he would be unable to replicate the magic of his first car company. In 1925, he gave up. He divorced his wife of 27 years, remarried, and moved to the sleepy orchard town of Orlando, Florida. Without Harry at the helm, both companies floundered. Only 3,001 cars had been built by HCS when both it and the fire engine company shut down in 1926.

Back at Stutz, a director at Bethlehem Steel, Charles M. Schwab, purchased the company in 1922. The company was also unable to avoid the recession and they reduced prices dramatically. With sales dropping, Schwab brought in a new president, Fredrick E. Moskovics, a talented engineer, and work began on the development of a new luxury car from the ground up.

In January of 1926, the new Stutz Vertical Eight, Series AA, made its debut. Featuring "safety glass," which had thin wires pressed between two panes of glass, he marketed the car as the "Safety Stutz." In the boom times of the mid 1920s, the car sold extremely well.

However, the boom was short-lived, as the stock market crash in 1929 decimated the luxury car market. Stutz was in a worse position than many manufacturers, as its prices were higher and they had no low-cost lines to pick up the slack. In May of 1931, Stutz started selling the DV 32, named for the 32 valves supporting its eight-cylinder engine; but in 1934, Stutz built only six cars.

In 1930, the company attempted to diversify by introducing a light delivery truck called the "Pak-Age-Car." With the car business failing, the company discontinued its automobile line in 1935 to build the trucks exclusively. Unable to grow in a depressed economy, the company failed in 1939 after a 28-year run. Harry himself passed away on June 26, 1930; he was buried at Crown Hill Cemetery.

After the Stutz Company vacated their factory, Eli Lilly and Company purchased the building and set up a packaging division, "Creative Packaging," in 1940 that stayed in the building for 42 years. Eli Lilly himself was a preservationist, and the company took good care of the facility. Indianapolis Developer Turner Woodward purchased the building in 1992 and created the "Stutz Business Center," dividing the building into offices that house not only small companies but also a growing community of artisans.

Investment banker James D. O'Donnell revived the Stutz name in 1968 when he created a new "Stutz Motor Car of America." In 1963, renowned designer and Vice President of Chrysler Corporation Virgil M. Exner published a series of concept designs in Esquire magazine for what Stutz, Duesenberg, Packard, and Mercer cars might look like if they were still around. Wanting to make the Stutz design a reality, O'Donnell set up a manufacturing plant in Italy and proceeded to both hand-build and heavily modify a series of General Motors full-sized cars, throughout the 1970s and 1980s, into super-luxury cars. Elvis Presley was one of the first customers in 1971, and the order list filled with entertainers and world leaders. Selling only about 50 of the hand-built cars a year, the company faded by 1988.

Today Stutz lives on not only in the factory building, but also in the hearts of car collectors around the world. Together with Packard, Duesenburg, and others, Stutz represents the golden age of automobile manufacturing, and another piece of "Lost Indianapolis."

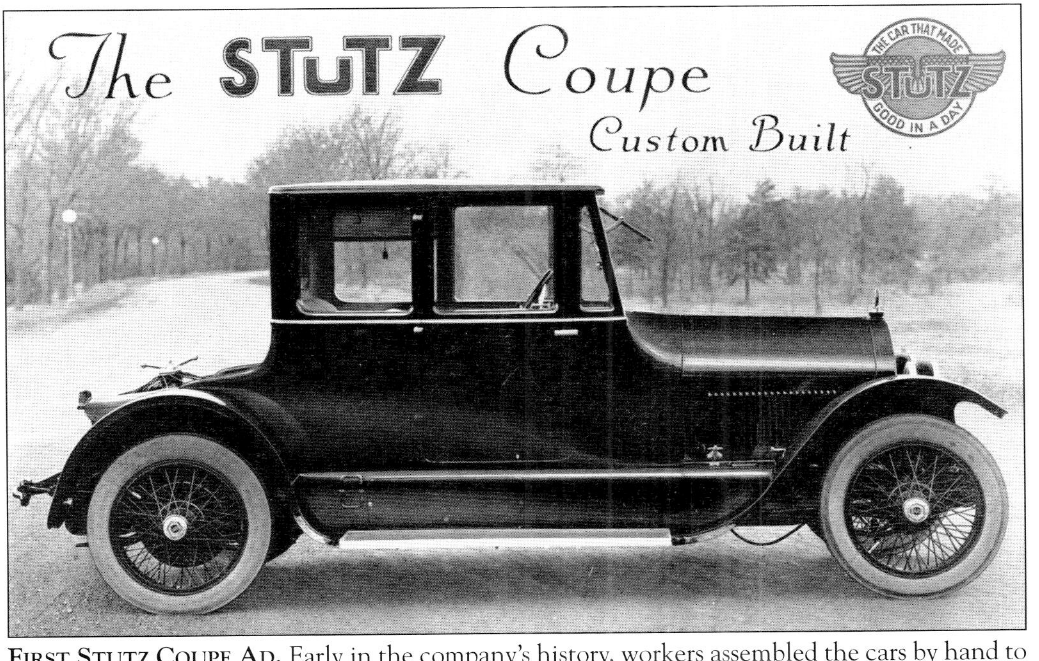

First Stutz Coupe Ad. Early in the company's history, workers assembled the cars by hand to each customer's specifications. (Indiana Historical Society Bass Photo Collection #5881.)

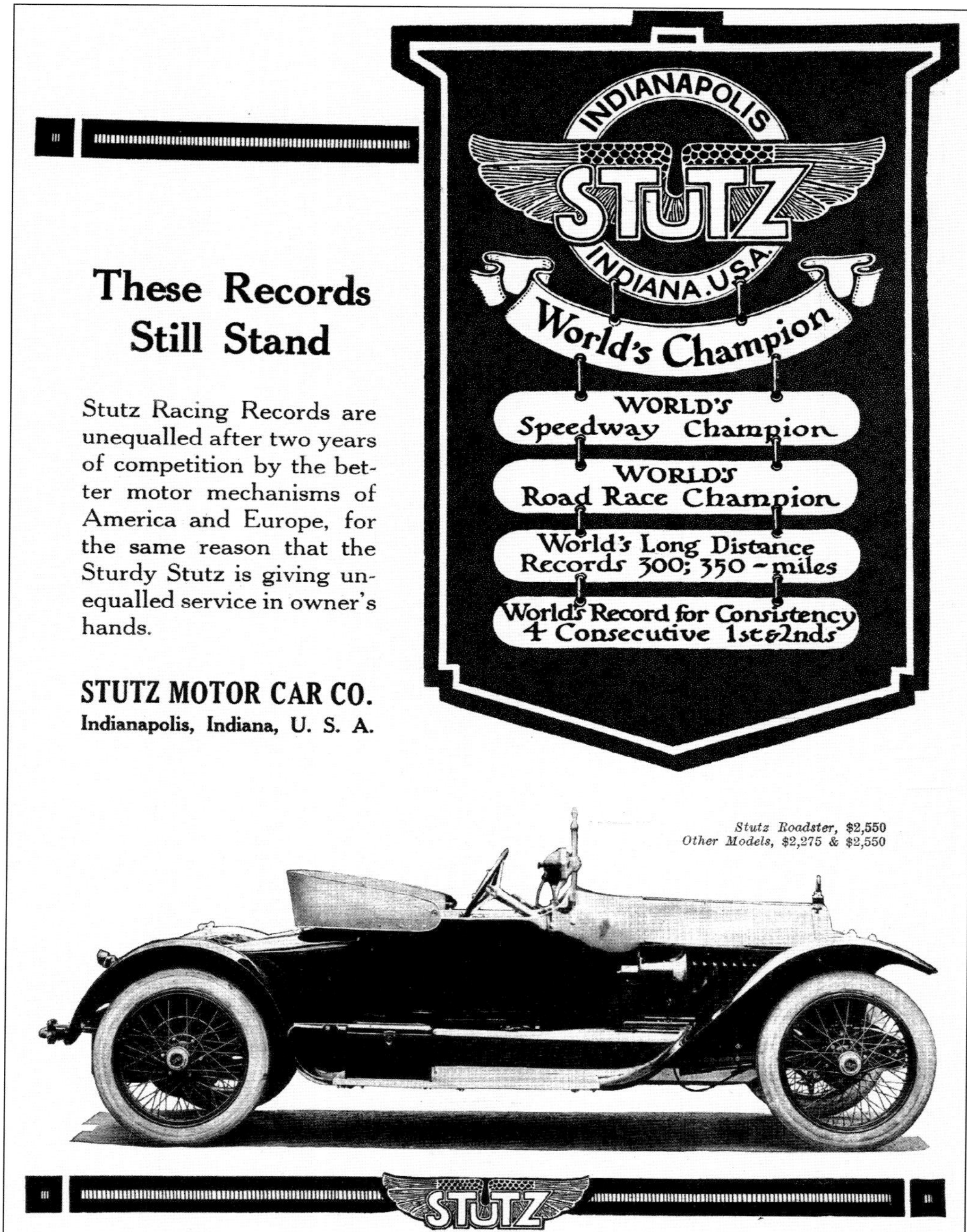

STUTZ ADVERTISEMENT—1916. Appearing in the October 26, 1916 issue of the now-defunct *Motor Age* magazine, this advertisement depicts a Stutz roadster, otherwise known as the "Bearcat," selling for $2,550. This was a giant sum money at the time, equivalent to over $42,000 today.

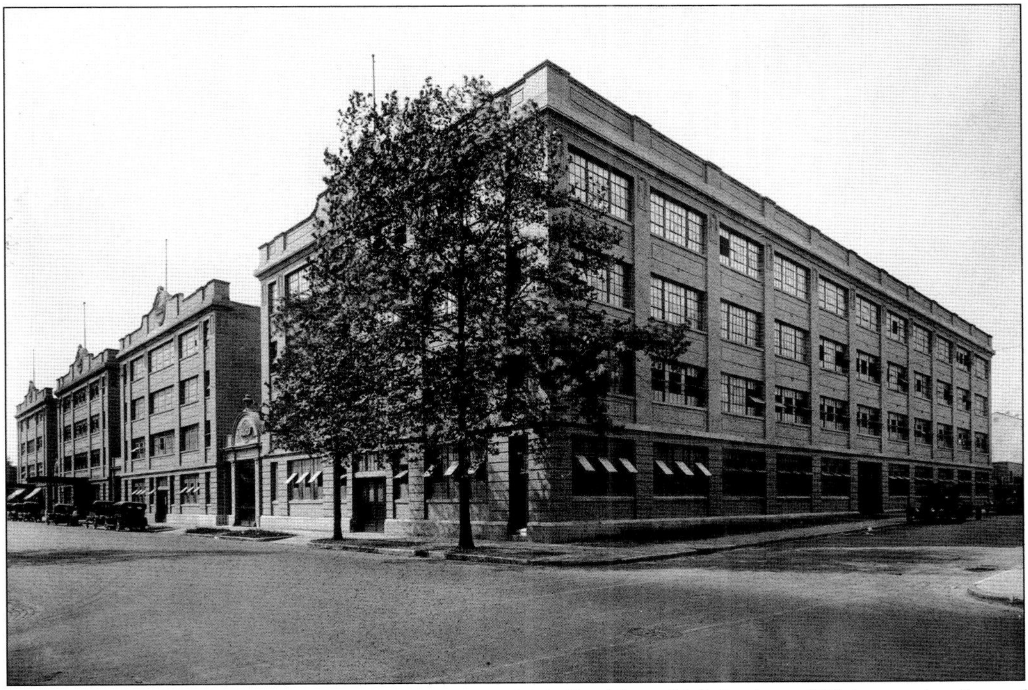

STUTZ MOTOR CAR COMPANY BUILDINGS—1920. Building "A", built in 1914, was the first of a series of similar buildings constructed along north Capitol Avenue in Indianapolis. (Indiana Historical Society Bass Photo Collection.)

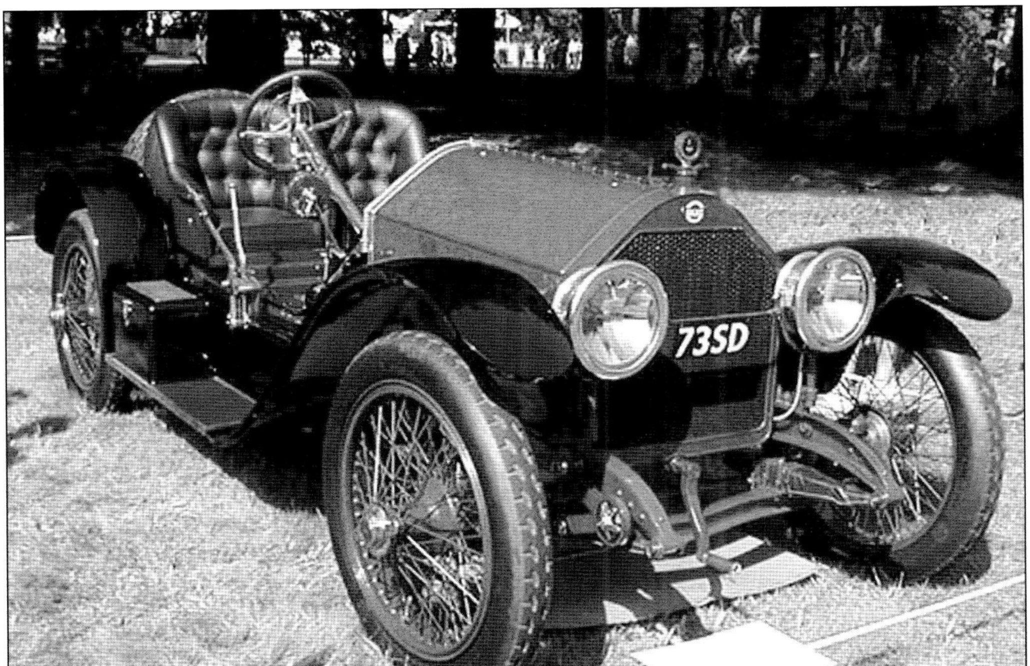

1917 STUTZ BEARCAT. One of the true classic automobiles.

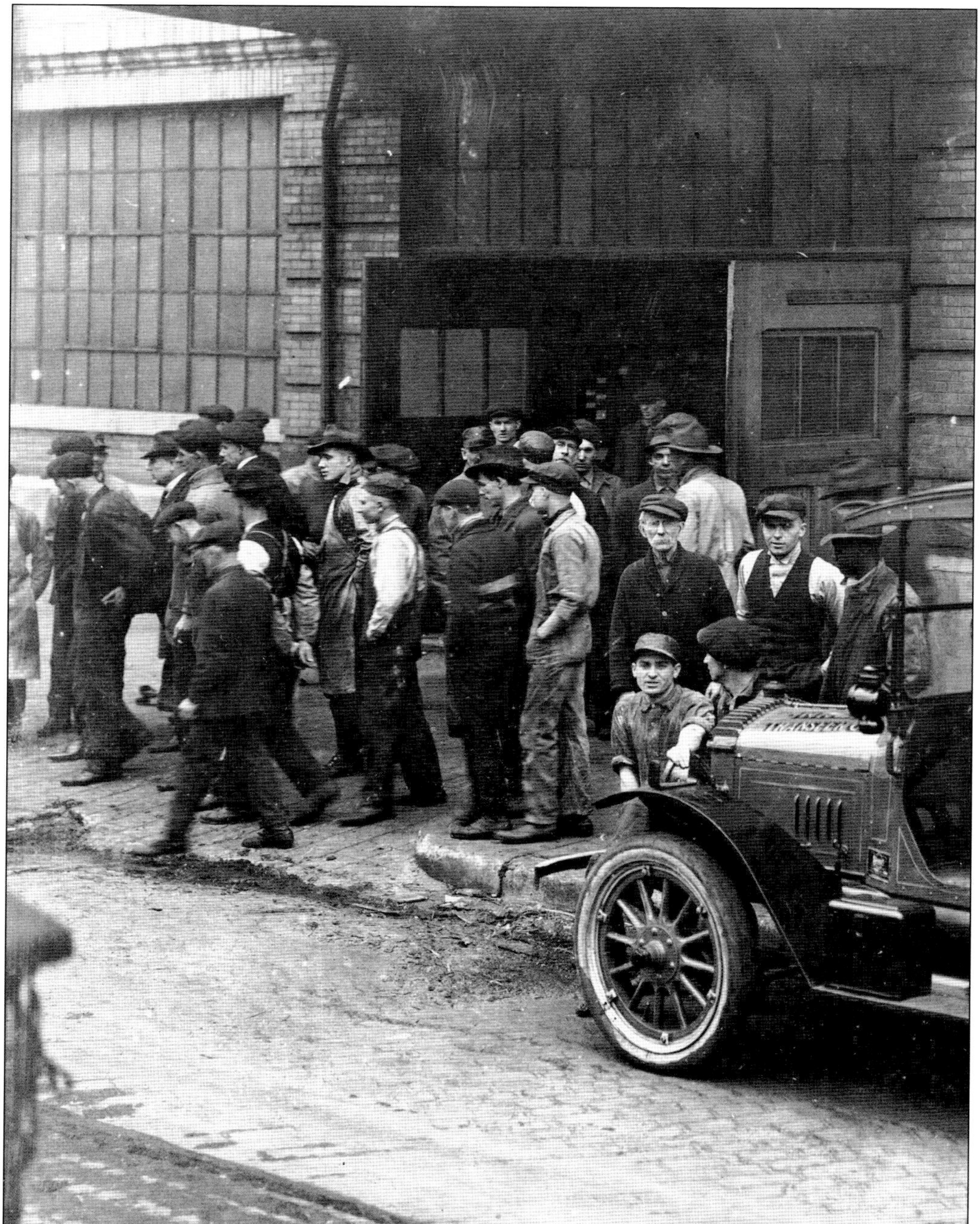

FACTORY WORKERS OUTSIDE STUTZ PLANT—1919. The end of the shift at the peak of the company's success. (Indiana Historical Society Bass Photo Collection #68695-F.)

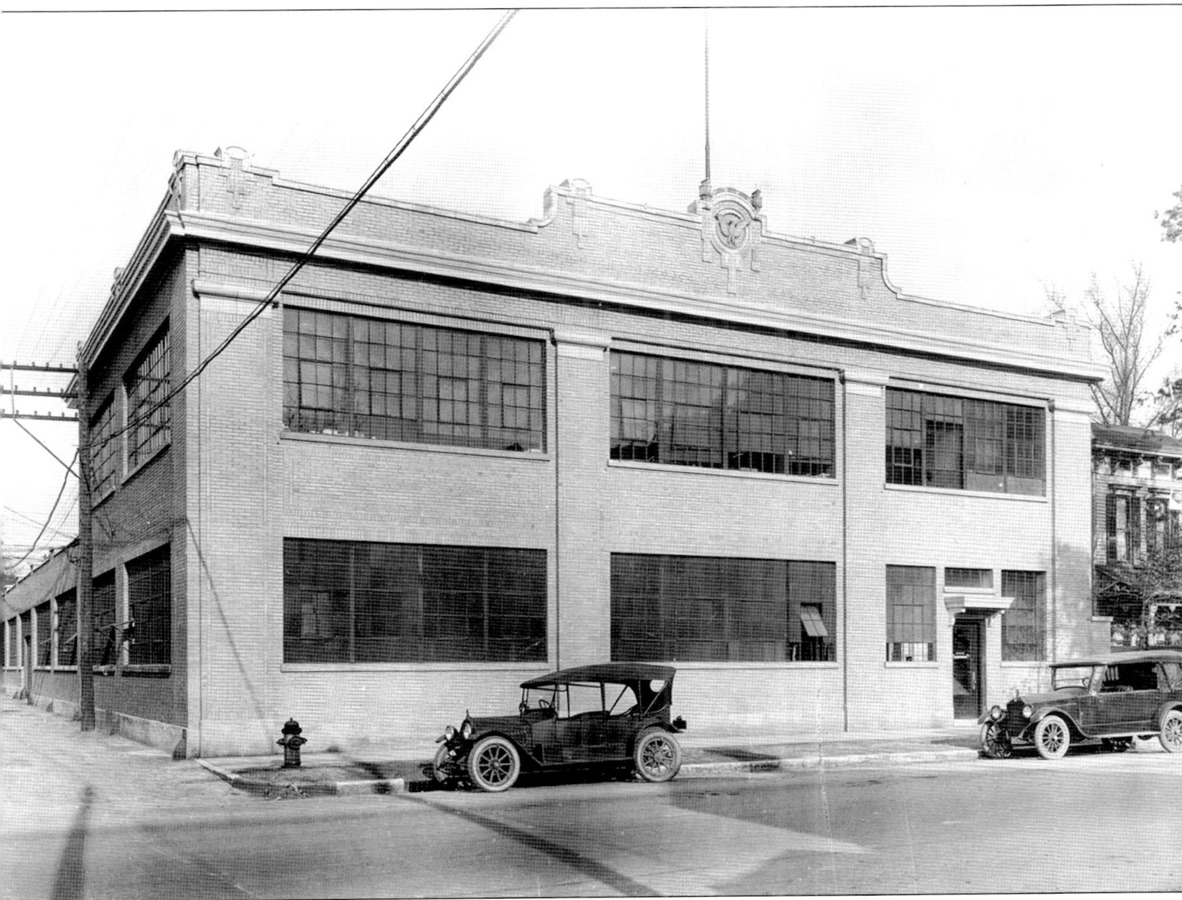

STUTZ FIRE ENGINE COMPANY—1920. (Indiana Historical Society Bass Photo Collection #70335.)

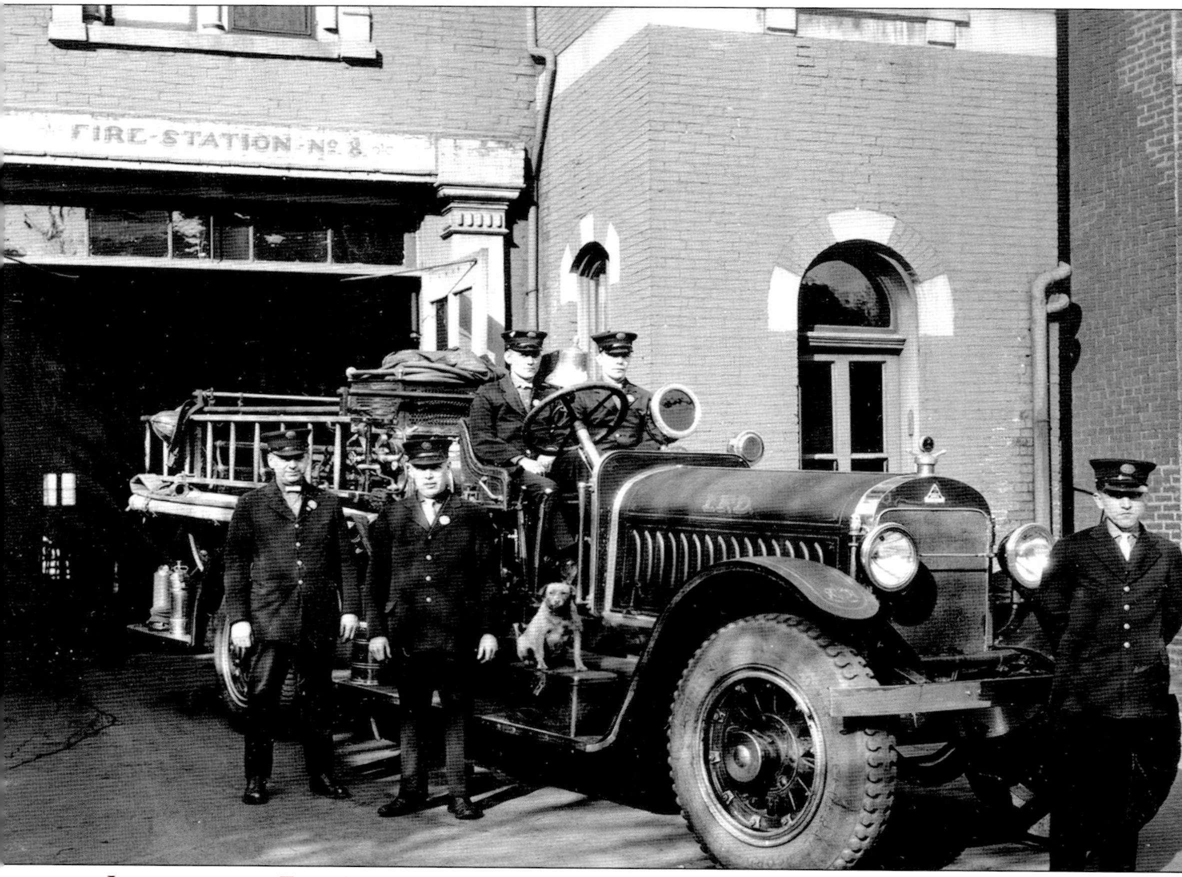

INDIANAPOLIS FIRE DEPARTMENT STATION 8—1926. Firefighters pose with their 1920 Stutz Pumper. Being a hometown company, Stutz supplied much of the Indianapolis Fire Department's equipment. (Indiana Historical Society Bass Photo Collection.)

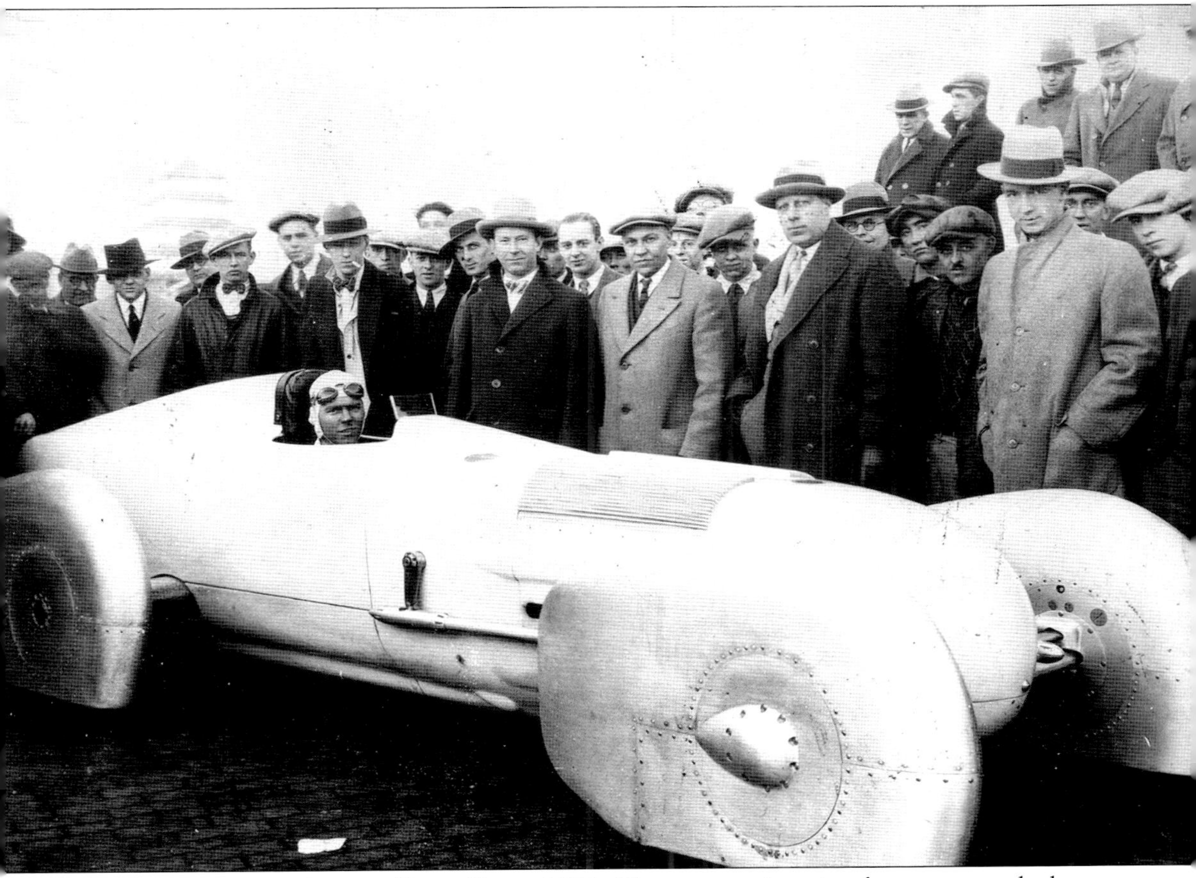

STUTZ BLACKHAWK SPECIAL RACE CAR—1928. The company's racing fortunes soured when Frank Lockhart, attempting to set a new land speed record at Daytona Beach, overturned at more than 200 miles per hour and died. (Indiana Historical Society Bass Photo Collection.)

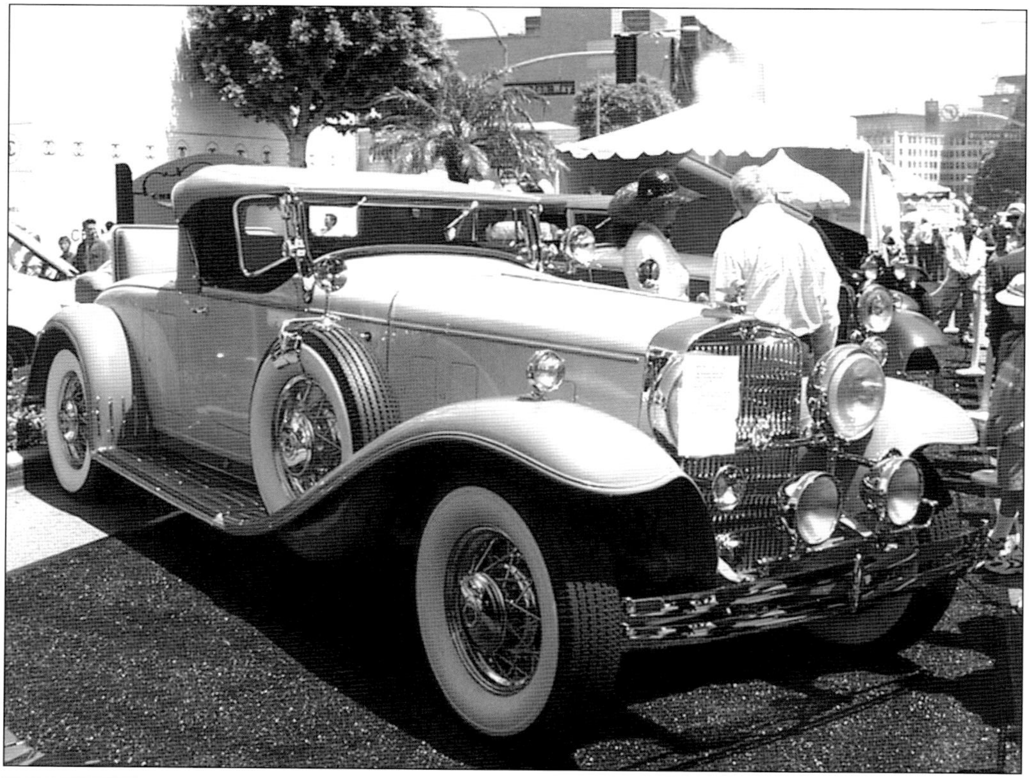

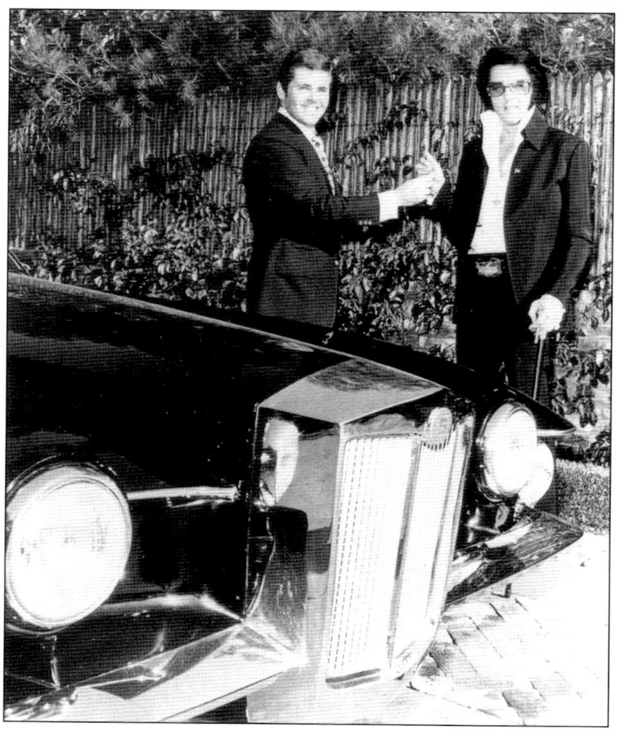

1933 Stutz DV Roadster. The DV 32 was the successor of the Bearcat, with a guaranteed top speed of 100 miles per hour.

Elvis Gets Keys to His Stutz—1971. Elvis eventually owned four of the hand-built luxury cars, and they were the only ones he personally drove.

Eight

Fisher Automobile and Prest-O-Lite

Shortly before his death, Carl Fisher liked to walk along the shoreline in Miami Beach, Florida, and reflect on the long journey that brought him there. It is the story of a true American original.

Fisher was born on January 12, 1874, in Greensburg, Indiana. It was difficult for Carl to pay attention in school because of a severe astigmatism, and he dropped out in 1886. He held a couple of jobs, including work as a newspaper and cigar salesperson on trains in and out of Indianapolis. About that time, a bicycle craze started to sweep America, and the enterprising Carl opened a very successful bicycle repair shop with his brothers in 1891. To promote his shop he started creating promotional stunts, which included a tightrope walk over Washington Street (in a padded suit, of course).

As the bicycle craze died down around 1900, another took its place—the automobile. Frequently these same bicycle shops turned to creating new devices, and Fisher's was no exception. He went into partnership with his friend, Barney Oldfield, and opened what was probably the very first auto dealership in America. Fisher began promoting Packards, Reos, Stutz, and Oldsmobiles in the same manner. At one point, he pushed a car off a building, started it up, and drove it off to demonstrate its durability.

Another time he actually strapped a car to a hot air balloon and flew it over the city—and then seemingly drove it back into town to mobs of cheering crowds. Actually, in order to make the car light enough, he had the engine removed, and drove a different, pre-planted car back into town.

1904 proved to be a watershed year for Fisher. The owner of a patent for a sealed, gas-filled automobile headlamp approached Fisher and convinced him to market the device. This was the first practical sealed beam headlight—before that time, gas flames and even candles had been tried as methods for seeing at night, as the bumpy roads would not allow the fragile filament of an Edison-style lamp to survive. Fisher brought in James Allison, his friend from the days of racing bicycles, and they called the company "Prest-O-Lite."

Soon, Fisher's firm supplied nearly every headlamp used on an automobile, along with refill canisters of gas, which made him very wealthy. Simultaneously he became business associates and friends with all of the great auto magnates of the time. He built plants in several spots around the country to supply the demand, with one of the in what would become Speedway, Indiana. Unfortunately, the gas that filled the lamps was highly explosive, which meant that Prest-O-Lite's factories frequently caught fire. After one such explosion at the plant in Omaha, Nebraska, frantic managers telegraphed Indianapolis with the message "Omaha left at four-thirty."

In 1911, the Union Carbide company bought Prest-O-Lite for the then-unbelievable sum of $9 million. In 1912, Fisher and Allison used some of their fortune to back a young Purdue

University graduate named John Esterline who had devised a reliable electrical starter system. Ironically, the widespread use of this starter would make an on-board electrical system standard on most cars, which in turn put their former company out of the head light business. Another popular use for the gas canisters was as power for welding torches—which you can still purchase to this day, under the brand name "Prest-O-Light".

In 1909, Fisher and Allison joined with another bicycling friend, Arthur Newby and a fourth person, Frank Wheeler, each putting up $250,000 to create a proving ground for automobiles in Indianapolis. At the time, Indiana was the heart of the automotive industry, with more companies based in Indiana than in Michigan. They created a two-and-a-half mile track, paved it with crushed stone and called it the Indianapolis Motor Speedway. The first race at the track was actually a motorcycle race, to which the public didn't respond. The first automobile race, held on August 19, 1909 was deadly—six people died, including two spectators.

Convinced the crushed stone was the problem, Fisher convinced Newby to purchase and install 3.2 million paving bricks over the next year and a half. This would create a new, durable, relatively smooth surface—one that allowed the first 500-mile race to take place on Memorial Day of 1911. People still call the track "The Brickyard," and a one-yard strip of the original brick forms the start/finish line of the track today.

As with the track, Carl again proved himself a master at convincing others to pay for his ideas. Fisher recognized that the poor road system in America would soon hamper the growth of his automobile industry. He wrote, "The highways of America are built chiefly of politics, whereas the proper material is crushed rock or concrete." On September 1, 1912 at a dinner party for automobile manufacturers, he unveiled his idea for a coast-to-coast road from New York City to California. Founded in July of the following year, the Lincoln Highway Association announced the highway's route in August of 1913.

As work began, Fisher took a vacation in Miami, Florida. He looked over a swampy, bug-infested stretch of land, and in his mind transformed it into the perfect vacation destination for his automobile industry friends—he called it "Miami Beach." In order to get there, however, he had to appeal to the governor of Indiana to start another highway project—this time one that would run from Chicago to Miami. On April 3, 1915 in Chattanooga, Tennessee, the "Dixie Highway" project was born, and just over one year later, the road was opened from Indy all the way to Florida.

As the economy boomed, so did Carl's playground in Florida, growing over 440 percent from 1920 to 1925. In 1925, at the height of the boom, observers estimated Carl's wealth at $100 million. Unfortunately, in 1926 the end began for Carl as he divorced his wife, Jane. About this same time, the press began to uncover shady land deals that had sprung up around Miami Beach, spawning the proverbial "if you believe that, I have some swamp land in Florida to sell you" phrase.

Carl had also started to develop what he called "the Miami Beach of the north"—at Montauk on the eastern tip of Long Island. In September, a hurricane struck and nearly wiped out Miami Beach—over 113 people died. Tourism dropped in 1927. The final blow came in 1929 with the stock market crash—there was no longer a market for high-priced vacation homes. Montauk flopped, and Carl's fortune was lost with so many others. He even had to sell his own house in Miami Beach and declare bankruptcy.

His former partners in the Miami Beach development gave him a salaried position as a publicist and promoter. Carl began to drink heavily, and by 1938 he had cirrhosis of the liver. The man Will Rogers said had done "more unique things, even before I heard of Florida, than any man I ever met," died on July 15, 1939. He had only $52,198 to his name according to an article in the Miami Herald the next day.

A local undertaker cremated him, and the urn stayed in Miami until 1943, when his friends placed it in the family mausoleum at Crown Hill Cemetery in Indianapolis, though not in the space originally reserved for him. Years earlier, on September 22, 1918, a Captain

Robert Hammond of the British Royal Flying Corps crashed during a war bond celebration at the Speedway. Since the family lived in England, Carl temporarily donated his place in the mausoleum until they could come and claim the body. They never did, and to this day, Captain Hammond is in Carl's original place in the structure.

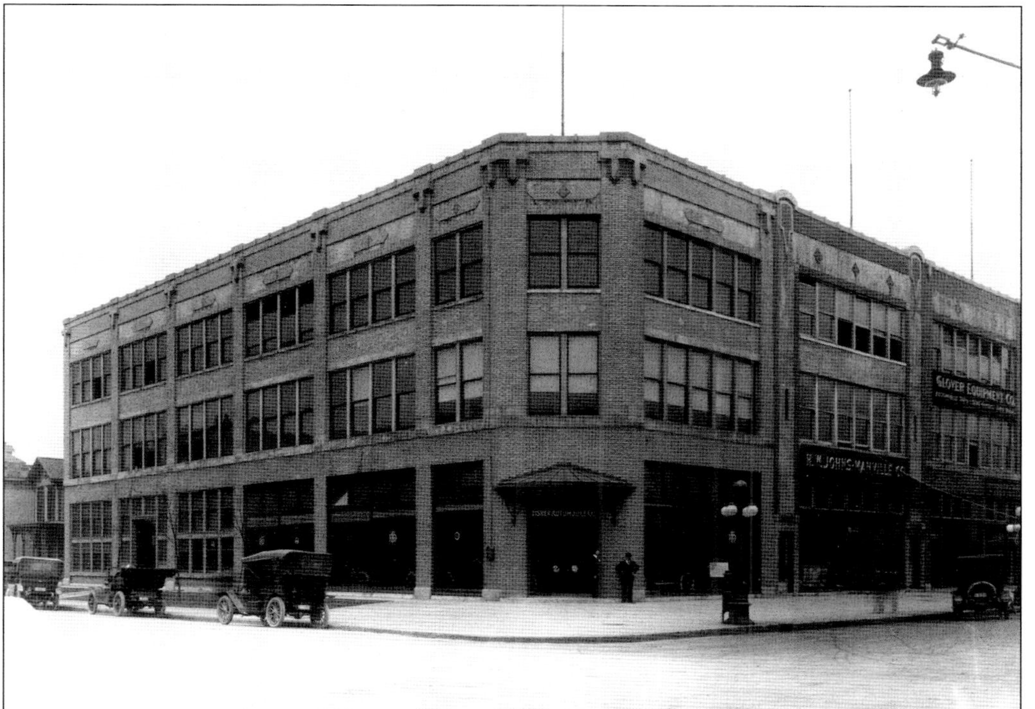

EXTERIOR OF THE FISHER AUTOMOBILE COMPANY—1914.

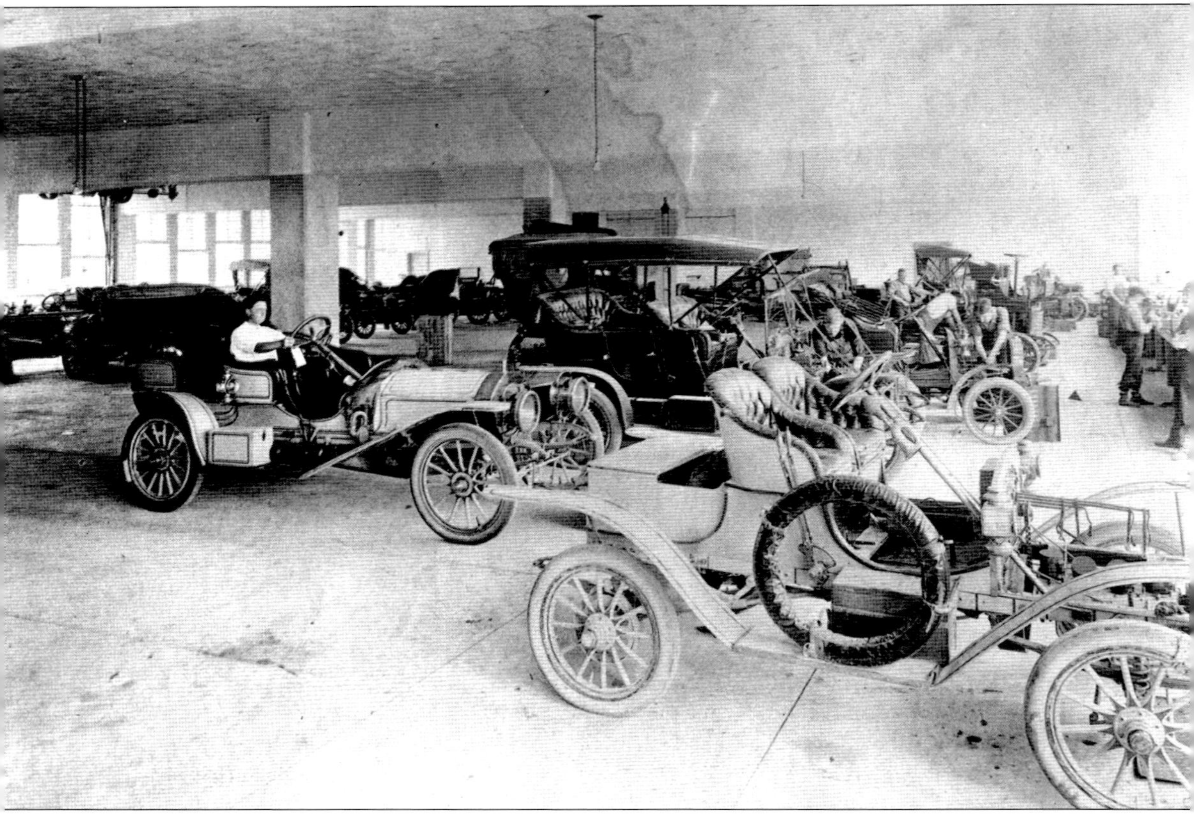

FISHER AUTOMOBILE COMPANY—1914. Constructed at 400 North Capital, this was most likely the first automobile "dealership" in the world. Carl carried Oldsmobiles, Reos, Packards, Stoddard-Daytons, and other brands. (Indiana Historical Society Bass Photo Collection #303671-2.)

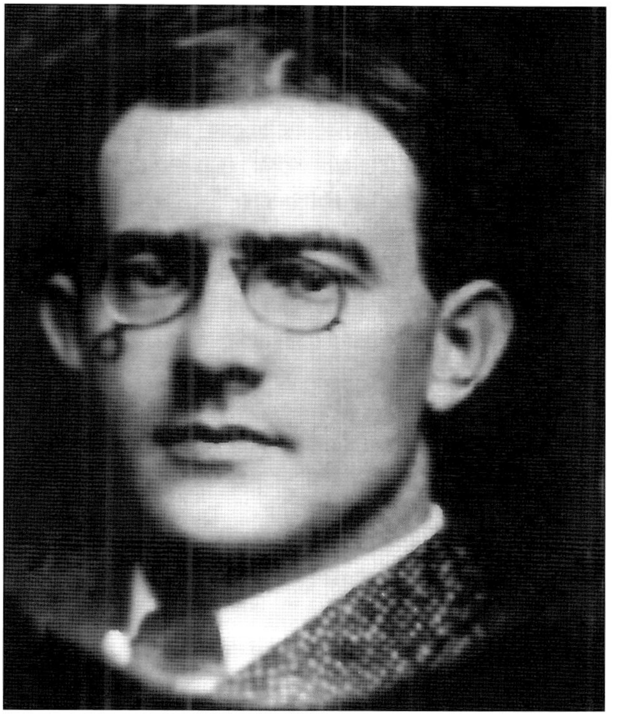

CARL FISHER—1909. This is likely his wedding picture. He was 35, and his bride, Jane Watts, was only 15. He had another fiancé at the time of the wedding, and a minor scandal erupted as a result.

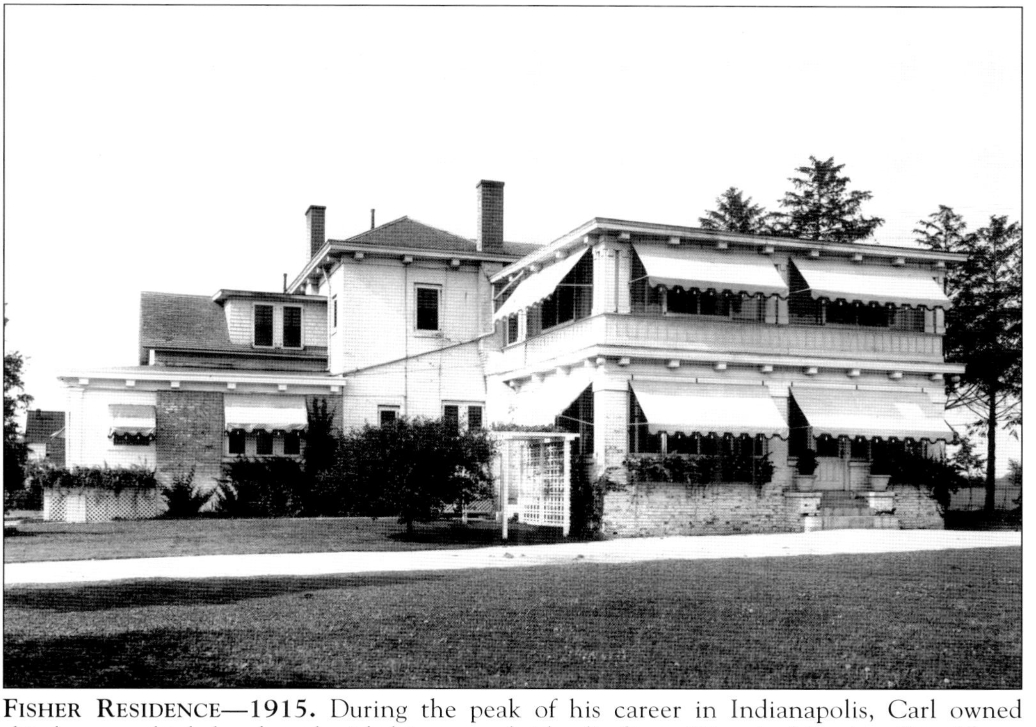

FISHER RESIDENCE—1915. During the peak of his career in Indianapolis, Carl owned this house, which he shared with his young bride. (Indiana Historical Society Bass Photo Collection #48503.)

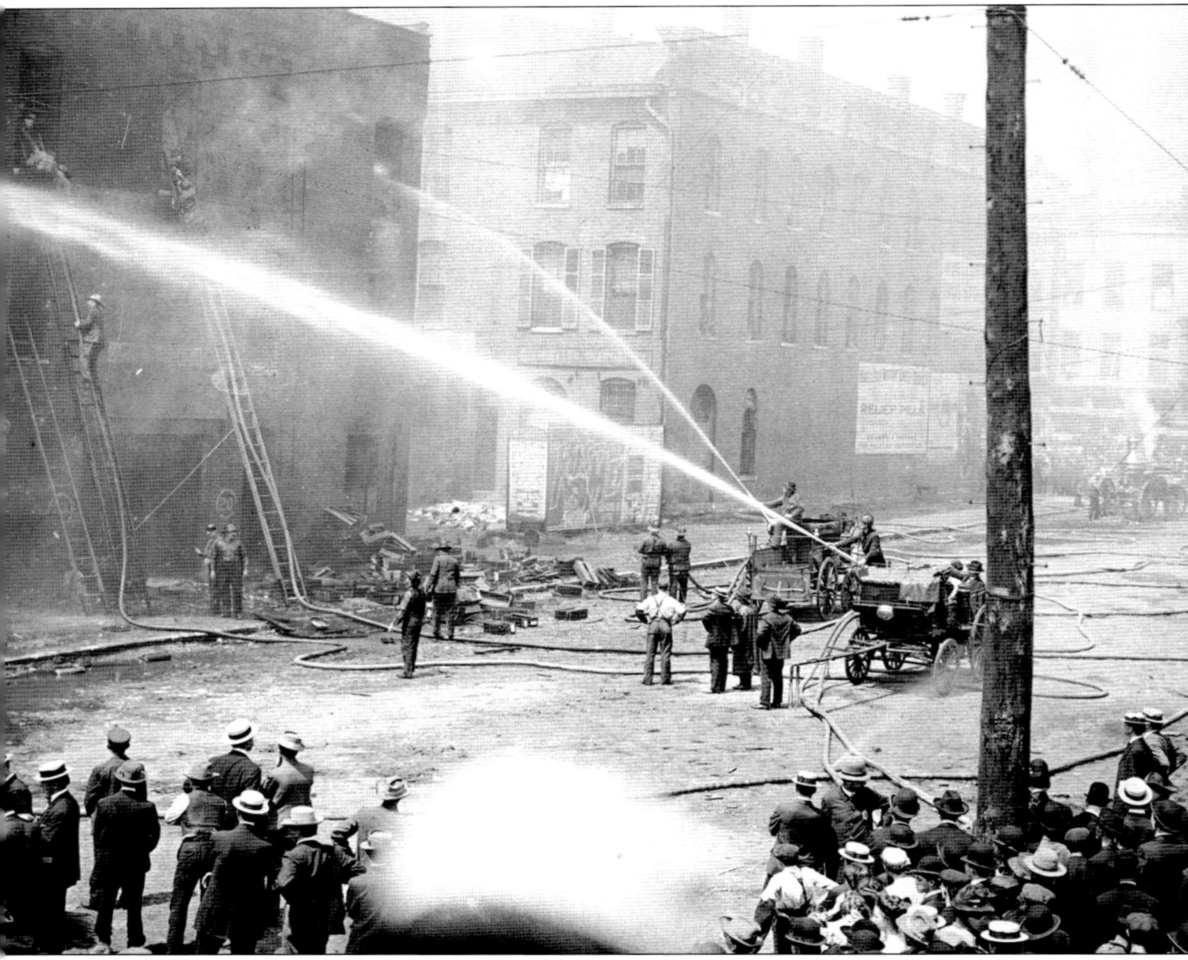

PREST-O-LITE FIRE—1907. The factory stood at 211 East South Street in Indianapolis. The explosion also blew up a sauerkraut plant nearby, spraying wet kraut all over the block. The city passed an ordinance forbidding the filling of the gas canisters within city limits, so Fisher built a giant new plant in what would become Speedway, Indiana. (Indiana Historical Society Bass Photo Collection #9490.)

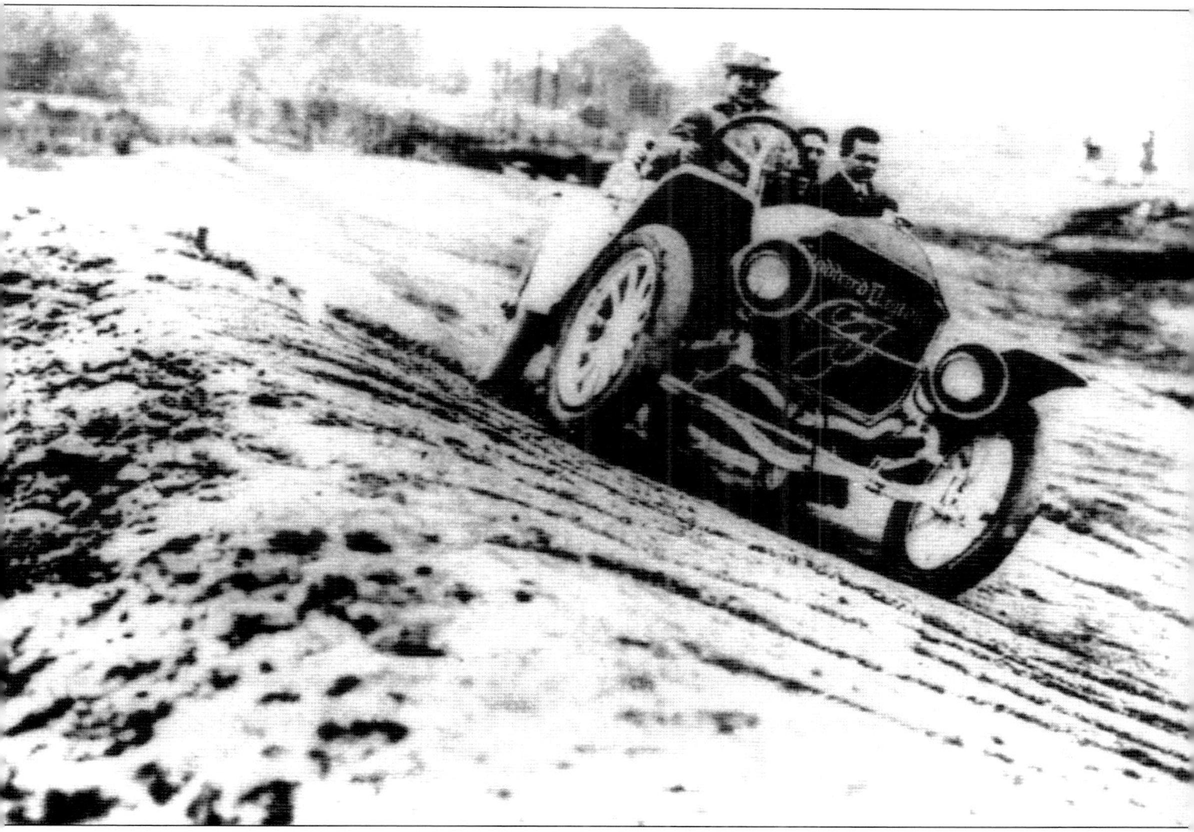

INDIANAPOLIS MOTOR SPEEDWAY. This grainy photograph depicts Fisher piloting his Stoddard-Dayton during one of the first trips around the newly built track in 1909.

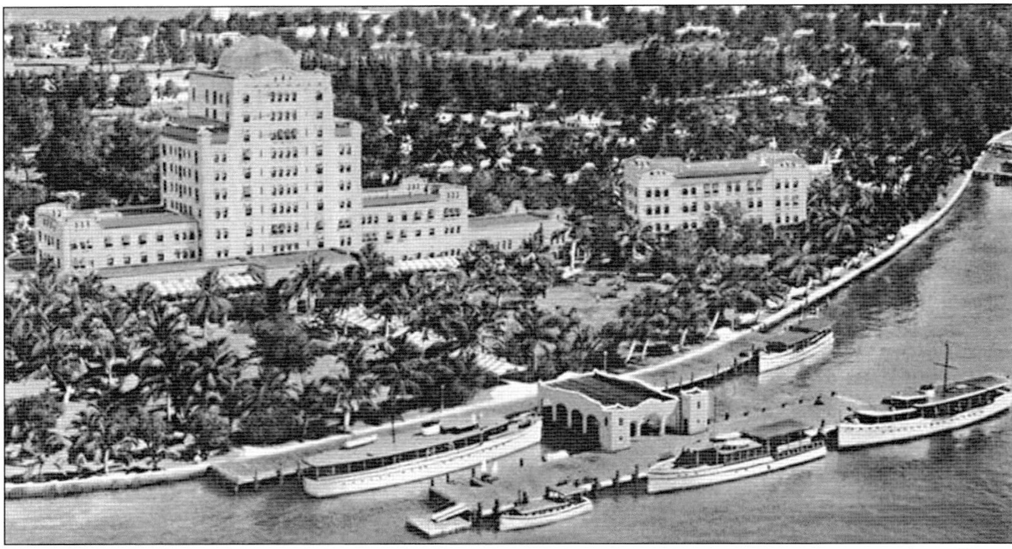

FLAMINGO HOTEL. In 1919, Carl announced plans to build a hotel in Miami Beach to house both celebrities seeking a vacation destination and potential lot buyers for his developments. He formally opened the $2 million facility on January 1, 1921, and had 200 rooms that went for $15 per night for a single. Sparing no expense, he even had 40 Guernsey cows sent from Wisconsin to provide fresh milk. He launched another brilliant Fisher marketing campaign in which he lured President-elect Warren Harding to town for a well-photographed golf vacation with a small elephant as his caddy. In February of 1922, the hotel turned away over 2,000 potential guests, so Carl expanded the hotel, opened the new Nautilus Hotel, and convinced other companies to build properties. At the peak in 1925, there were over 50 hotels in Miami Beach. After Carl lost control of the hotel in the stock market crash of 1929, it changed hands and was eventually torn down in the late 1950s to build the Morton Towers, a residential development. Today workers are renovating the Morton Towers and they are to be renamed the "Grand Flamingo" in honor of the hotel that once stood there.

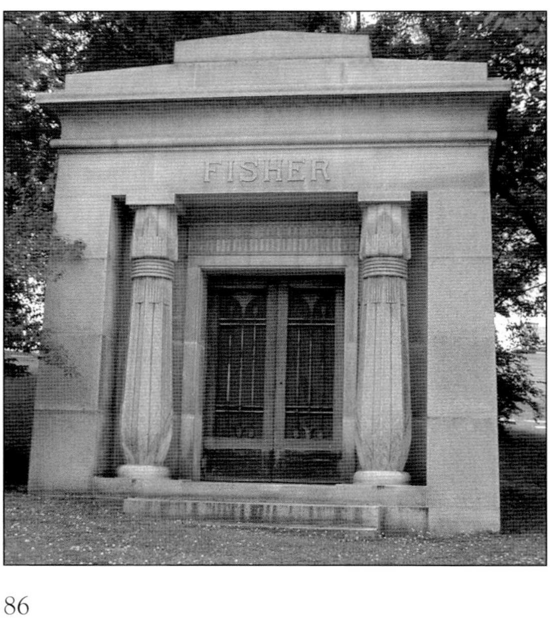

FISHER FAMILY MAUSOLEUM—2001. Carl's cremated body lies in this mausoleum in Section 13, Lot 42 of Crown Hill Cemetery in Indianapolis.

Nine

Riverside Park

Riverside Park is really the story of two parks: one public, one private, both with an intertwining history.

The public park begins with a man named Thomas Taggart. Born in Ireland in 1856, he immigrated in 1861, and by 1877 he had moved from Xenia, Ohio, to Indianapolis to run the restaurant at Union Station. He immediately became involved in local Democratic politics, and in 1886 won the election for Marion County Auditor. Upon completion of that term, party members elected him State Chairman in 1892, a post he held until 1894.

In 1895, Taggart ran for mayor of Indianapolis and won. During his term in office, which lasted until 1901, he worked for street paving and track elevation, to alleviate a big city issue whereby trains leaving and entering Union Station completely blocked city streets for hours at a time.

His biggest legacy to the city, though, was his love of public parks, and during his term he bought more land for parks than any mayor had to date. One of his most ambitions projects was a tract of land bordering the White River on the city's extreme northwest side. At the time, there was nothing but farmland in the area south of Crown Hill Cemetery and west of the city, but in 1898, the far-thinking mayor directed his Bureau of Parks to pay $230,000 to secure the land. Soon, park patrons were strolling along the river, playing sports in the wide-open spaces, or launching a boat out onto the water.

The street railway company extended their lines from downtown to the park, and a surge of visitors every weekend raced out to get away from the city for a while. In that crowd were three wealthy Indianapolis executives, J. Clyde Power, Albert Lieber, and Bert Feibleman. Together with some investors from Pittsburgh, they purchased a triangle-shaped plot of land just north of the main park area along Thirtieth Street east of the White River.

On that spot, the group would create the Riverside Amusement Park, which opened in 1903. Initially there were only a few rides, including a toboggan, as well as some food stands and games. Nevertheless, business was brisk, and soon they were adding new rides and attractions at a breakneck pace. In order to encourage traffic from the nearby public Riverside Park, admission to the Amusement Park was free—owners charged only for riding the rides. That meant that an entire family could spend time in the park, even if only a few brave souls wanted to take part in the thrills. To keep traffic up even at night, the park built a dance hall, which was converted in later years into a roller skating rink.

In 1919, Lewis Coleman gained control of the park, having served as the company's lawyer and taking his pay in stock for many years. He launched the Riverside Exhibition Company and issued new stock to raise capital to improve the facility. He added the roller coasters and a miniature railroad as traffic at both the public and private Riverside Parks continued to swell. A young Frank Thomas, who would go on to invent the soft-serve ice cream machine and who's son would play a major role in the creation of another Indianapolis institution, Burger Chef, built and patented the first "fun house" ride at Riverside during this time.

The area around the parks was changing, too. David Parry, owner of the Parry Motor Car Company, had purchased a large tract of land west of the river for his own private residence. Upon his death in 1915, his family subdivided the land, and some of the wealthiest and most prominent residents of Indianapolis built homes in the area known as "Golden Hill." Development of the majority of the land occurred in the 1920s, and the area was the heart of middle-class Indianapolis in the years before World War II.

In 1900, Taggart would go on to national prominence, serving on the Democratic National Committee and as its Chairman during the election of 1904. Simultaneously he developed the French Lick Springs Hotel, a resort for the rich and famous that would serve as the unofficial headquarters of the Democratic Party for many years. In 1916, he left the committee to serve out the unexpired U.S. Senator term of Benjamin Shivley, but was defeated for reelection in 1920.

Taggert passed away quietly on March 6, 1929, after serving his city and country for decades. He left a considerable estate and a significant legacy for the residents of Indianapolis.

After the war, change was in the air. Though Riverside Amusement Park would see over one million visitors in 1952, the desire of the middle class to move out of older areas of town into the suburbs was hitting the area hard. Property values diminished, as there were more sellers than there were buyers. Coupled with properties that were, in many cases, 40–50 years old and in need of repair, the area took a hit in the public perception.

Accelerating this flight by white residents to the suburbs was the rate at which African-Americans were moving into the area in the still very segregated and racially charged city. In the 1950s the white population decreased by almost 60 percent while the African-American population grew by almost 120 percent.

Amazingly, the amusement park doggedly stuck to its policy of "whites only," which had been in place since its inception. This policy was deadly in this new era. Coupled with the suburban white impression that the neighborhood had become dangerous, attendance at the Amusement Park dove while the residents happily continued to enjoy the public city park to its south.

By 1960, another great force influenced the neighborhood. The state mapped the proposed Interstate 65 through the middle of the area, dividing the residents living along the canal from those living along the river. The primary effect of this was to discourage new home purchases, and as more people left the area, property values sank even further.

By the mid-1960s, Riverside Amusement Park's "whites-only" policy was gone, but it had done irreversible damage. The owners of the park deferred maintenance as it was losing over $30,000 a year. At the same time, large regional amusement parks were growing in popularity, raising the cost of new rides beyond what many smaller operators could afford.

At the end of the summer of 1970, Riverside Amusement Park closed for good. The rides, the roller rink and the buildings sat vacant and deteriorating for several years, becoming the home to vagrants and an illegal dumping ground. Several newspaper articles from the mid-1970s detailed dangerous buildings where neighborhood children would routinely play. In order to erase the decay, the city ordered the balance of the buildings razed in 1978.

As a final slap in the face, an outbreak of the rare disease histoplasmosis occurred between September 1978 and August 1979 in Indianapolis. Some epidemiologists tracing the progression of the disease believe that the process of removing the amusement park disturbed the soil and released the fungus that causes the disease. Outbreaks of the disease continue to occur occasionally in Indianapolis, and today it is still a leading complication for residents who contract AIDS.

In the mid-1980s, the city made a significant investment in the public Riverside Park, turning the indoor pool and gymnasium building into the Riverside Family Aquatic

Center. Today families drive for miles to visit this new jewel of the park system. The city also developed part of the park's land into the Major Taylor Velodrome for the 1986 Pan American Games, and renovated the two golf courses.

In the early 1990s, a private developer launched a plan to reuse the amusement park land for new single-family homes. Though there was some public protest based on the fear of reigniting the histoplasmosis epidemic, the "River's Edge" development began. Today, residents drive along streets where once sat carnival rides, next to a park that lives on today.

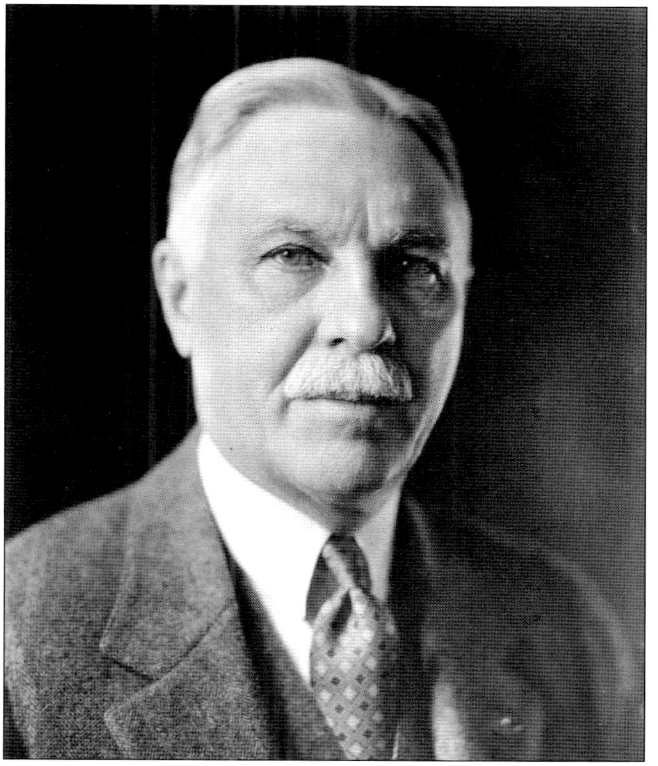

THOMAS TAGGART—MARCH 1928. (Indiana Historical Society Bass Photo Collection #225554-F.)

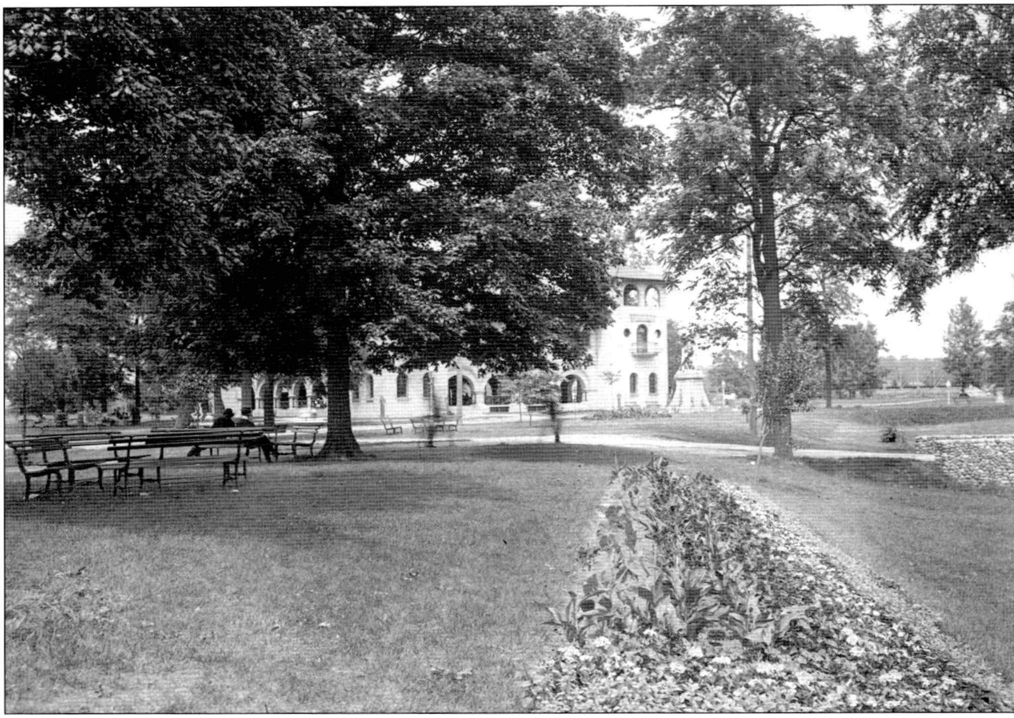

Shelter at Riverside Park—1906. (Indiana Historical Society Bass Photo Collection #7149.)

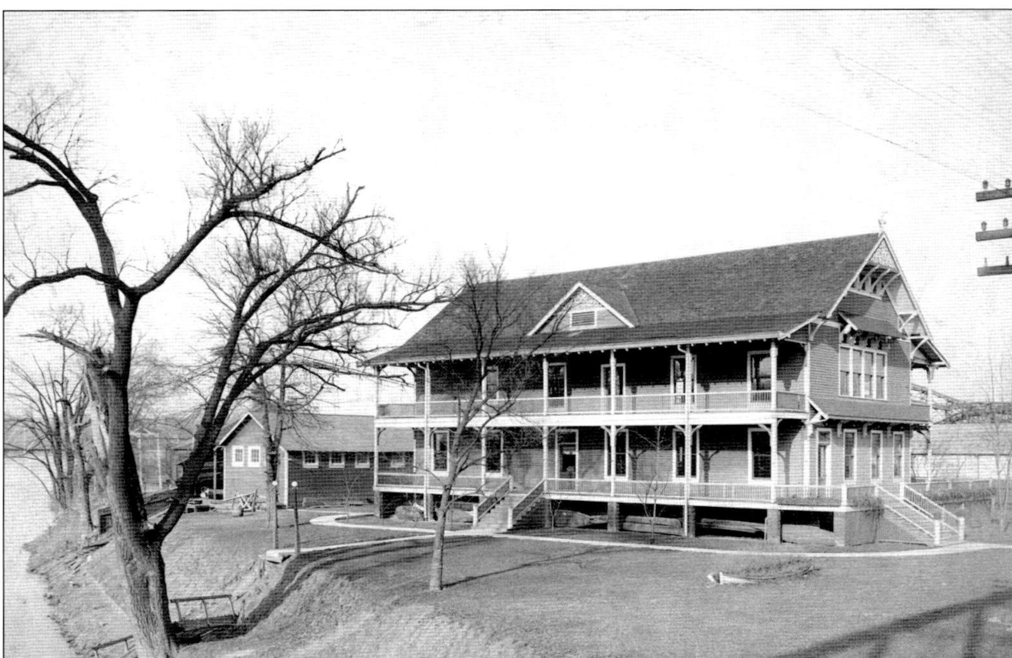

Canoe Club at Riverside Park—March 1907. (Indiana Historical Society Bass Photo Collection #8782.)

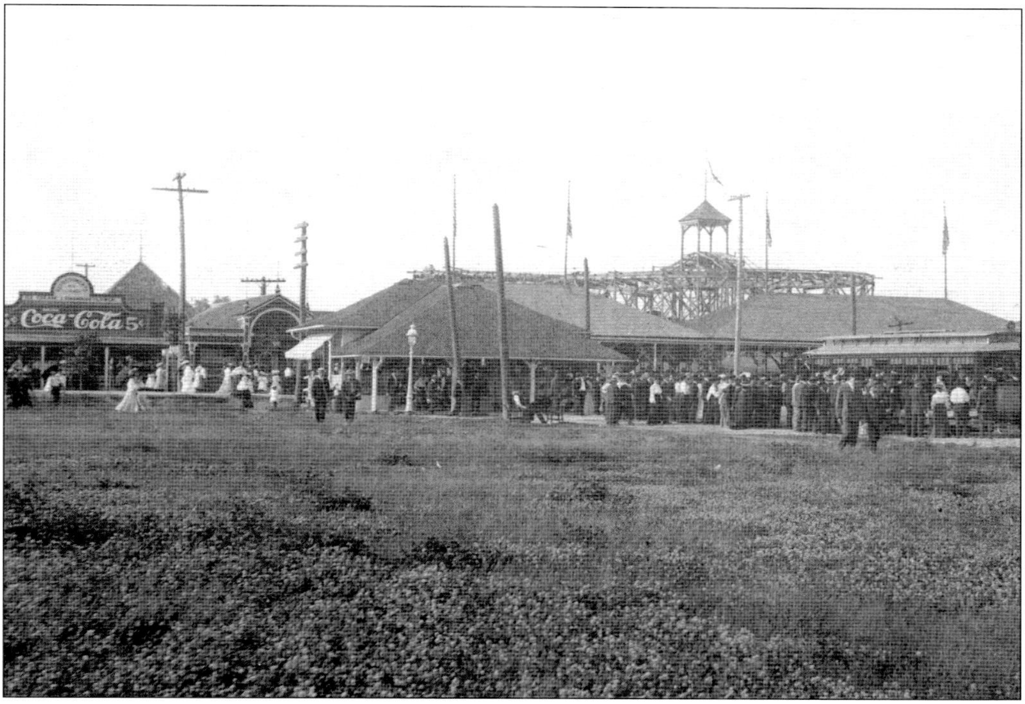

EARLY PHOTO OF RIVERSIDE AMUSEMENT PARK. Crowds wait to board the interurban back to Indianapolis. A roller coaster looms in the background, and 5¢ Coca-Cola was available in the booth on the left. (Indiana Historical Society Bass Photo Collection #4702.)

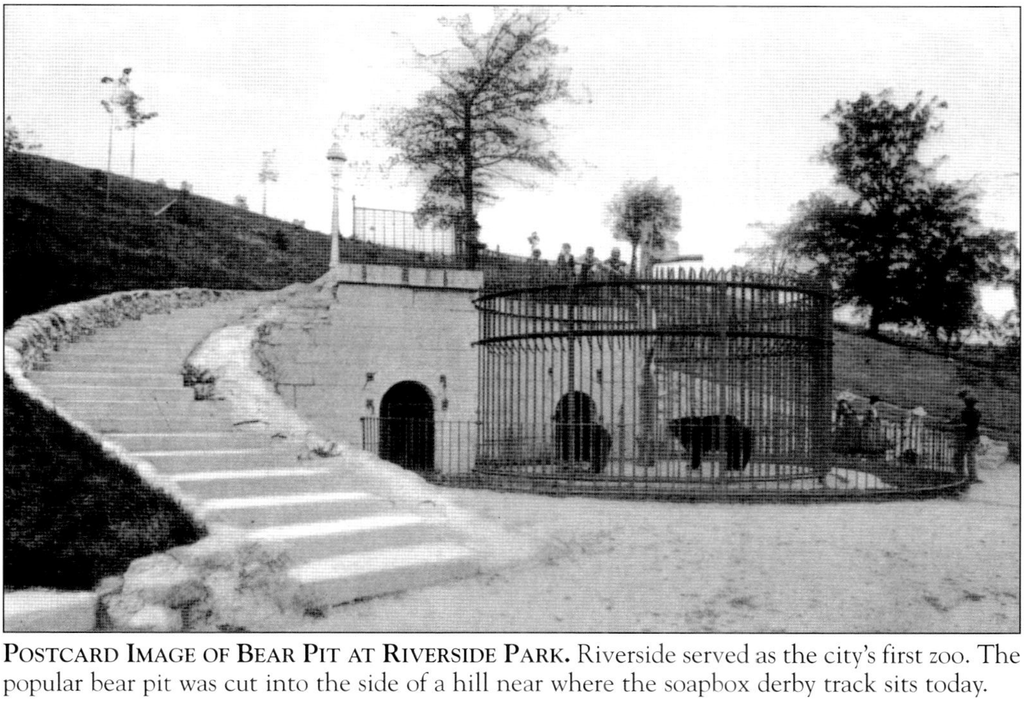

POSTCARD IMAGE OF BEAR PIT AT RIVERSIDE PARK. Riverside served as the city's first zoo. The popular bear pit was cut into the side of a hill near where the soapbox derby track sits today.

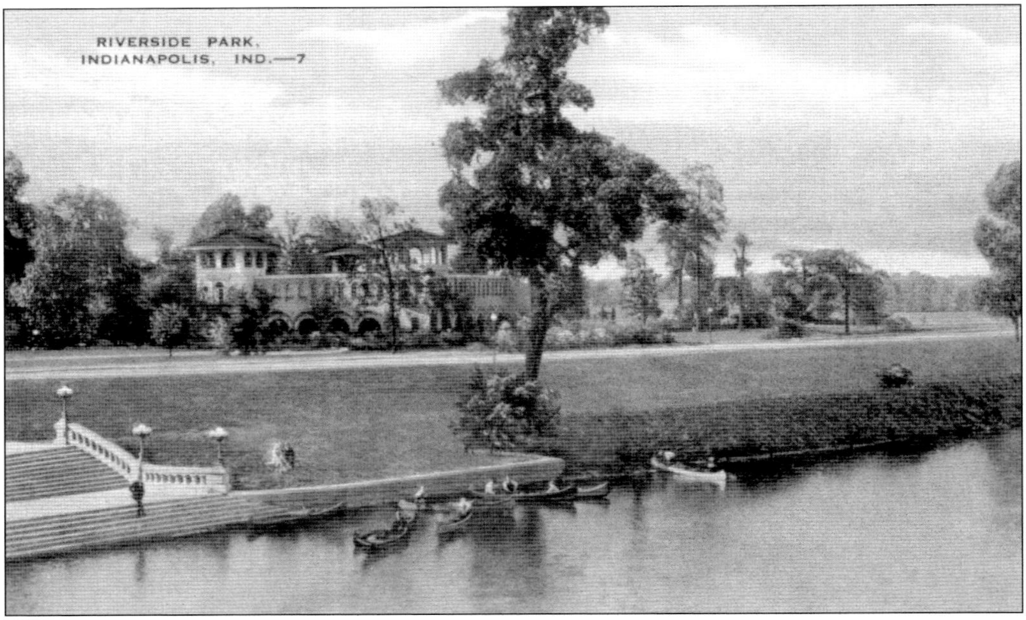

POSTCARD OF BOAT LAUNCH. Taking a canoe out on the river was a popular pastime for park visitors.

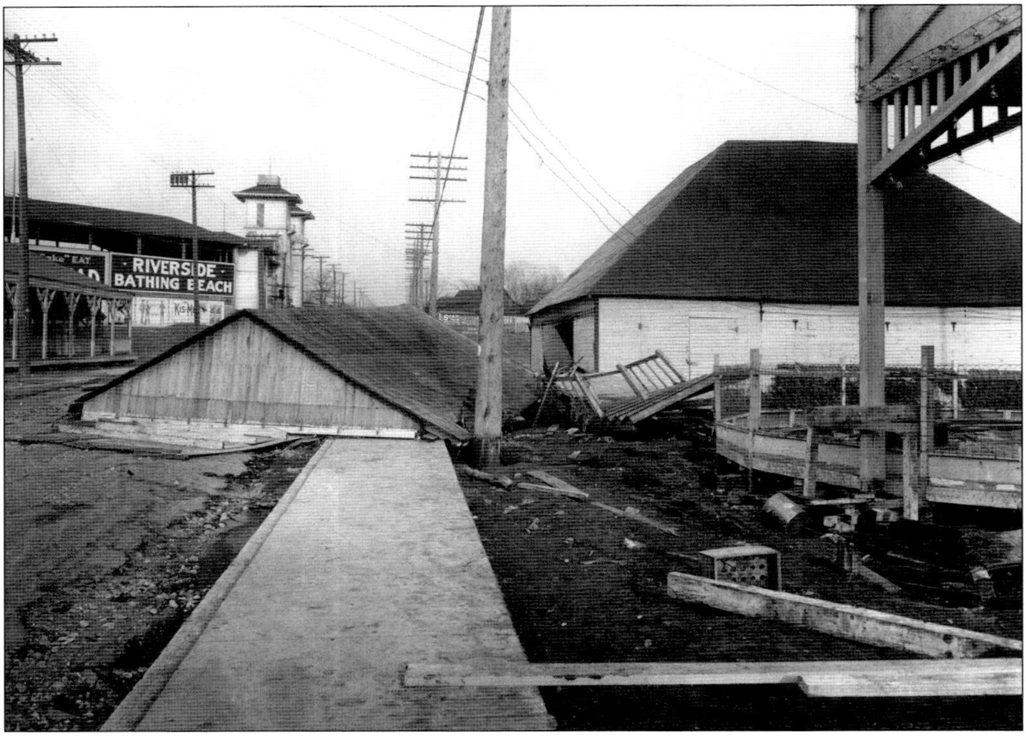

STORM DAMAGE—1913. A small tornado caused damage at the amusement park that summer. (Indiana Historical Society Bass Photo Collection #32581.)

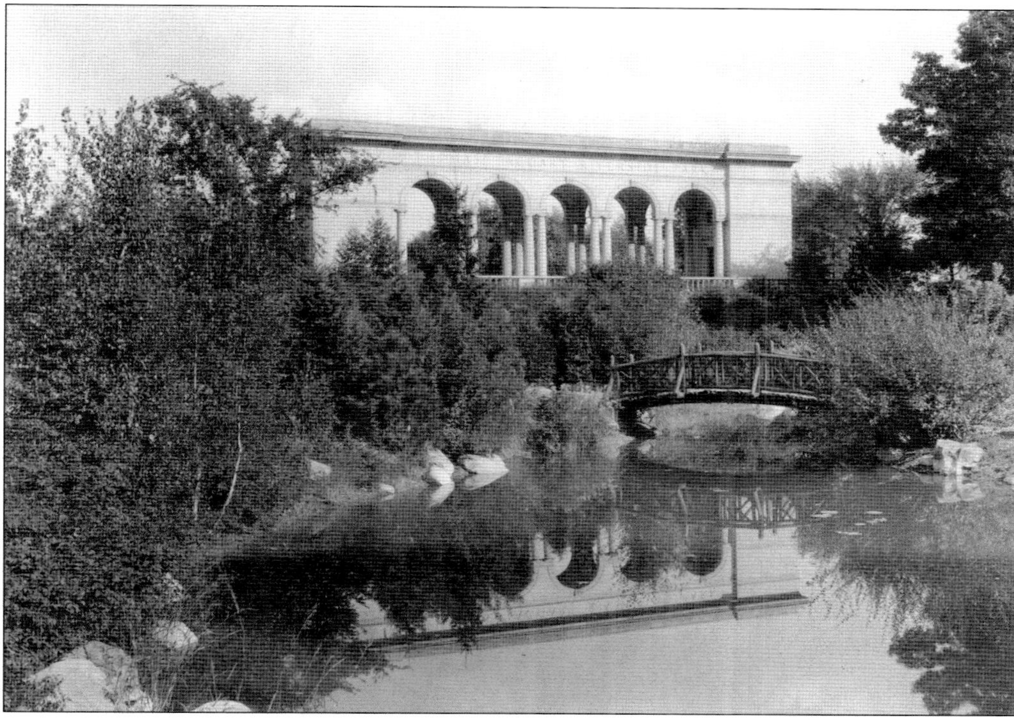

THOMAS TAGGART MEMORIAL—1936 AND 2002. This memorial used to sit amidst a lushly landscaped garden. Today the reflecting pond is gone, the plants are missing, and a fence keeps vandals off the structure that is undergoing cleaning and rehabilitation. (Top photo Indiana Historical Society Bass Photo Collection #235681-F.)

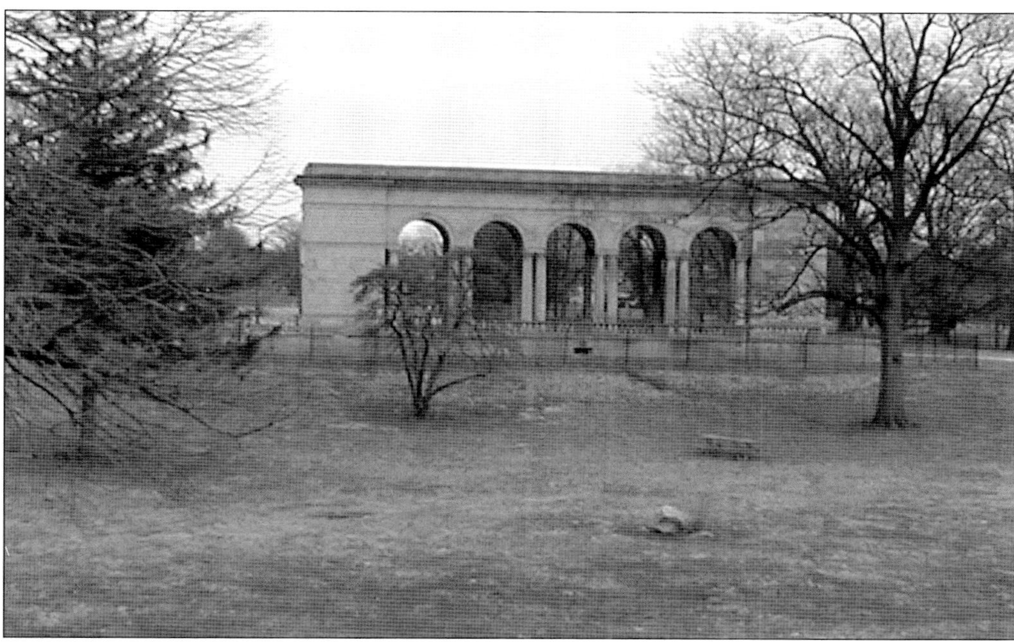

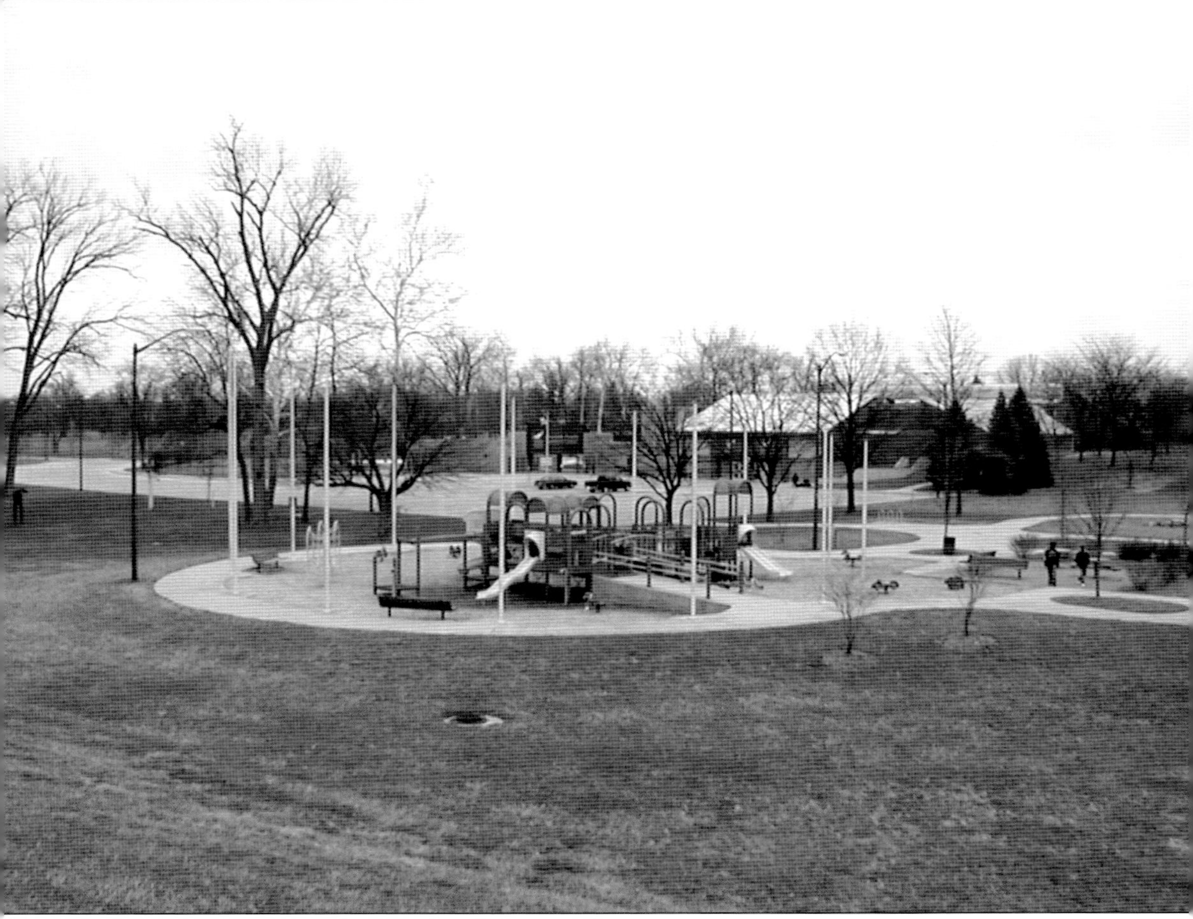

RIVERSIDE PARK AQUATIC CENTER—2002. The family-oriented pool, playground, and gymnasium sit immediately north of the old sunken gardens surrounding the Thomas Taggart Memorial on the east side of the White River.

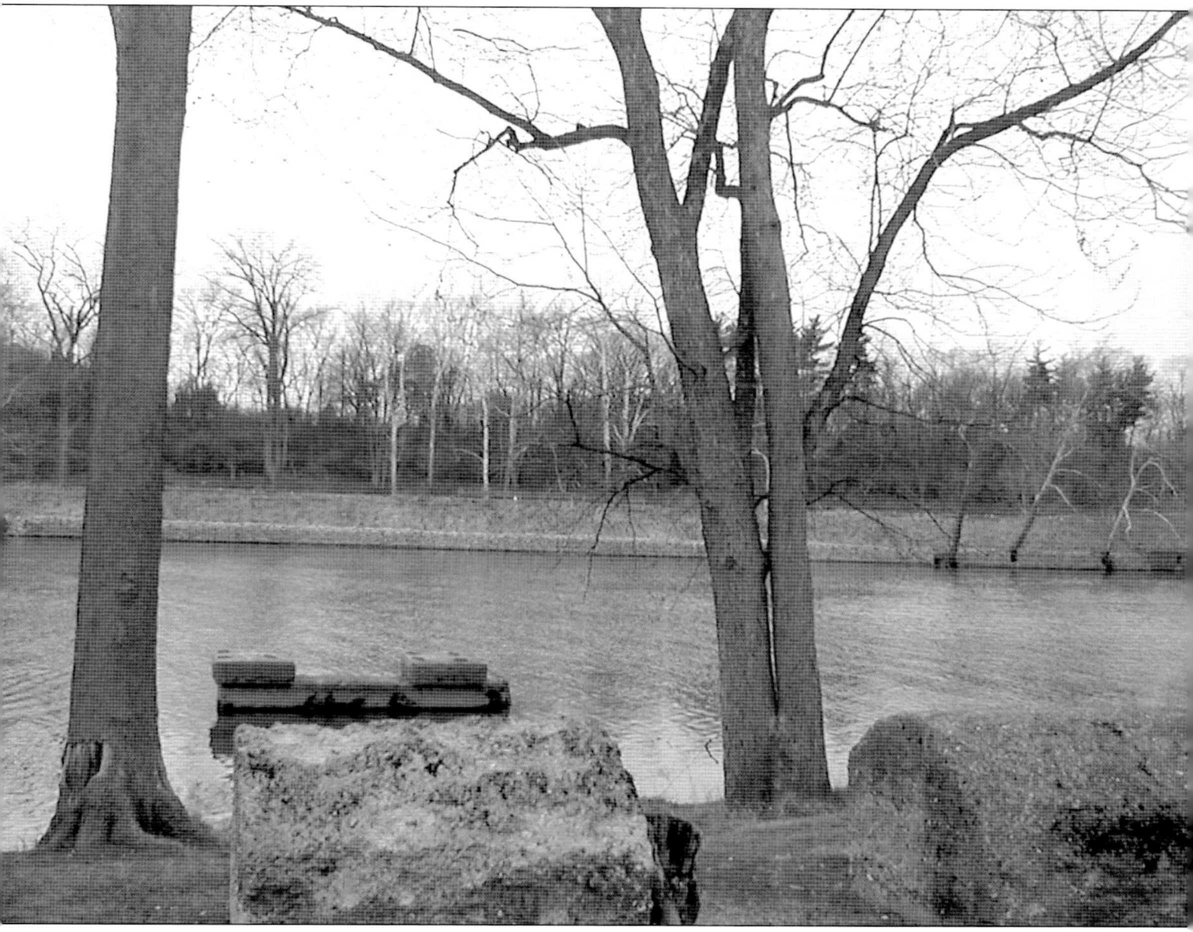

WHITE RIVER INSIDE RIVERSIDE PARK—2002. The remains of a pier bear silent witness to what once was the city's premier recreation area.

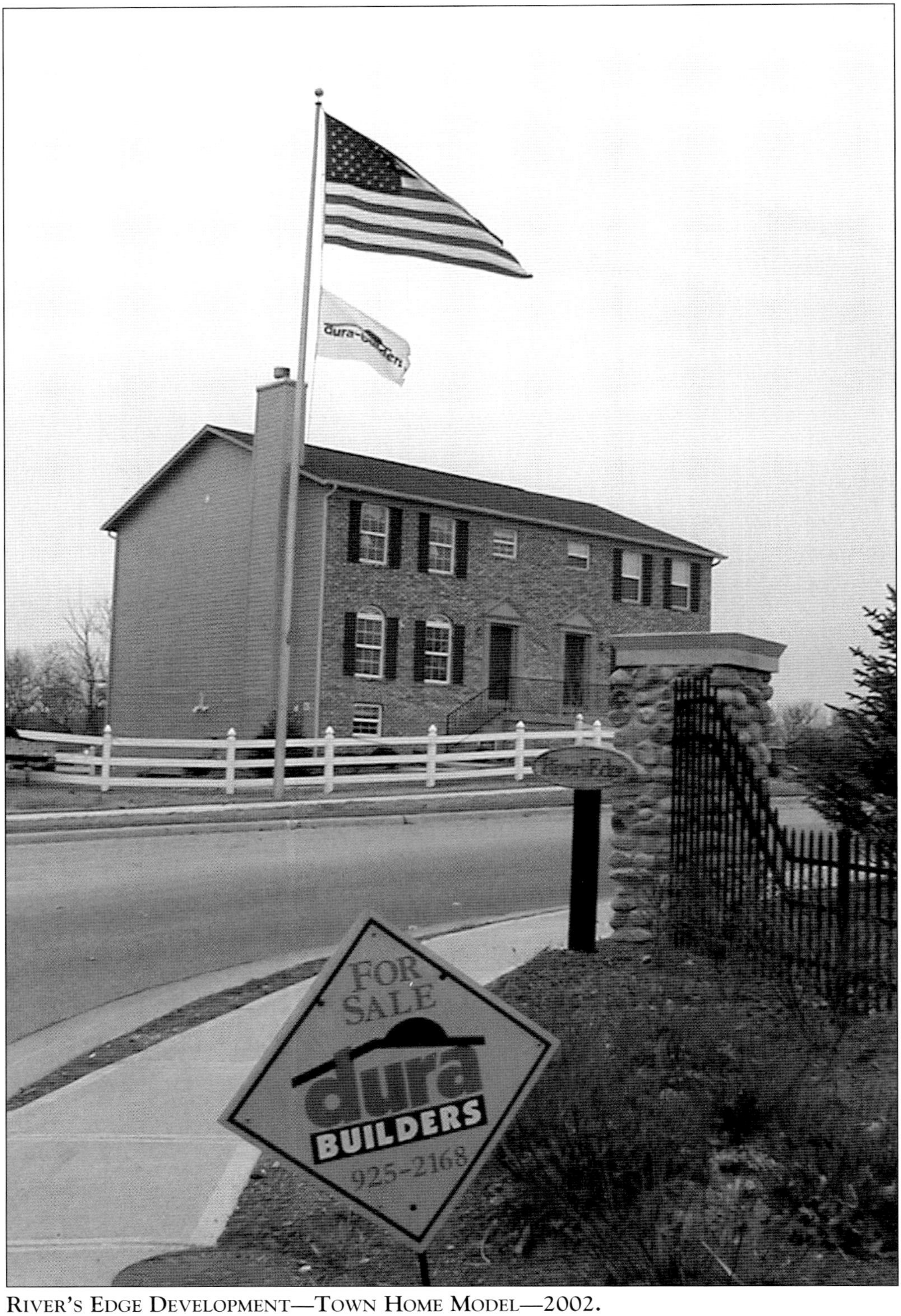

RIVER'S EDGE DEVELOPMENT—TOWN HOME MODEL—2002.

Ten

Burger Chef

It was the summer of 1930, and although Frank Porter Thomas Sr. was broke, he was glad to be back in Indianapolis. A carpenter by trade, he had started as an apprentice at age 14 to avoid working on his father's farm near Peru, Indiana. In 1910, while building elephant barns for the circuses that wintered there, he built one of the first roller coasters in Indiana at a park somewhere between Peru and Wabash. This led to a series of similar construction projects and by the late 1920s he was building rides all over, including Cedar Point in Sandusky, Ohio, Palisades Park in New Jersey, and Coney Island in New York. He even patented the first "fun house" on May 13, 1926, built in Indianapolis' Riverside Park.

As the Great Depression hit, he took one final chance—rehabilitating a defunct hotel in Corpus Christi, Texas, to become the center of a new amusement park of his own creation. Knowing his future was on the line, he made every effort to promote the facility. He built a giant pier for marathon dancing, which was all the rage. He hired a flagpole sitter. He had his young son, Frank Thomas Jr. and his cousin Morris tack up posters all over south Texas and northern Mexico for two weeks. He even hired a man to ride a motorcycle in a giant "motodrome," or circular cage, while being roared at by an old lion. With high hopes, opening day came—and went.

The park was a flop.

Thomas packed his family into their Packard in the middle of the night and drove back to Indiana—not stopping until they were over the border into Oklahoma, one step ahead of the sheriff.

Frank was now back in Indianapolis, but without a penny to his name. He wandered past the new "North Pole" stand operated by "Pop" Spencer on Illinois Street next to the Central Canal. They were serving a new treat called "Frozen Custard," and the machine that turned it out fascinated Frank. Frank asked where one could purchase such a machine, and, fearing competition, Mr. Spencer ripped the manufacturer's plate off the device and refused to tell.

Frank had seen all he needed, though, and his mechanical mind set about creating a new version of the device, one that was simpler and made of the new material "stainless steel." He went right back to the "North Pole" to show his creation. So vastly improved was it that Mr. Spencer threw out his old machine and bought Frank's to replace it!

The US Patent Office granted Frank a patent on his frozen custard machine, and he began selling them around the area. The second one went to the "Tee Pee" drive-in at 38th Street and Fall Creek Road. Since mechanical refrigeration was not yet in wide use, the original device used rock salt and ice for cooling. That rock salt contained sand, which would eventually clog up the pump circulating the brine. It became the job of 14-year-old

Frank Thomas Jr., to "service" the machines by driving around in his 1925 Model "T" Ford and cleaning out the pumps.

Frank Jr. relayed to his father that by installing an impeller to stir up the brine they might be able to keep the pumps from clogging. His father agreed, and Frank Jr. had, at the same time, made his own first invention and put himself out of a job. For many years thereafter, he would help his father in the business, even running a frozen custard stand at the Indiana State Fair during the Depression. He went off to Purdue to study Chemical Engineering in 1937, switching to Mechanical Engineering in his junior year and becoming a protégé of a leading researcher in mechanical refrigeration.

Upon graduation in 1941, he received a fellowship at Lehigh University in Pennsylvania, but at the end of the first semester, while home for Christmas, his mother handed him his draft call-up card, and he was off to war. He eventually rose to the rank of major, and returned home to his sweetheart, Jill, in November of 1945.

Using the money he had saved from his paychecks and several down payments on orders, Frank Jr. and Frank Sr. restarted the business, calling it General Equipment Company. Having gotten off to a good start again, Frank Sr. retired, handing the company over to his son. After the war, Frank Jr. brought in his brother, Don, and his brother-in-law, Bob Wildman, to continue in the frozen custard machine business.

In 1946, they received a call from a salesperson in California asking them if they could produce a soft-serve ice cream machine that could compete with Dairy Queen. At the time, Dairy Queen was a dominant franchise company, but they granted exclusive territories, locking potential entrepreneurs out of the market. The salesperson reasoned that if the company were able to produce an alternative soft-serve machine, drive-in owners could compete with Dairy Queen without having to join their franchise system. Frank, Don, and Bob took the challenge, shipping a machine they called a "SaniServ." The new product took off like a rocket, thanks to a cover story in Billboard magazine - at the time the journal of fairs, circuses, amusement parks, and carnivals, but now the magazine of the music industry. By 1950, they had built a new manufacturing facility to handle the orders that were flooding in.

In 1952, Frank Jr. walked into a nearby diner and ordered a hamburger and a chocolate shake. The two men sitting on each side of him heard the order and asked for shakes, too. The server started to cry, went to the manager, and announced that she was quitting, because "when I dip the ice cream it's so hard it hurts my thumb, and when I put the can on the beater the machine shocks me." Frank heard this, and went back to the office to modify their frozen custard machine to deliver milk shakes fully made direct from a spout. After significant work with several universities to develop the perfect mixture that would not freeze too quickly, by 1953, they began to market the very first automatic milk shake machine in the world.

This machine got the attention of James McLaramore and David Edgerton, who had opened a few 15¢ hamburger stands in Miami. They had designed a conveyor-belt device that would cook hamburgers by sliding them past electric heating rods. Impressed by the milk shake machine they had seen, they approached General Equipment to see if they might be willing to manufacture their machine, too.

Frank saw a few problems with the machine and reworked it, replacing the electric rods with gas jets and laying the patties flat on a chain. McLaramore and Edgerton bought the first of these new "flame-broiler" machines for their chain, which they had named "Burger King."

Meanwhile, General Equipment decided to build a "demonstration restaurant" to display their new flame-broiler and milk shake machines to potential customers. They selected a long-closed frozen custard stand at the defunct Little America Amusement Park across Keystone Avenue from the new Glendale Shopping Center. Ironically, this stand, constructed in the shape of a series of small "igloos," was one of the shops Frank Sr. had set up when he started out in the frozen custard business himself. After extensive remodeling, the new test store opened in 1957.

Frank and others noticed the quick success of McDonalds, who by 1958 had about 250 stores. Much of that growth had come through Ray Kroc's use of franchising, a business arrangement that allowed independent entrepreneurs to open a store that benefited from a solid, proven "system" and brand, while sharing a small portion of the profit with the parent company. General Equipment began to get inquiries from people seeking not only to buy equipment, but an entire franchise.

The taste of the "flame-broiled" hamburgers that came out of their machine was unique, they reasoned, and business was so good at the demonstration store that they decided to jump in and try it for themselves. They created Burger Chef Systems in 1958, and contracted a design company to come up with a unique building shape, and Grant Sign Company of Illinois to design a marker that would distinguish it from roadside competition. The first store, at 1300 West Sixteenth Street opened in 1958, and by the end of that year, they had eight stores.

The chain grew fast. By 1960, there were 73 restaurants. In 1965, they built a new corporate headquarters at 1348 West Sixteenth Street, adjacent to the original store. The building served both as an office and a warehouse for the extensive material required to startup and maintain a new store. In time, they opened a training center across from the Indiana State Fairgrounds, as well as a printing shop.

By 1966, they opened the 500th restaurant at 2200 North Meridian Street in Indianapolis. They experimented with different designs, opening the "Downtowner" Burger Chef at 6 East Washington Street that year in a converted narrow restaurant and office building. In 1966, they also renamed General Equipment Company to "SaniServ" and made it a division of Burger Chef. By 1968, there were 800 restaurants in 39 states.

The industry started to attract the attention of some deep-pocketed food conglomerates seeking to diversify. In 1964, McDonalds made an initial public offering of stock, making its chairperson, Ray Kroc, an instant millionaire. In 1966, Burger King sold out to Pillsbury Corporation. Burger Chef, too, was in need of a corporate partner to continue their growth. Borden made several overtures, but it was General Foods, a major competitor of Pillsbury, which had spent several months in Indianapolis studying the books, that would eventually make an offer in 1968.

The selling price was around $16.3 million. The original investors, including Frank, Don, and Robert took their share of the proceeds, and Frank agreed to stay on as head of the new division for a time. In 1969, they opened the 1,000th store in Treasure Island, Florida, but there was trouble on the horizon.

Frank's original boss departed, and would be replaced three more times over the next two years. General Foods was unable to set a consistent strategy. They tried different logos and store designs, even moving the "executive offices" from Indianapolis to White Plains, New York, in 1971, only to move it back in 1977. One story tells of having to ship ten complete store equipment packages to Atlanta for only five stores, the rest stolen or lost in shipment.

Frank had enough, leaving the company for good in 1970. He focused on community and charity work, including the Taylor Foundation, which he and his wife, Jill, organized to help vision-impaired children. He also became an avid pilot, finally settling in Taos, New Mexico.

The chain peaked at 1,050 stores in 1973, but mismanagement and lack of direction had the franchises in open revolt. General Foods wrote down the value of the division by $47 million and announced plans to close hundreds of under-performing stores. In 1977, the company finally brought in a president with extensive fast food experience, Terry Collins, and the chain began to experience improvements. They introduced a new, modern logo and a store design that clicked with customers. They also benefited by tying in promotions to a low budget space film starring mostly unknown actors titled *Star Wars*.

Unfortunately, even with these improvements, the chain never really did better than break-even for General Foods, and by 1981 they had enough, selling the remaining 679-store operation to Montreal-based Imasco Corporation, owner of the Hardee's restaurant chain. One-by-one the stores were converted into Hardee's locations or closed, but not before a $14 million lawsuit brought by a group of franchises that accused General Foods of wrongfully forcing franchises to undertake expensive renovations while simultaneously seeking to sell the chain.

Right up until 1996, one Burger Chef remained open because of this lawsuit—in Cookville, Tennessee—but the settlement reached with its owner, Bill Mitchell, meant that upon his retirement that year, the last store slipped into history. Phillip Morris purchased General Foods shortly after they sold off Burger Chef, only to merge with Kraft in 1995. In 1997, CKE Restaurants, owners of the west coast Carl's Jr. Chain, purchased Hardee's from Imasco, thus practically obliterating any record of a separate Burger Chef Systems company.

CKE still owns the logos and trademarks associated with Burger Chef, and in 2000, selected Hardee's restaurants brought back the "Big Shef" to celebrate the addition of flame broilers back into the Hardee's system. Throughout the country, many former franchises continue to operate their stores, many with few or no changes to the menu. If you look carefully, you can still find small echoes of this piece of "Lost Indianapolis."

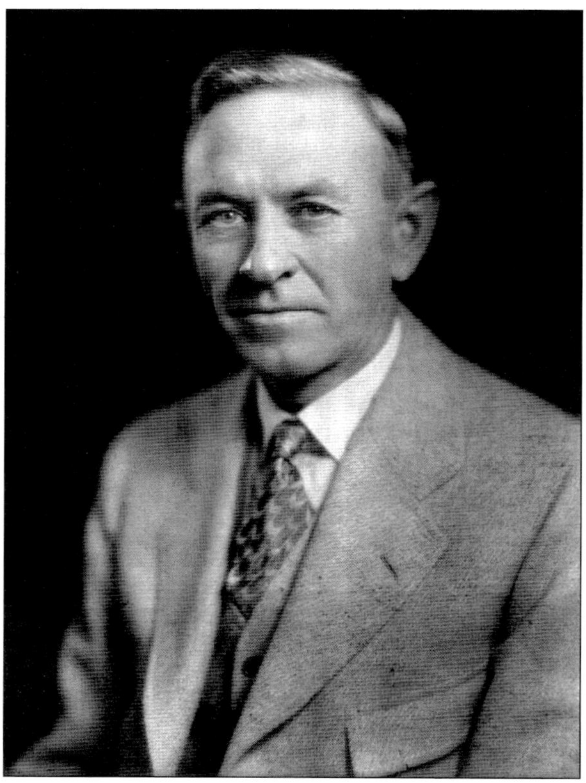

FRANK THOMAS SR.— 1927. Taken at age 52, just before the Depression and his invention of the soft-serve ice cream machine. (Photo from Frank Thomas Jr.)

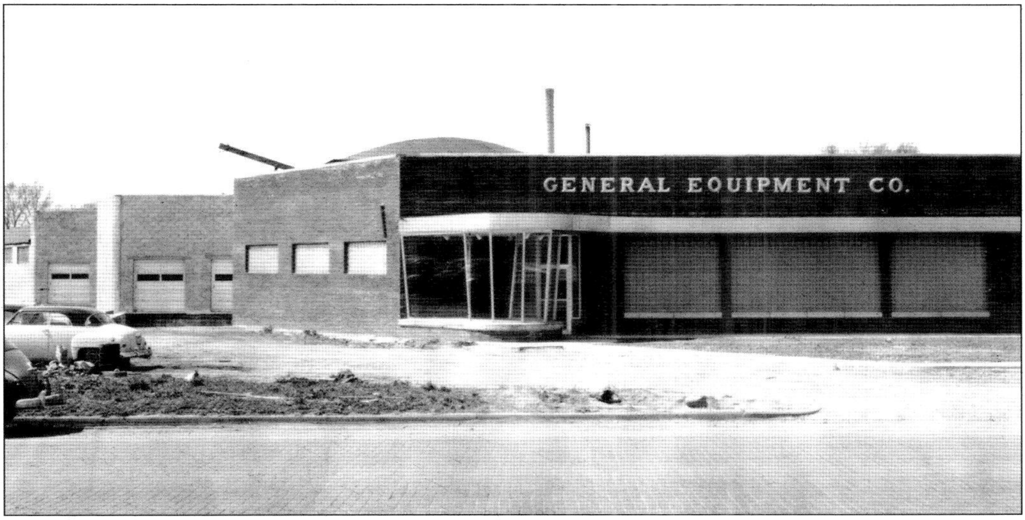

GENERAL EQUIPMENT COMPANY. The top photo is of the newly completed headquarters and shops built in 1950 at 1348 Stadium Drive by Frank Thomas Jr., Donald Thomas, and Bob Wildman to house their growing soft-serve ice cream machine business. Note that Stadium Drive was still paved with bricks at the time. The Ceramics and Sculpture facility and a warehouse for IUPUI now stand on the site. The bottom photo shows Frank Thomas Jr. (right) standing at the production line in 1947. (Photos from Frank Thomas Jr.)

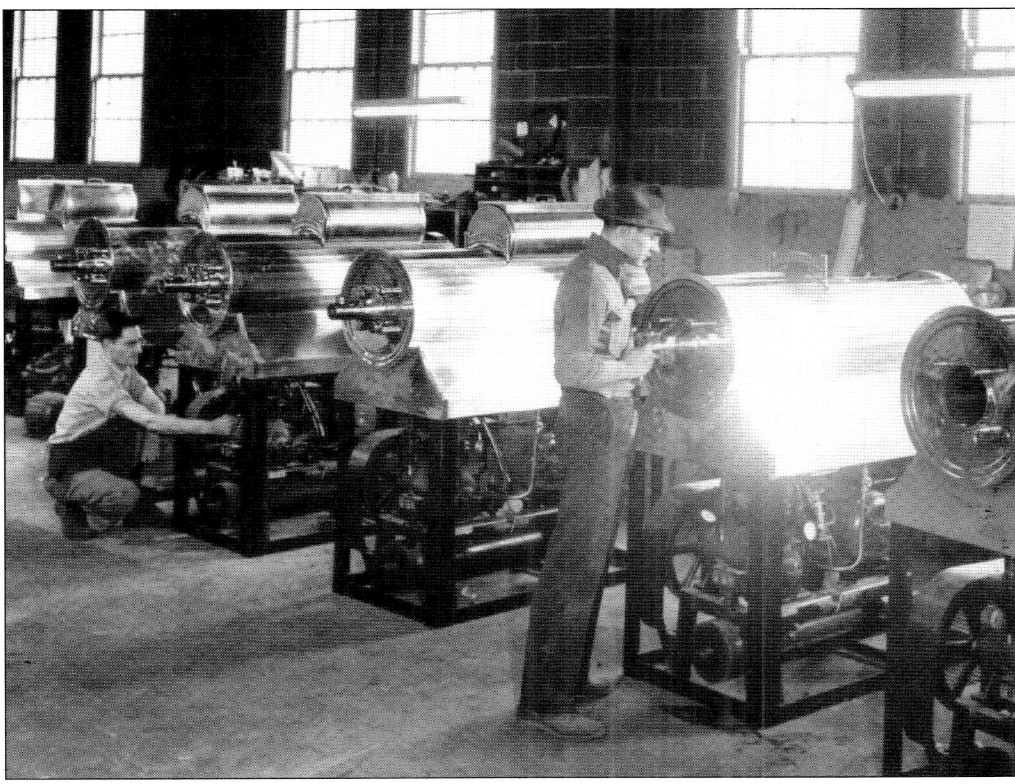

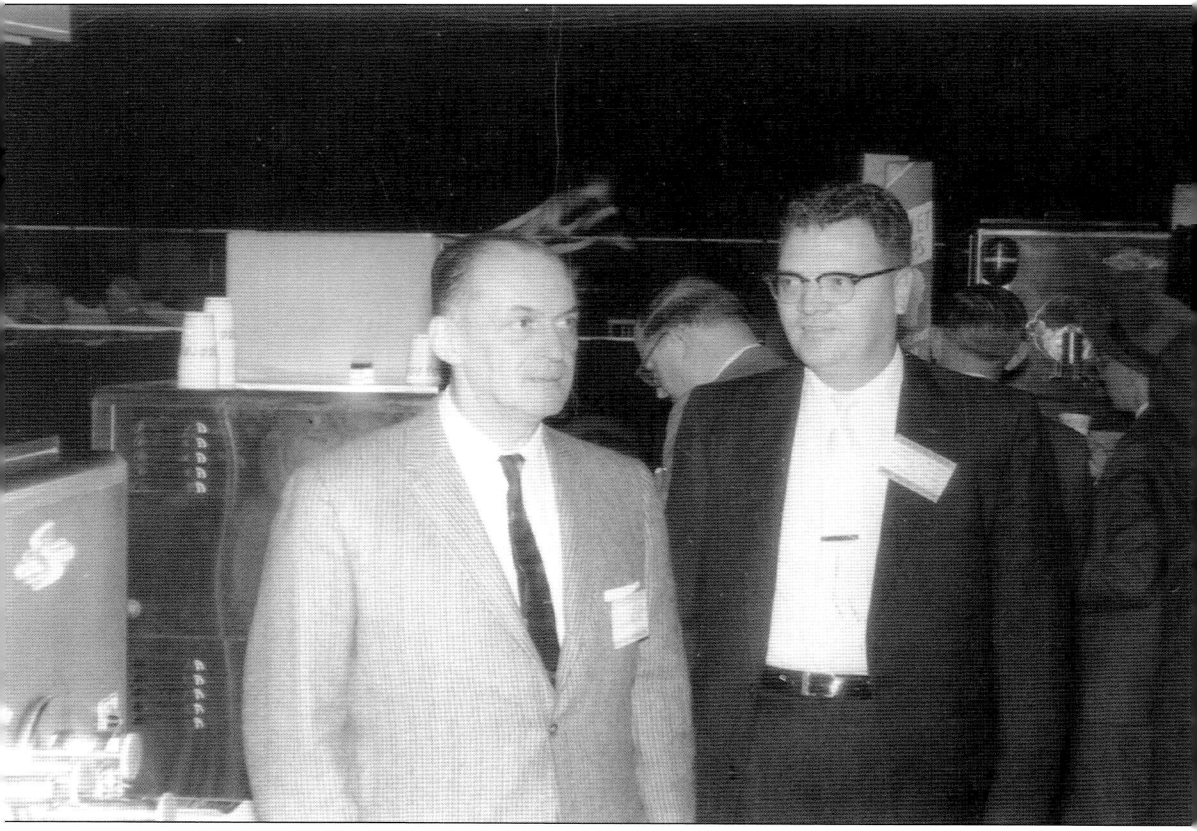

RAY KROC AND BOB WILDMAN—1956. This photo shows the General Equipment Company booth at the Chicago Restaurant Equipment Show in 1956. For years, Bob, Frank, and Don tried to convince Ray to drop the Multimixer in favor of their automatic shake machine, but he never bought, especially after Burger Chef became a direct competitor. (Photo from Bob Wildman.)

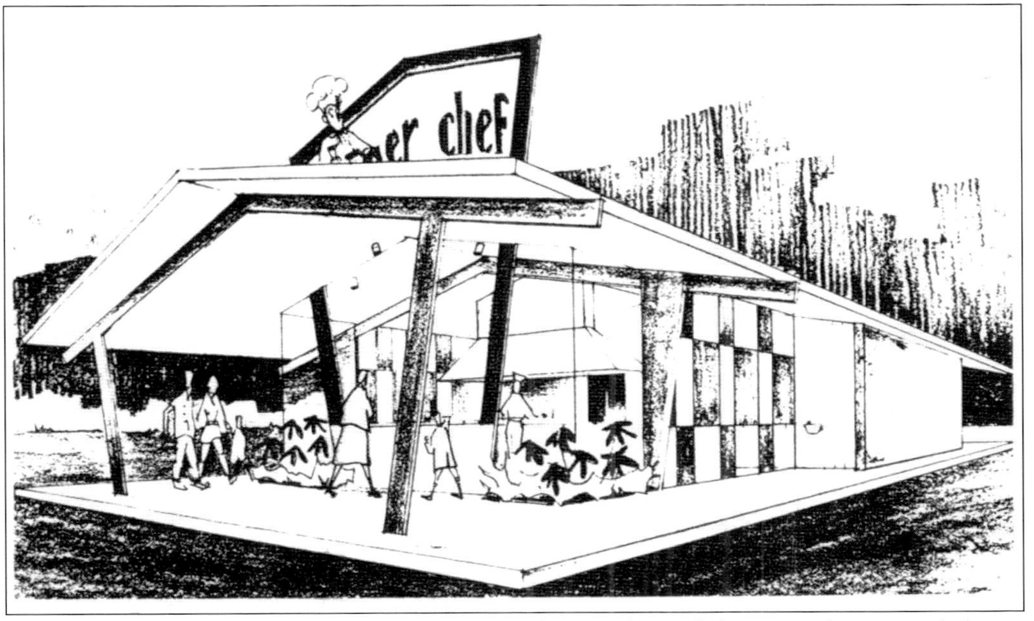

Conceptual Store Design—1957. Very much a product of the time, the original design featured a tall, arch shaped canopy and an open, glass front where customers could watch their food being prepared.

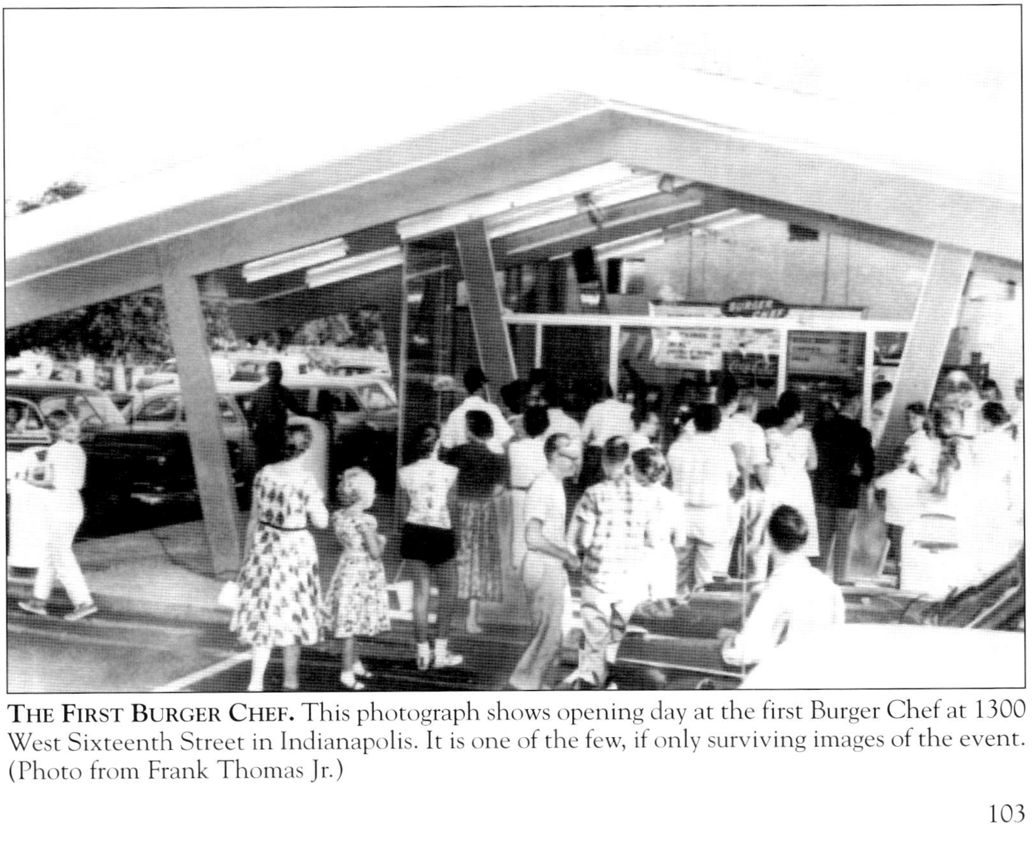

The First Burger Chef. This photograph shows opening day at the first Burger Chef at 1300 West Sixteenth Street in Indianapolis. It is one of the few, if only surviving images of the event. (Photo from Frank Thomas Jr.)

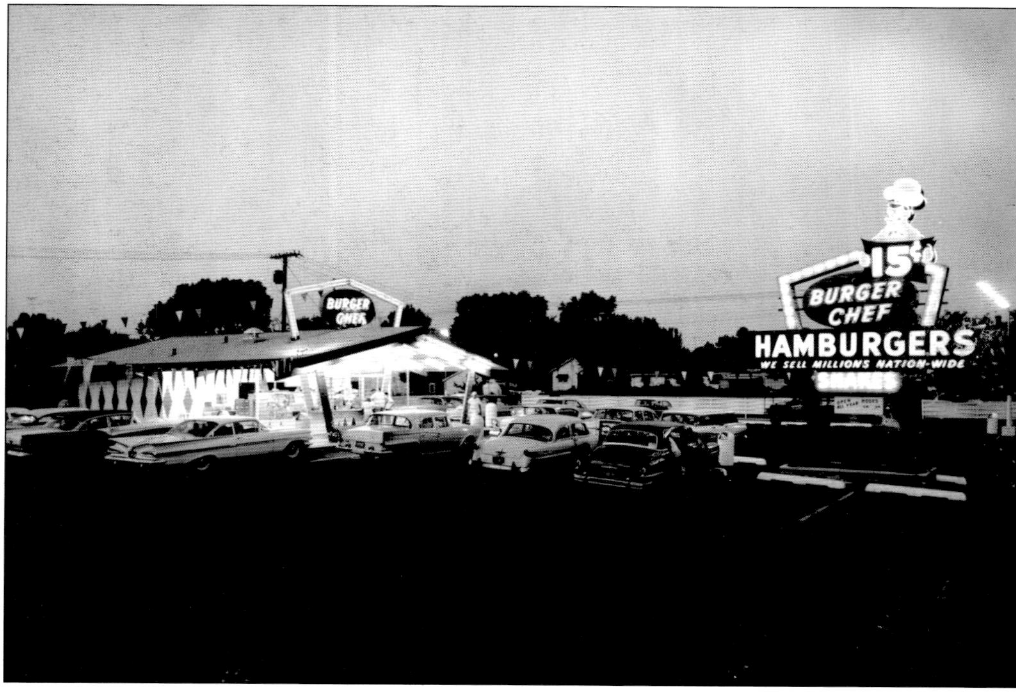

LAFAYETTE STORE AT DUSK—1958. Fifteen cents was the expected price of a drive-in hamburger at the time, and the sign made sure the motorist knew that Burger Chef was no different. Eventually the company had to cover the 15¢ neon price with a plastic housing as costs increased. Later designs would enclose the front portion of the store to protect customers from the elements while ordering—indoor seating would also follow. (Photo from Frank Thomas Jr.)

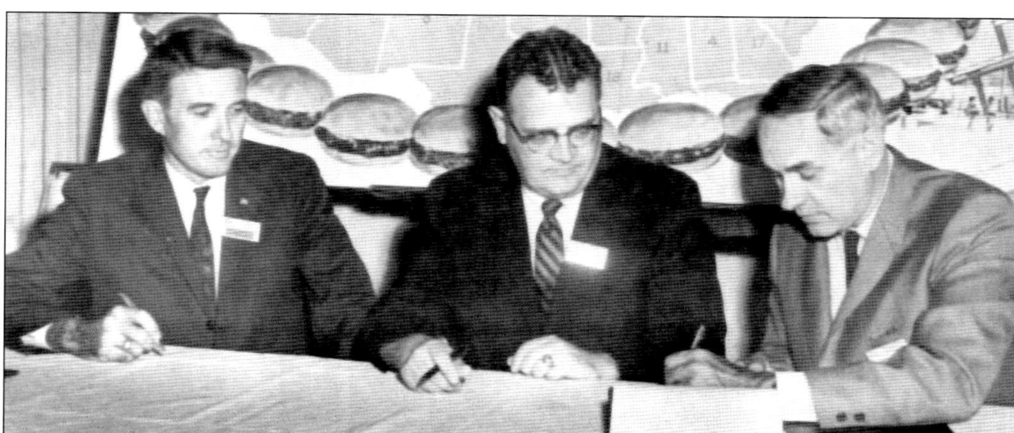

SIGNING THE LEASE ON STORE 500—SEPTEMBER 3, 1965. This store stood at 2200 North Meridian Street in Indianapolis. From left to right: Donald Thomas—Vice President, Robert Wildman—Executive Vice President of Franchise Development, and Frank P. Thomas Jr.—President.

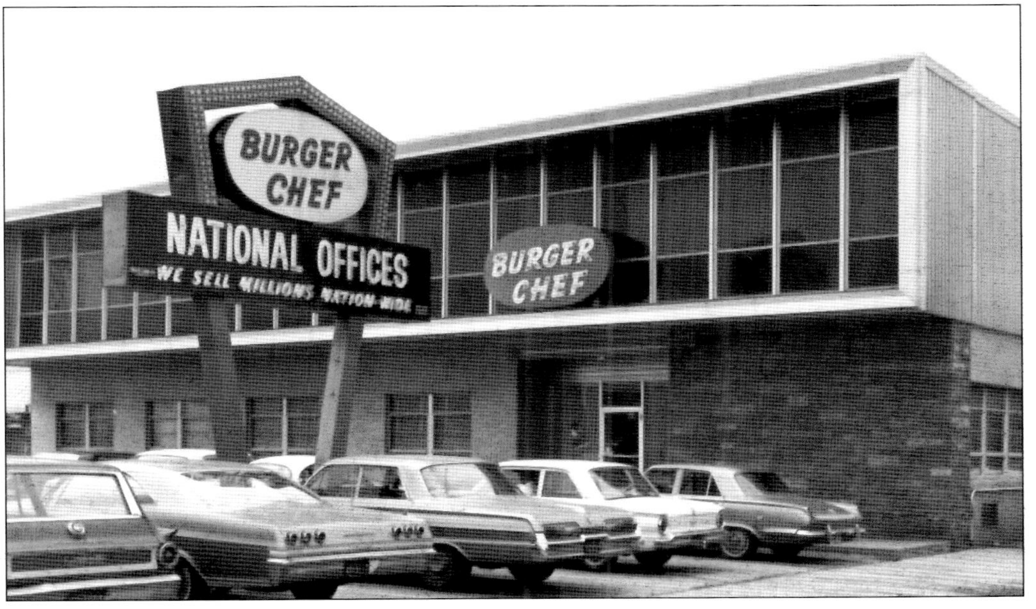

CORPORATE HEADQUARTERS—1967 AND 2002. This building, at 1348 West Sixteenth Street, served as the corporate headquarters from 1965 until 1971 when General Foods moved their executives to White Plains, New York, as a part of their acquisition. Today the Kirby Risk Supply Company next door uses the rear portion as a large warehouse. The original store location—1300 West Sixteenth Street—is now the home of the Indianapolis branch of Greybar Electric Supply Company.

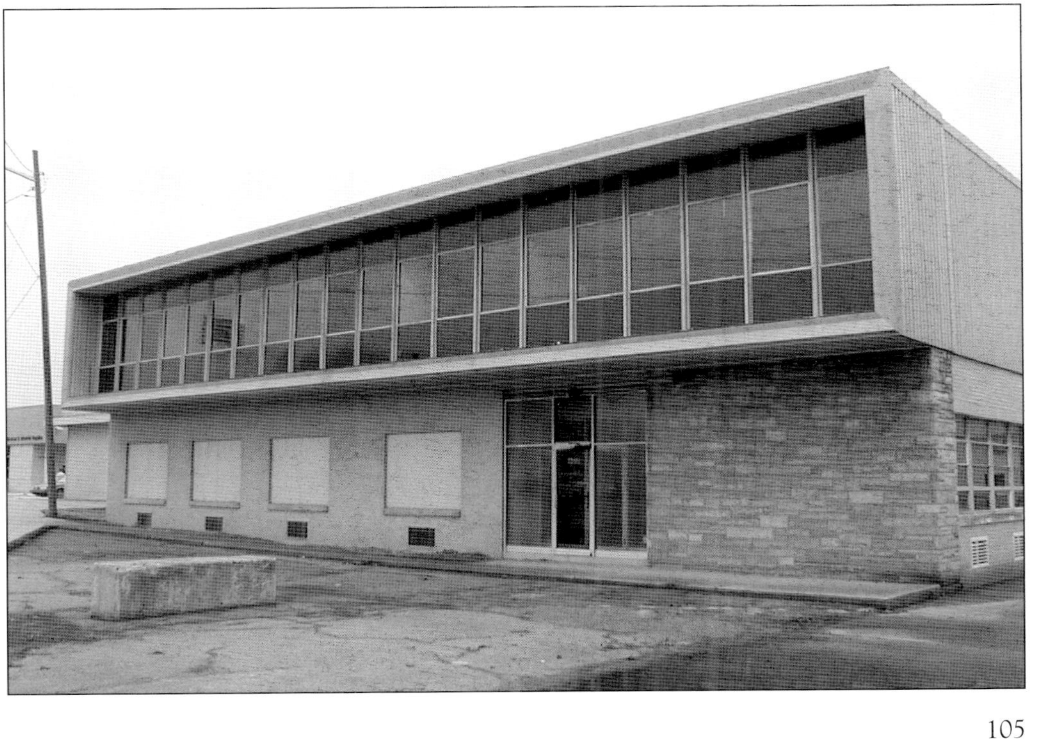

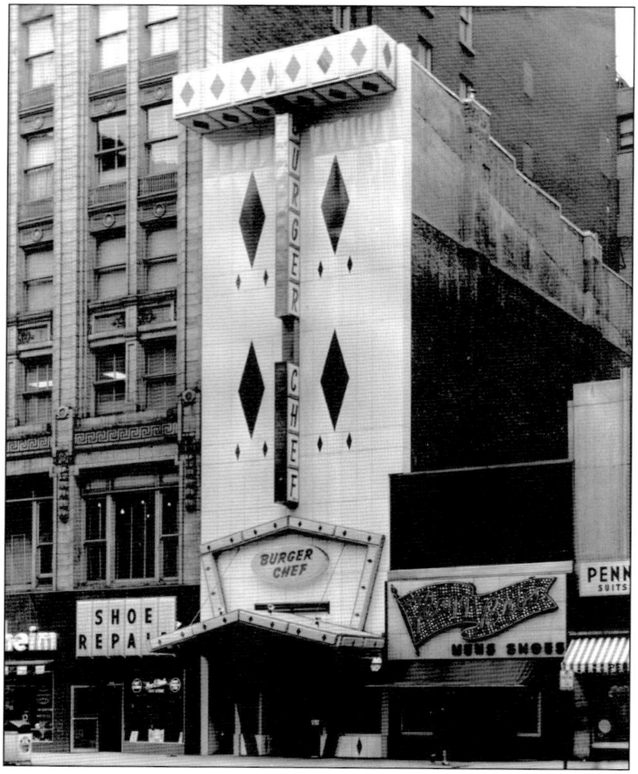

SIX EAST WASHINGTON. The company took over the location of Craig's Restaurant, who had been at this address for 90 years before moving to Glendale. To keep customers moving through, they created a self-serve cafeteria line with a moving conveyor belt that moved your tray along at a pace of 700 customers per hour. Carry out patrons exited the store in the alley behind. The company slightly adjusted their menu to cater to downtown lunchtime customers by adding salads to the burgers, fries, and milkshakes. Left photo shows the newly completed renovation. Bottom photo shows the location in 2001—it was converted, along with the rest, into a Hardee's before it was closed. Workers razed the building in February of 2002. (Photos from Frank Thomas Jr.)

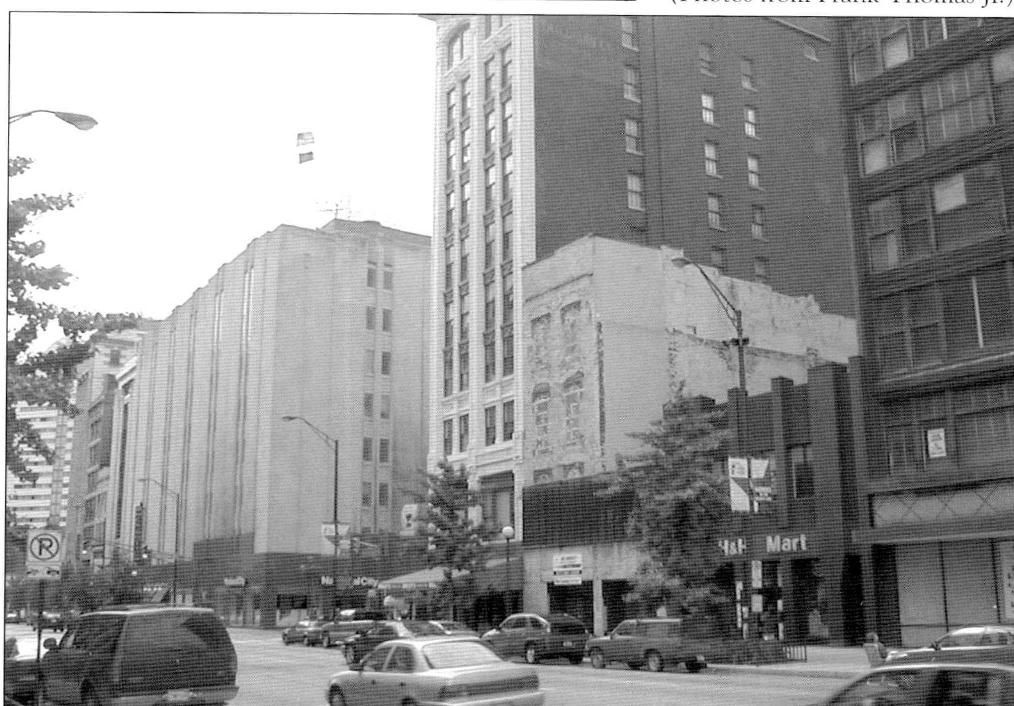

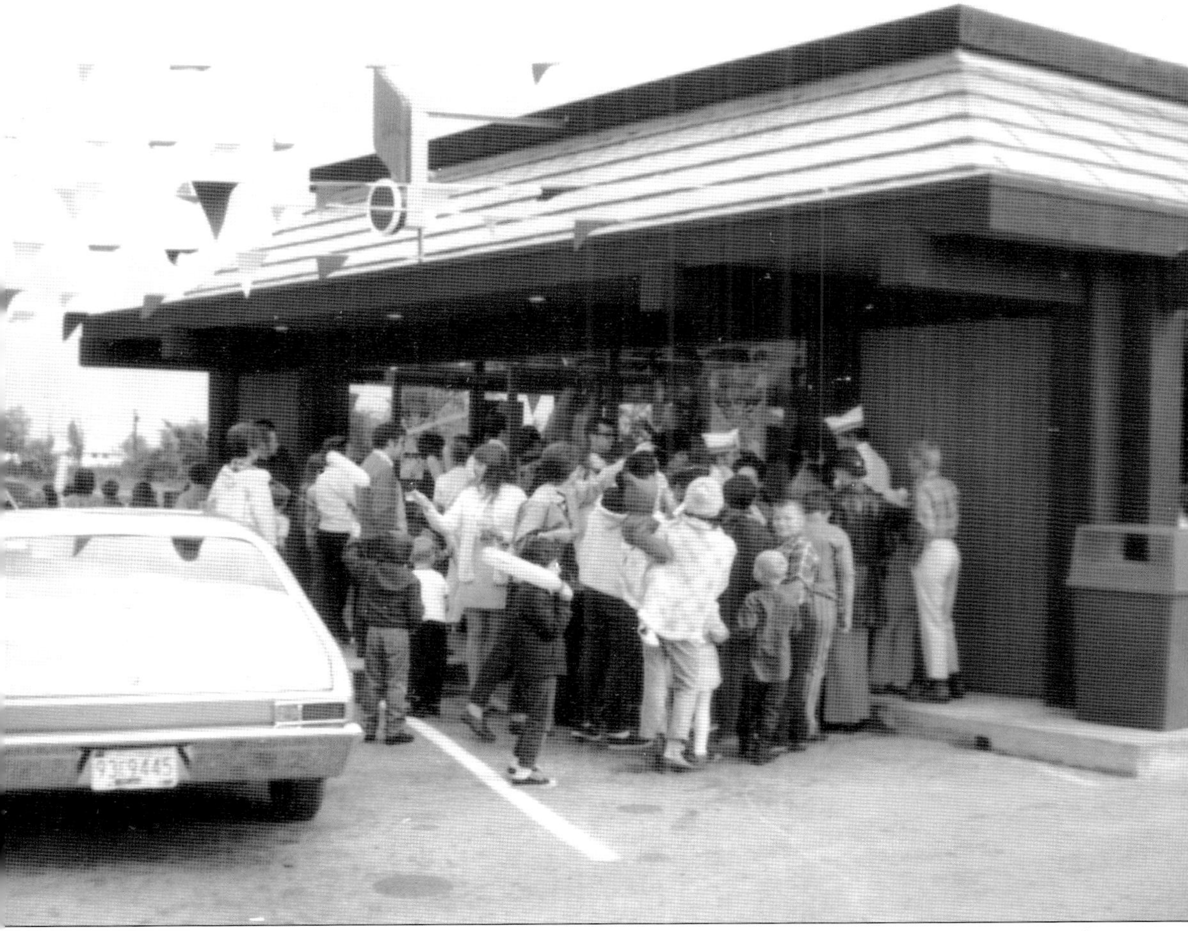

GREENBRIAR—EARLY 1970S. This picture shows crowds outside the store at Eighty-sixth and Ditch Road in Indianapolis on opening day. General Foods created this store and logo design, used from 1970 to 1972. Though substantially remodeled, the store is still a Hardees. (Photo from Rick Patton.)

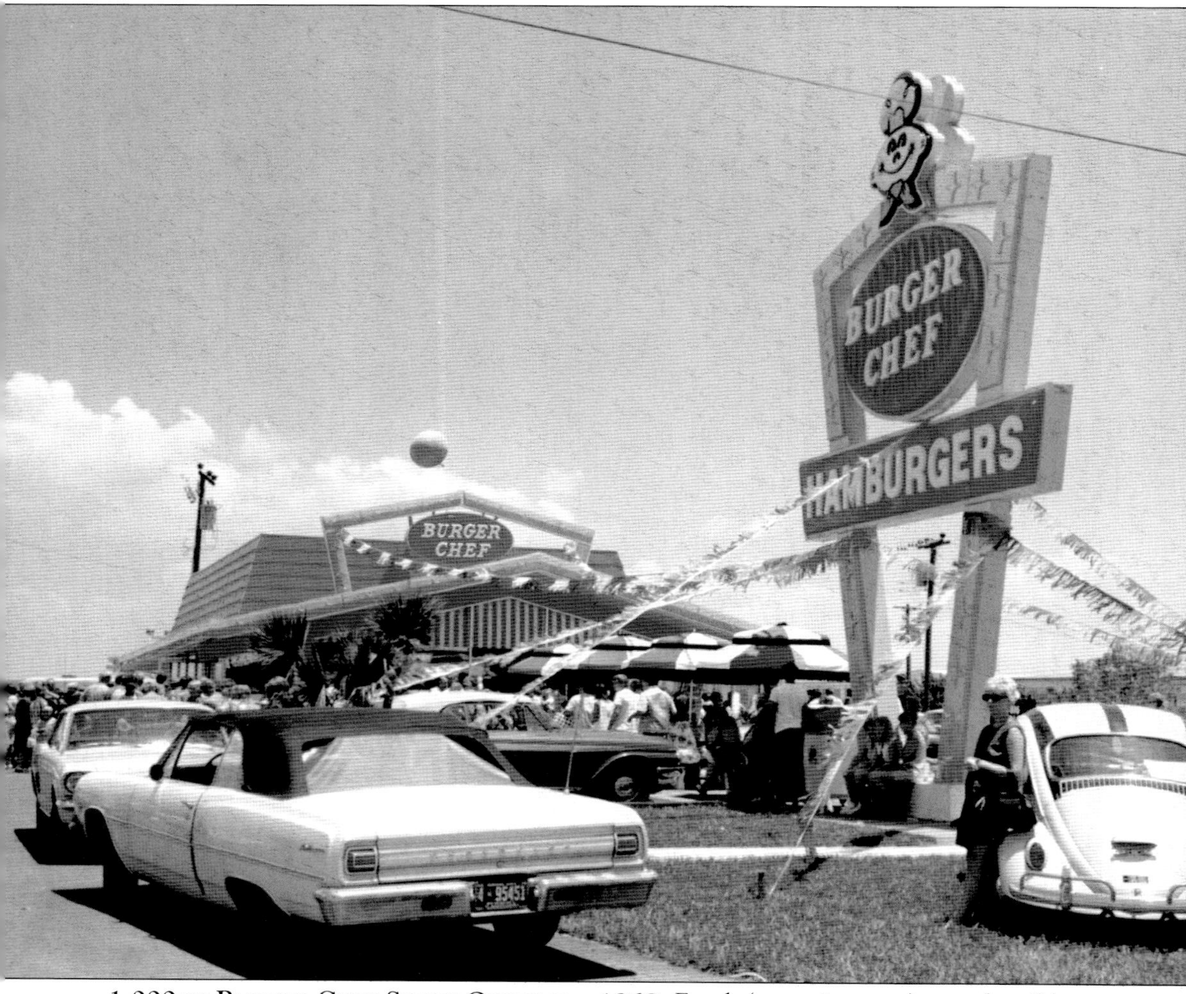

1,000TH BURGER CHEF STORE OPENING—1969. Frank (opposite page) cuts the ribbon on the 1,000th Burger Chef in Treasure Island, Florida on August 9, 1969. By this time, the

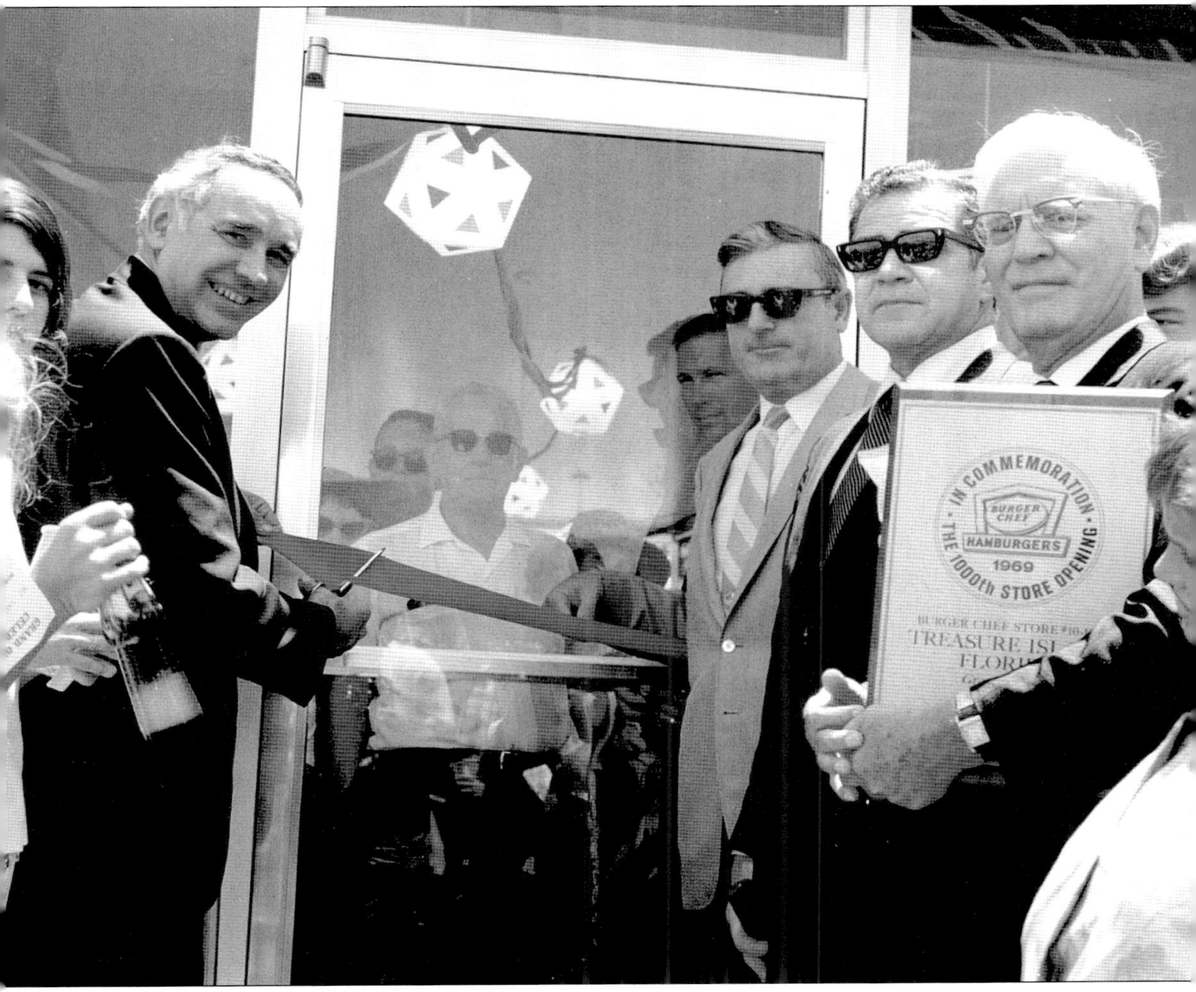

company was a division of General Foods.

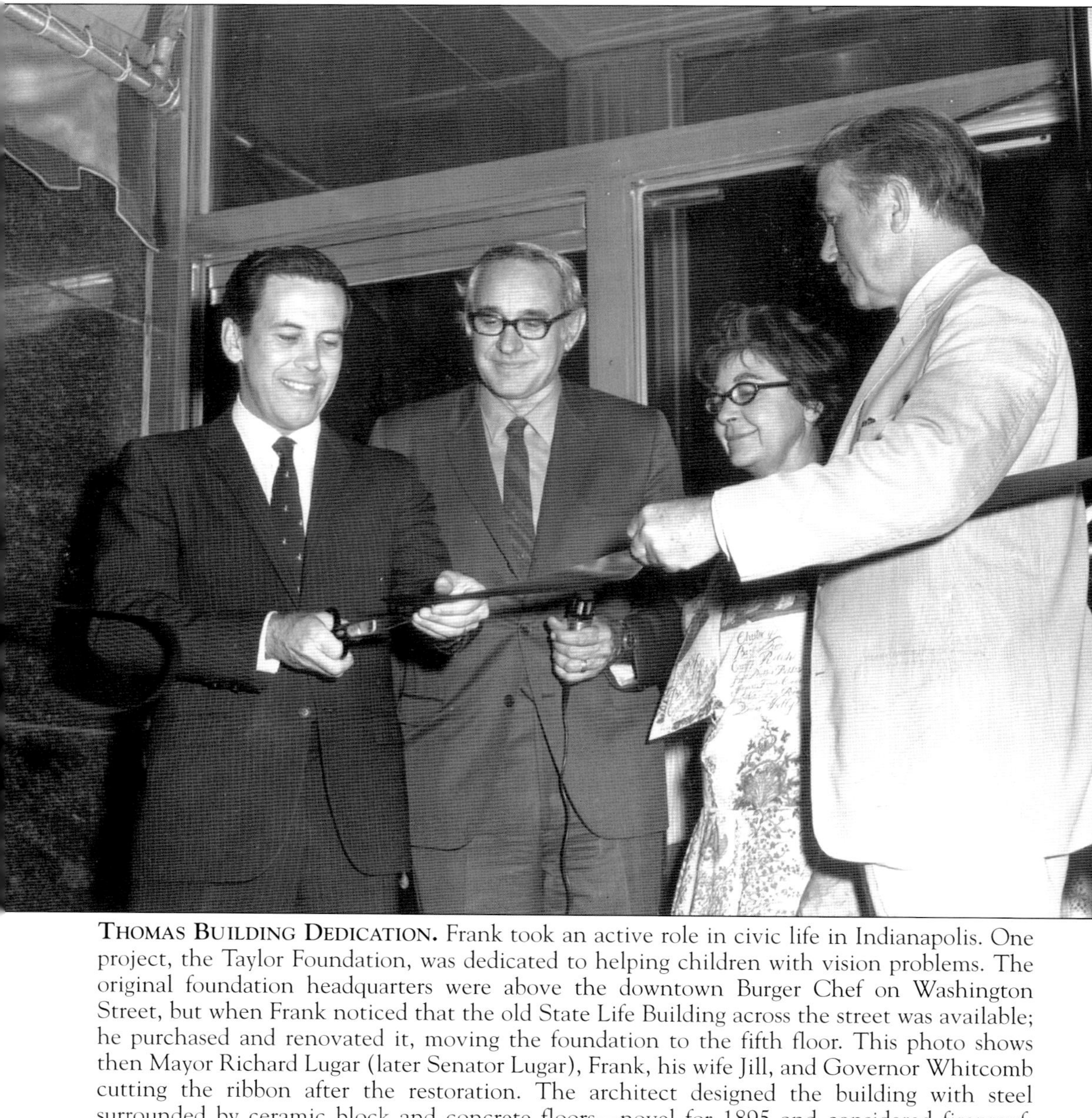

THOMAS BUILDING DEDICATION. Frank took an active role in civic life in Indianapolis. One project, the Taylor Foundation, was dedicated to helping children with vision problems. The original foundation headquarters were above the downtown Burger Chef on Washington Street, but when Frank noticed that the old State Life Building across the street was available; he purchased and renovated it, moving the foundation to the fifth floor. This photo shows then Mayor Richard Lugar (later Senator Lugar), Frank, his wife Jill, and Governor Whitcomb cutting the ribbon after the restoration. The architect designed the building with steel surrounded by ceramic block and concrete floors—novel for 1895 and considered fireproof. Unfortunately, a blaze broke out in a construction site next door in 1973, producing a fire so hot that it caused the steel to warp and twist. After a judge dismissed a multi-million-dollar lawsuit against Thomas by the tenants, workers tore the building down. Frank shortly thereafter decided to resign from most all of his civic appointments and retire.

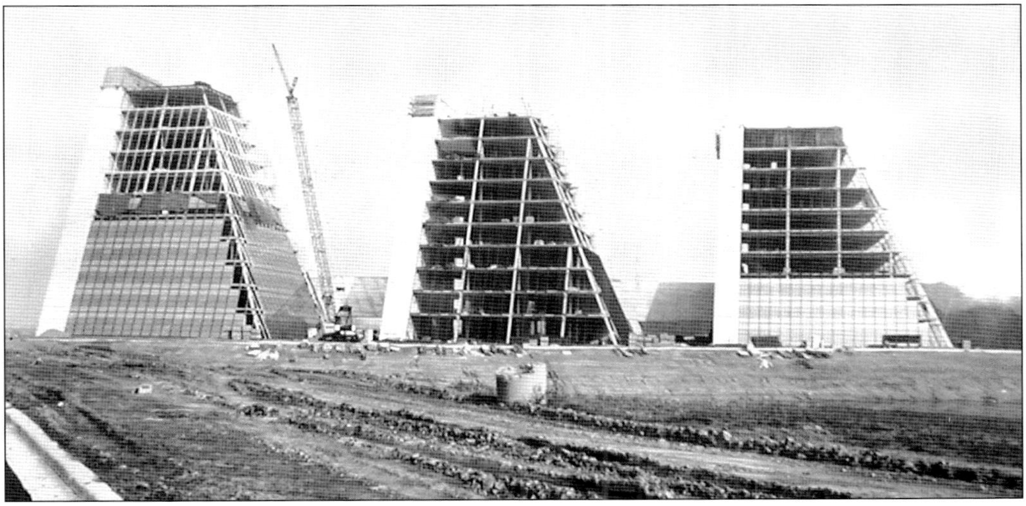

COLLEGE LIFE INSURANCE COMPANY HEADQUARTERS—NOVEMBER 1970. Better known as the "Pyramids," they were the first three of a planned nine buildings constructed to house the records of the growing insurance firm. The advent of computerized record keeping meant there would now be room to sublease, and when General Foods moved the divisional headquarters back to Indianapolis, they would move into Tower 2, 6th Floor.

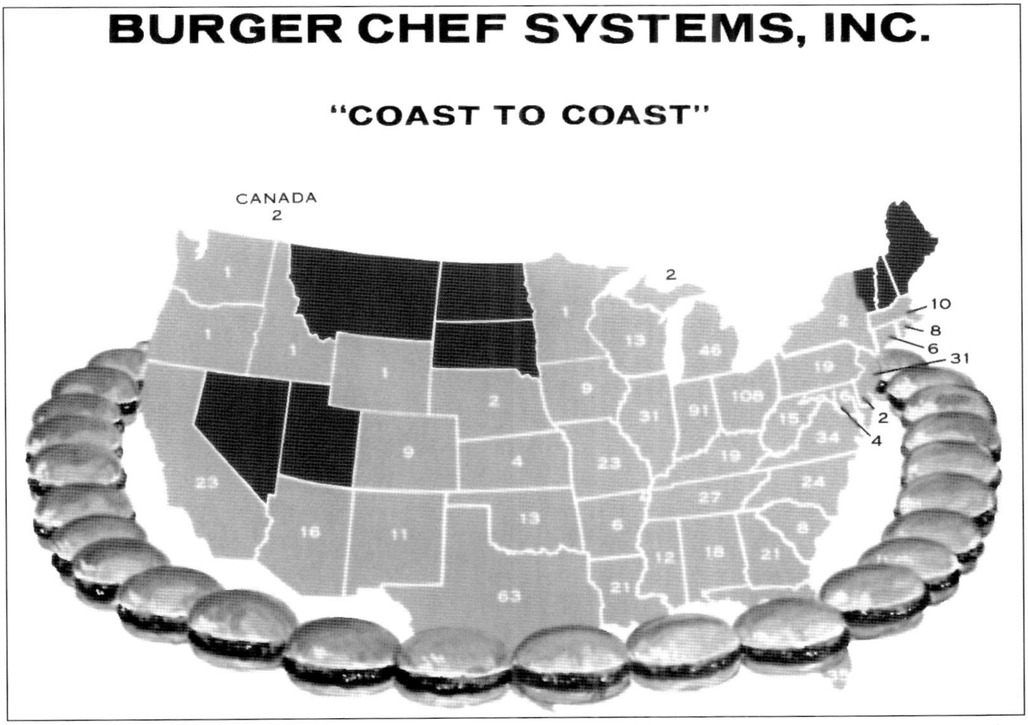

FRANCHISE FOLDER COVER—1967. There were over 775 stores in the chain when this graphic was created. Burger Chef was an aggressive recruiter, and developed a substantial set of materials for potential franchises. Field sales managers were a key to their growth—but one of the first groups of people let go when General Foods took over.

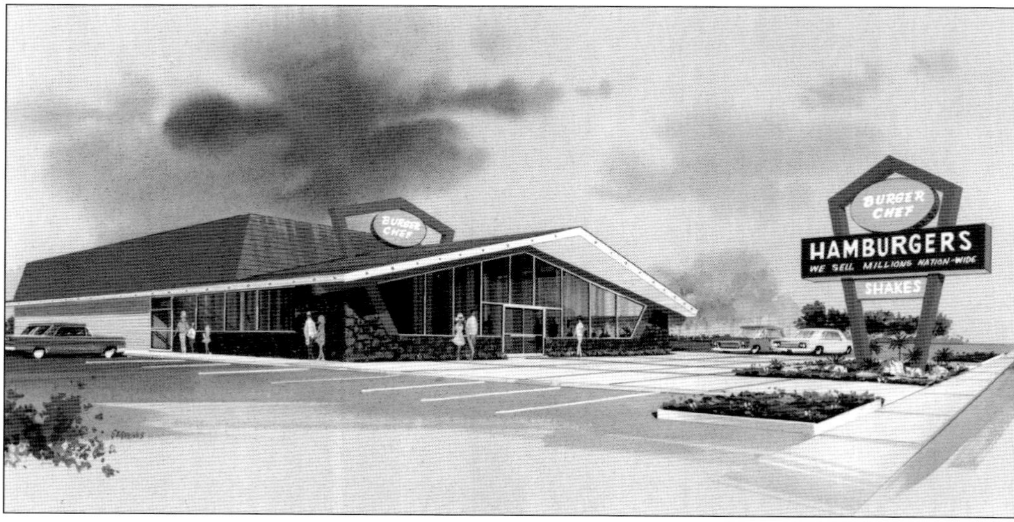

Cosmo II Conceptual Drawing. In the late 1960s, the company commissioned a new store design, built to minimize the "drive-in" look and make Burger Chef compete better with the family restaurant.

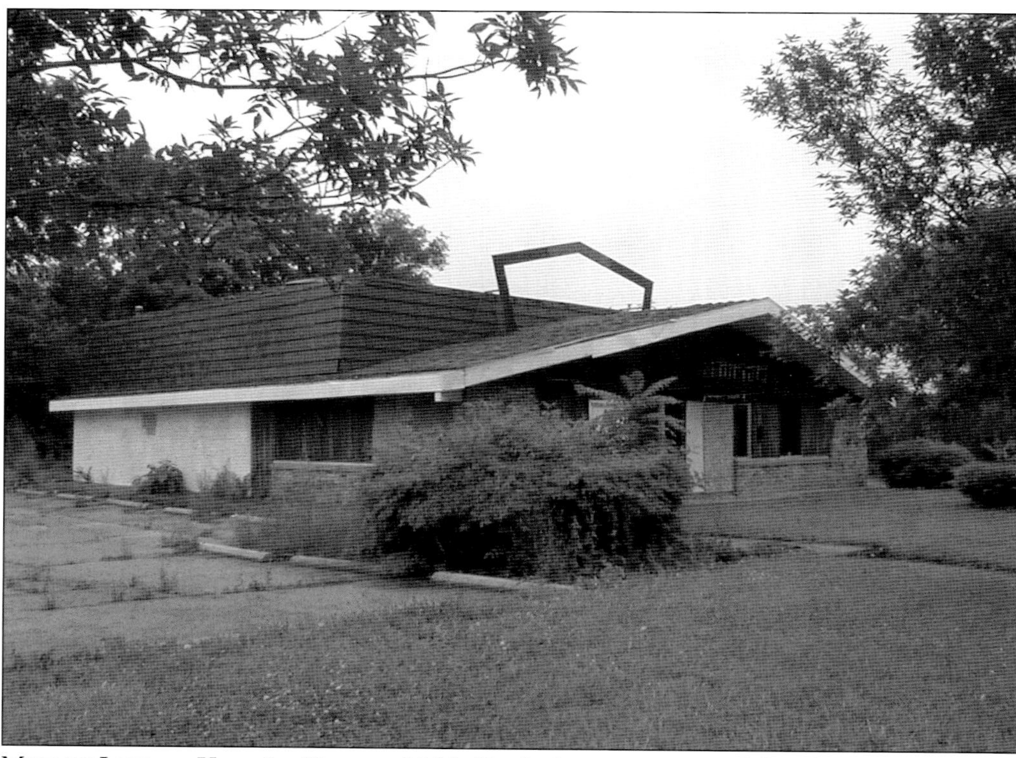

Martin Luther King Jr. Drive—2002. Hardee's never converted this abandoned location, and it is a great example of a "Cosmo II" style building. It still has the "arch" on top, and the original orange roof tile color is showing through the black paint in spots.

Eleven

Market Square Arena

A lonely traveler is driving his car on I-70 through Indianapolis on a sleepy Sunday morning just after dawn. Up ahead he notices several police cars with flashing lights block the road. He slows to a stop, reaches for his coffee, and jumps at the sound of a loud explosion as a huge cloud of dust fills the sky. Is it a bad truck accident? Is it a train derailment? No. It is the end of an Indiana original, Market Square Arena.

Market Square Arena was demolished at 7:00 a.m. on July 8, 2001. Thousands have memories created in the building—from graduations, to high school championships, to lazy Saturdays spent watching the Lipizzaner Stallions. Market Square Arena was where Elvis played his last concert before his death, where Wayne Gretzky first skated out onto the ice to start his pro hockey career, and where Michael Jordan made his first comeback from retirement in 1995. It was where Andre the Giant defeated Hulk Hogan for the World Wrestling Federation title during the first televised wrestling match since 1955. However, it is basketball that is really the story of Market Square Arena—one that runs deep into this hoop-happy state's history.

Basketball wasn't invented in Indiana—that honor goes to Springfield, Massachusetts where, in 1811, James A. Nasmith nailed a pair of peach baskets to the wall at his YMCA and threw an old soccer ball out onto the floor. However, most believe the game was perfected the game in Indiana. Rev. Nicholas McKay brought the game to his Crawfordsville YMCA in 1894 and had a blacksmith create a pair of metal hoops to hang on the wall to make the ball easier to retrieve. In 1925, James Nasmith himself visited the state finals game that year and wrote, "Basketball really had its origin in Indiana, which remains the center of the sport."

Despite this history, though, in 1967 there was no major league professional team playing in Indiana. There had been a few in the past—including the Zollner Pistons who played in Fort Wayne between 1941 and 1957, and later move north to become the Detroit Pistons. A few civic and business leaders got together to buy a franchise in the new American Basketball Association—a league created in response to the slow expansion of the NBA in the 1960s. They thought that a separate league might force an NBA expansion into markets that could clearly support a professional team. They named the team the "Indiana Pacers," "Indiana" in the hopes of drawing more support than from just Indianapolis, and "Pacers" from the pace car in a race.

The early years were not very glamorous—the team played games in the drafty old coliseum at the Indiana State Fairgrounds. The teams really did not have decent locker rooms, but the crowds were good and the team ended the first year with a decent 38-40 record.

In the second season, the Pacers began to build some momentum. The team brought in Bobby "Slick" Leonard, a fiery coach that led the team for the rest of its stay in the ABA.

(Leonard is now the color radio announcer for the team.) They also traded for Mel Daniels, who eventually became a two-time ABA MVP and the ABA's all-time leading rebounder. In the 1969–1970 season, the team was 59-25 and they won the first of three ABA championship titles (the others would come in 1971–1972 and 1972–1973). The Pacers lost in Game 7 of the 1974 championship, almost becoming four-time champions.

It was in this environment that the ABA powerhouse began to find its surroundings somewhat inadequate. Indianapolis was a small town trying to become a city—many called it "Naptown" or "India-no-place." Mayor Richard Lugar, who eventually became an Indiana senator, realized that the Pacers were just the sort of thing that the city needed to keep. The problems were huge, however: the city's downtown was dying due to suburban flight, so leaders wanted to find a way to put the arena there to stimulate commerce rather than the spot the Pacers had picked out on the growing northwest quadrant of the city. However, buying land and demolishing buildings would add millions to the cost of a project that the small city was not sure how it was going to pay for in the first place.

Out of these problems was born a unique civic-private partnership that became the model for future projects in Indianapolis as well as other cities. On April 12, 1971, Mayor Lugar announced that a new 18,000 seat multipurpose arena would be built, including two 12-story office buildings and three parking garages. In order to get around the land problem, the plan included a parking garage on both north and the south sides of Market Street, west of Alabama Street, with the arena perched on top of the garages, straddling Market Street, which would run under the building. The city would fund one-third of the original $32 million price tag, with the balance paid for by a private investor group backed by Fred Tucker, an Indianapolis Realtor and J. Fred Risk, president of Indiana National Bank. The city bought the two small plots of land, the investor group, named "Market Square Associates" constructed the garages, and the city built the arena on top of them. Market Square Associates then leased the arena from the city and operated it on behalf of the Pacers.

Two Ball State University students, Joseph Mynheir and Terry Pastorino, partially devised the innovative solution as an architectural class project in November 1970. General contractor Huber, Hunt & Nichols (who would go on to build Cleveland Browns stadium, Pacific Bell Park in San Francisco, and the new Conseco Fieldhouse in Indianapolis, among others) took the plans drawn up by Architects 4, a group of four firms who collaborated on the design, and built the stadium. Groundbreaking occurred on October 20, 1971. Construction took almost two years, with the first event, a Glen Campbell concert, held on September 15, 1974. The arena held the first regular-season ABA game on October 18, 1974, against the San Antonio Spurs, which the Pacers lost in overtime, 129-121. Only 7,473 attended.

Alas, the days of the ABA were running short. Key players started leaving for the NBA. Most of the original owners had anticipated an early merger, not a protracted battle, and they simply began to run out of money. During the summer of 1976, the four strongest teams—the Pacers, the Denver Nuggets, the San Antonio Spurs, and the New York Nets—joined the NBA by each paying $3.2 million in fees. The other ABA teams died, unable to pay this tribute. The New York Nets (who would become the New Jersey Nets) paid an additional $4 million directly to the New York Knicks as penalty for lost revenue. A fifth team, the St. Louis Spirits, was turned away from the NBA, but in tribute the other four teams have been forced to pay one-seventh of their TV revenues to the former owners—in perpetuity. Many of the rules that made the ABA so exciting would also join the NBA, including the 30-second shot clock and the three-point line. The Pacers' home in the NBA would continue to be Market Square Arena.

Times were tough for the Pacers—they actually had to hold a telethon to raise enough money to continue the team. Many memorable events occurred in the building around this time, including the final concert of Elvis Aaron Presley, held on June 26, 1977, in front of over 18,000 people. He died in the early morning on August 16, 1977.

During the 1980s, the team continued to struggle, but underwent a resurgence in the 1990s under the leadership of players like Reggie Miller and Coaches Larry Brown and Larry Bird. In fact, they reached the NBA Eastern Conference Finals for the first time in the franchise's history in 1994, only to lose in seven games to the New York Knicks. They would again reach the Conference Finals in 1995, 1998, and 1999 before Coach Bird led the team all the way to the NBA finals in 2000, where the Pacers lost in six games to the Shaquille O'Neal-led Los Angeles Lakers.

Many of the features that made the Market Square Arena unique eventually led to its undoing. Since the building was literally perched above a city street, there was only one small loading ramp on the back of the building. Trucks setting up for a concert could only come up the ramp one at a time, and then there was no real place for them to park while the show was on. The city took to carefully parking them on Market Street's median, under the building, bumper to bumper. The building was extremely steep with narrow paths through the stands; ask anyone who tried to walk down the steps why so many would lose their orientation and fall. The final blow came when the team declared the stadium unable to support the new private boxes that have become a major new revenue stream for NBA teams. Instead, the same public/private partnership would build a new crown jewel—Conseco Fieldhouse—in the shadow of the old arena.

The last Pacer game was held on October 23, 1999—a preseason exhibition game against the Utah Jazz—a team who themselves owe their existence to the ABA Utah Stars who proved Utah could support a professional basketball team. Coach Larry Bird handed Bobby "Slick" Leonard, the man most associated with the Pacer's ABA days, a ball at the end of the last practice. Bobby sunk the shot—and thereby made the very first and the very last baskets at Market Square Arena.

Though perhaps unsuitable for basketball, it seemed to many that the city might use the building for another purpose. Citizens attending a public hearing in September of 1999 opposed the demolition 3 to 1. In fact, the building held concerts and special shows for years, and many felt conversion into a full-time hockey arena for the Indianapolis Ice was possible. Unfortunately, none of the ideas came along with funding—it cost the city over $1 million per year simply to heat the building, and its nearly 30-year-old escalators and air conditioning equipment were in dire need of replacement. On November 22, 1999, just one month after the final event, the city announced it would seek bids to demolish the building and turn the spot into two parking lots—with Market Street still running through the middle.

Work began in April of 2001 as the wrecking ball removed most of the parking garages on which the arena sits. By demolition day, workers had cut away the majority of the roof, exposing the open beams that supported the dome. On May 14, workers accidentally started a small fire when they did not realize that paper insulation lined the back of the roof material. The city contracted Controlled Demolition of Baltimore, MD, a world-renown firm, to implode the main structure. All throughout June of 2001, workers strategically weakened the building's structure as they wired 800 pounds of explosives to a central command post. In the days before the event, workers hung thick black curtains from the buildings surrounding the site to protect windows from debris. They draped one small bail bond building only a few hundred feet away entirely in cloth.

At 5:30 a.m. on Sunday, July 8, 2001, police began to enforce a "safety zone" around the building, which was designed to protect onlookers and discourage people from showing up for fear of being too far away to see anything. Unlike other cities who have thrown large parties surrounding the demolition of large buildings, Indianapolis chose to downplay the event. Reportedly, someone even had to persuade the mayor to attend. At 6:45 a.m. police shut off all I-65 and I-70 leading into and out of downtown—it was felt that traffic traveling on these roads early on a Sunday morning would be dangerously surprised by an arena imploding a few hundred yards away.

The end came in only 12 seconds. At precisely 7:00 a.m., Controlled Demolition set off a series of loud bangs—blasting caps that started chain-reaction explosions. The first large explosion started the roof dome collapse, and a second smaller explosion cut the steel support ring around the building into segments. Only seven windows were broken in the buildings next door, which workers replaced the very same day. By that afternoon, the city washed the streets clean of hundreds of pounds of dust and paperboard insulation—ending a new chapter in story of "Lost Indianapolis."

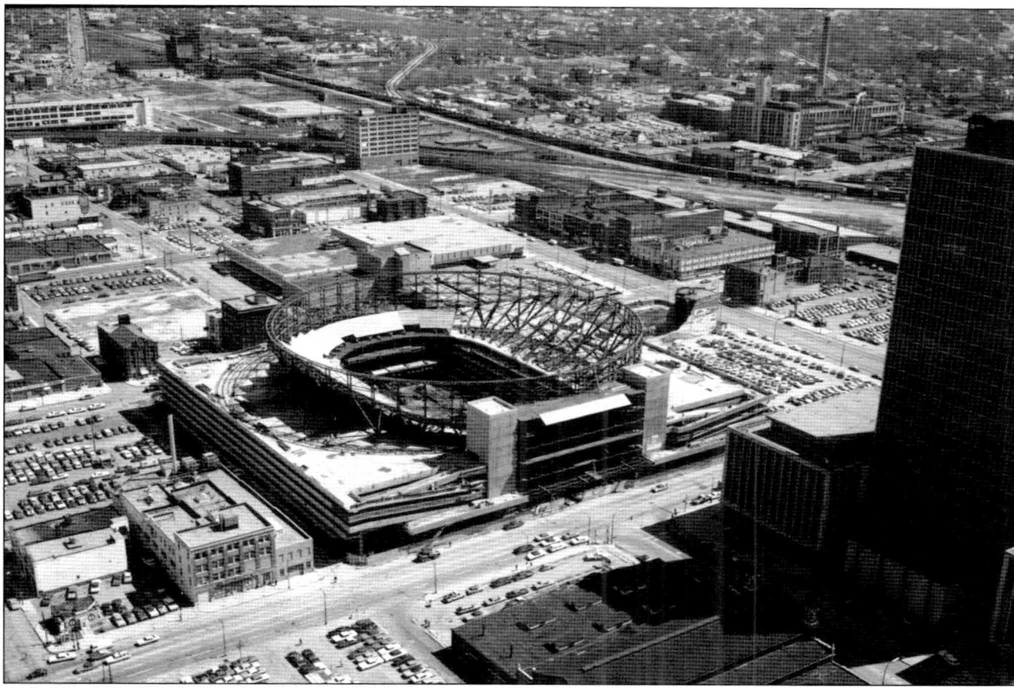

MARKET SQUARE ARENA UNDER CONSTRUCTION—1973. The photographer took the top photo from the Indiana National Bank Building (now the Union Planters Building). Ironworkers are placing temporary supports for the construction of the dome—the steel ring around the upper edge entirely supported the dome when completed. The bottom picture is of Market Square Arena shortly after opening in 1974. (Indiana Historical Society Bass Photo Collection.)

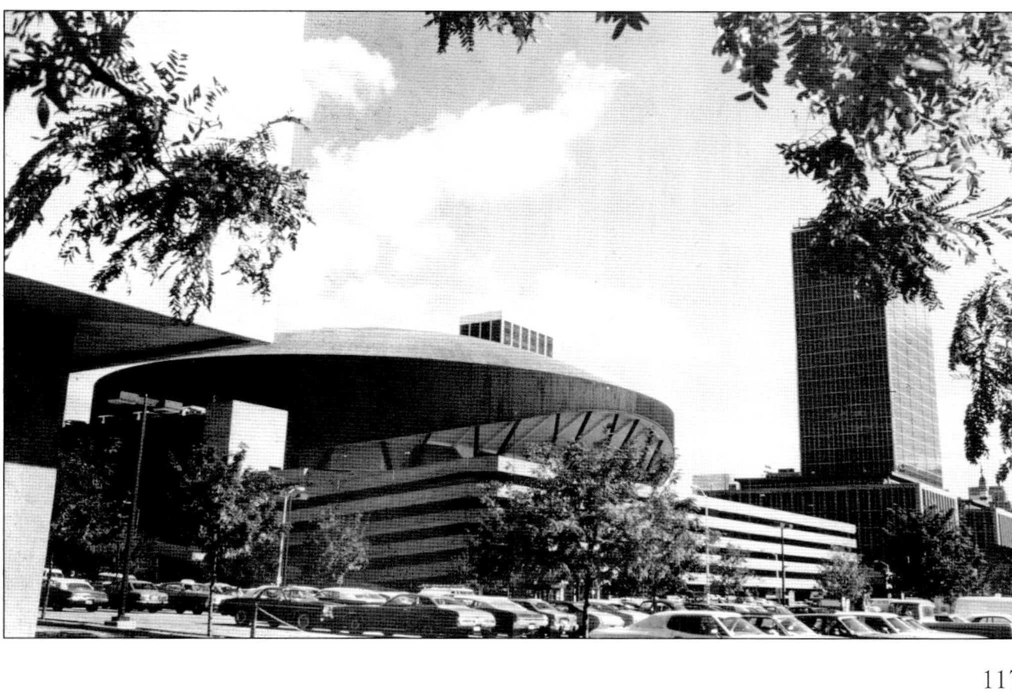

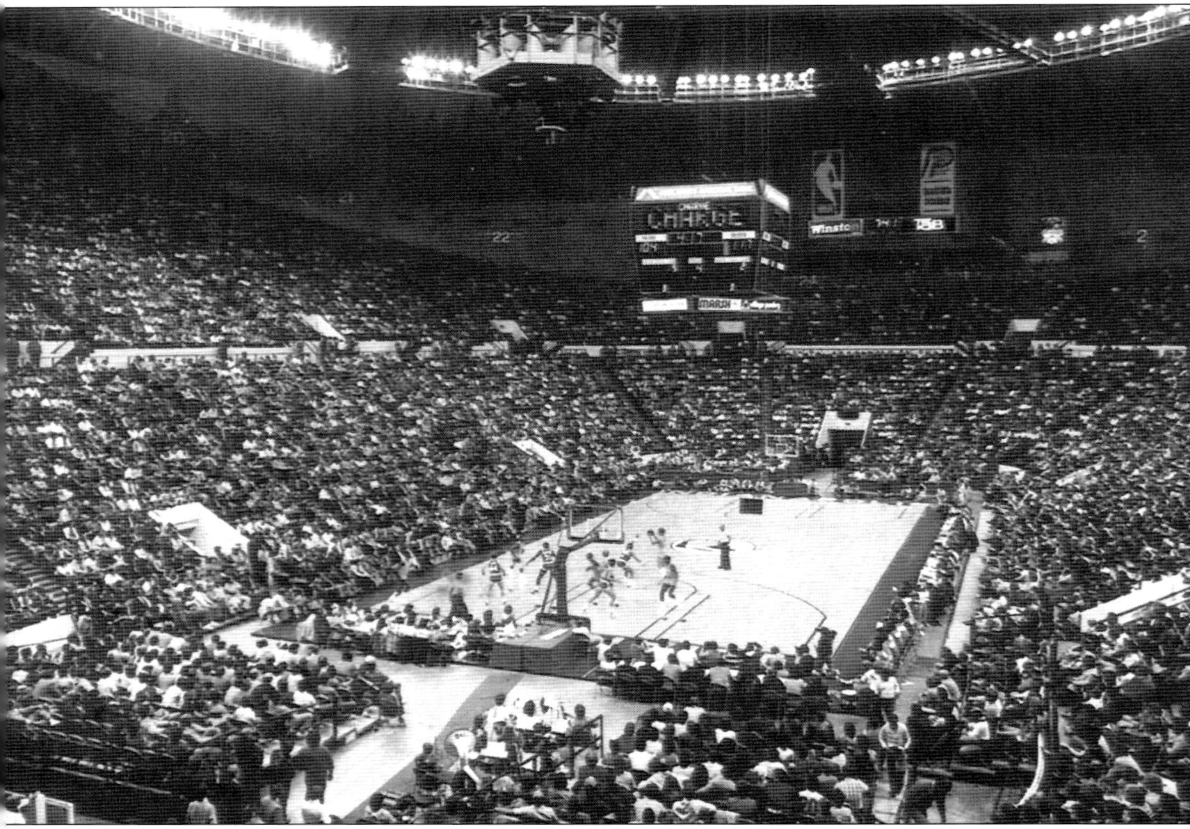

BASKETBALL AT MARKET SQUARE ARENA. The left photo shows the last 4.17 seconds of a game between the Indiana Pacers and the Boston Celtics in the early 1980s. Future Pacers

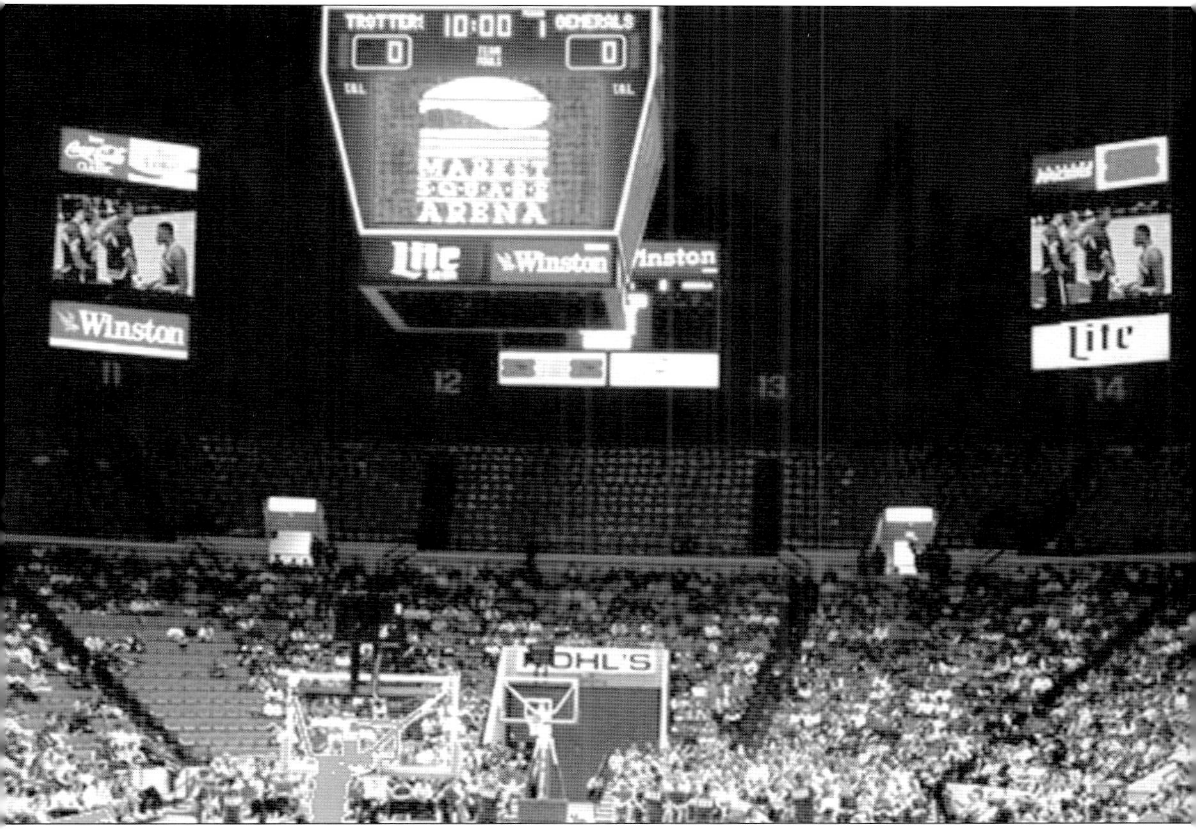

coach, Larry Bird, is on the floor. The above picture shows the start of a Harlem Globetrotters game in the late 1990s. Note the new scoreboard and large video screens added late in its life.

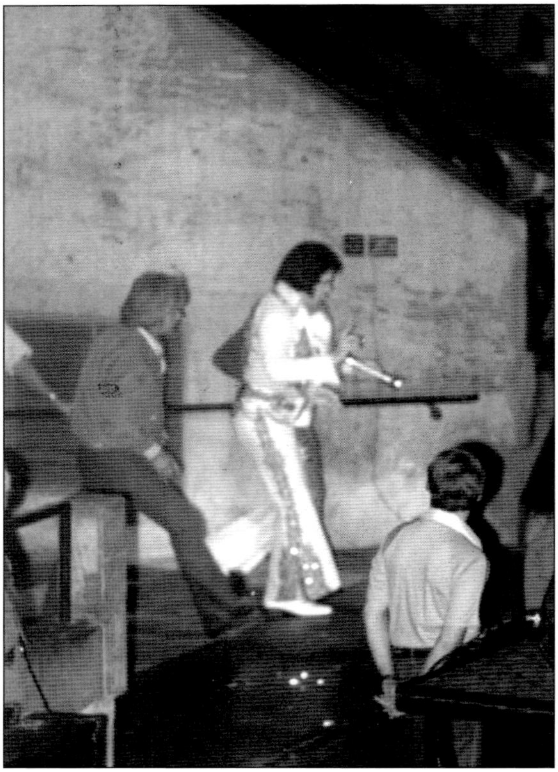

ELVIS' LAST CONCERT. The King walks onto the stage for the last time on June 26, 1977. Part of a Midwestern concert tour, Elvis departed for a break at Graceland after the concert, and passed away before ever performing again. Ironically, a camera crew had been following him from city to city, but neglected to film the stop in Indianapolis. Reportedly, many of the crew became ill from food poisoning after this performance.

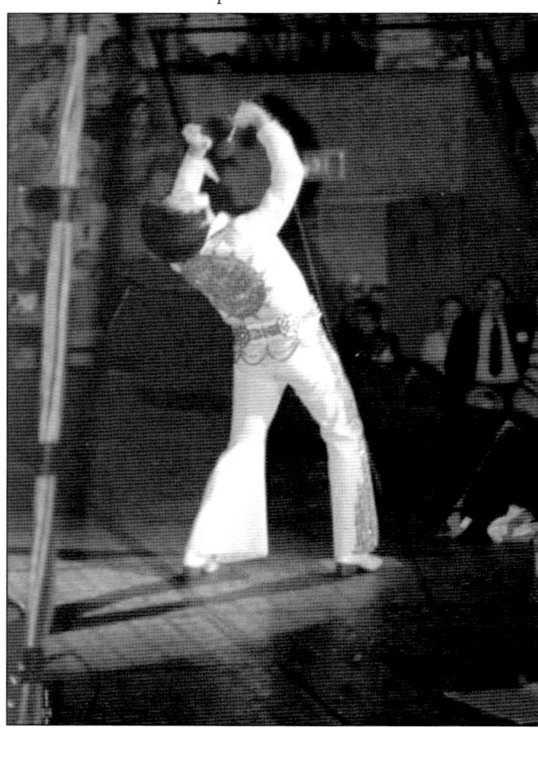

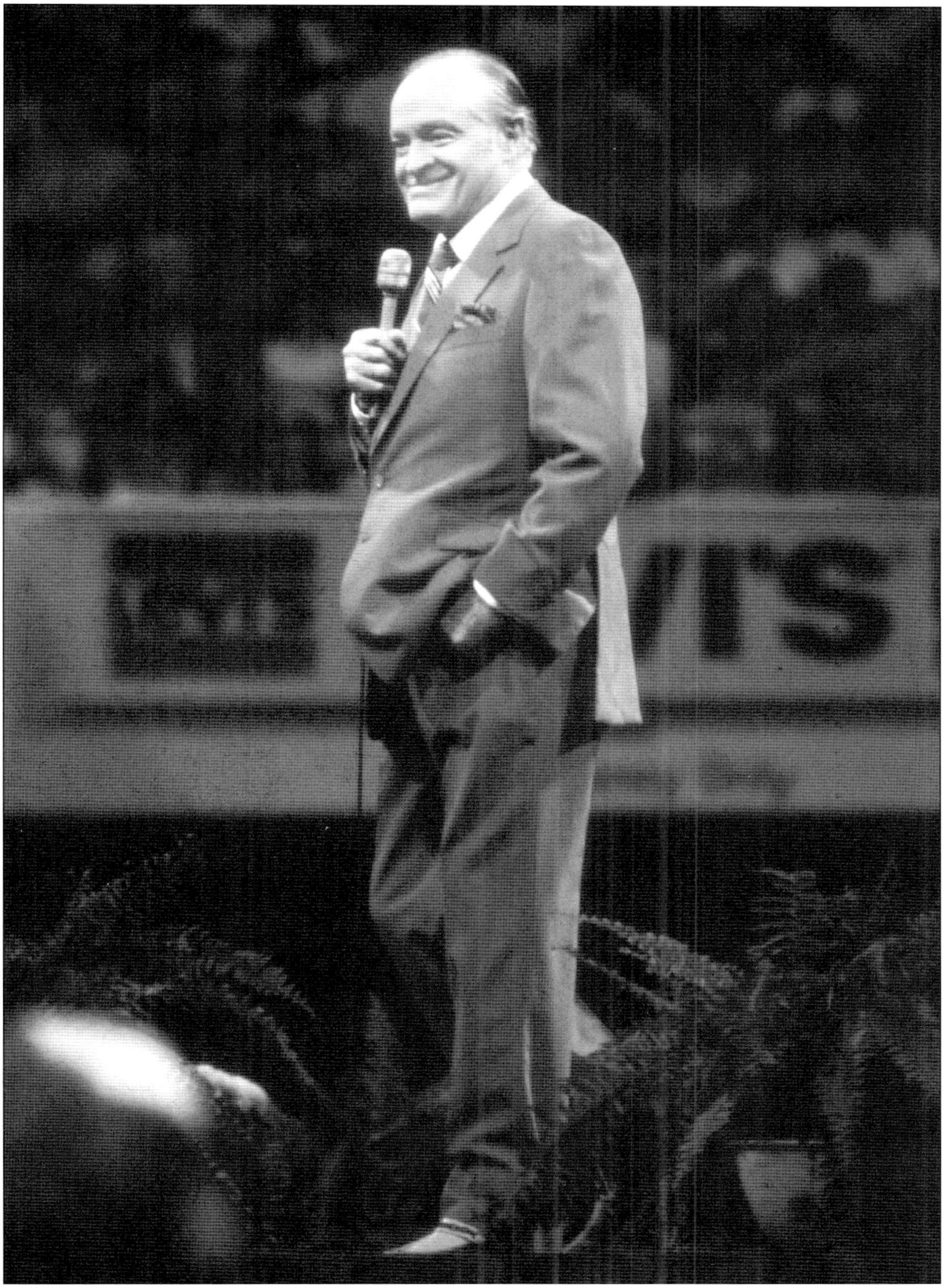

BOB HOPE AT MARKET SQUARE ARENA—1982. Many other events occurred at Market Square Arena beyond basketball games. Here Bob Hope opens the 1982 National Sports Festival, now the U.S. Olympic Festival. (Photo by Mark Wick/Eyes of Mark Wick.)

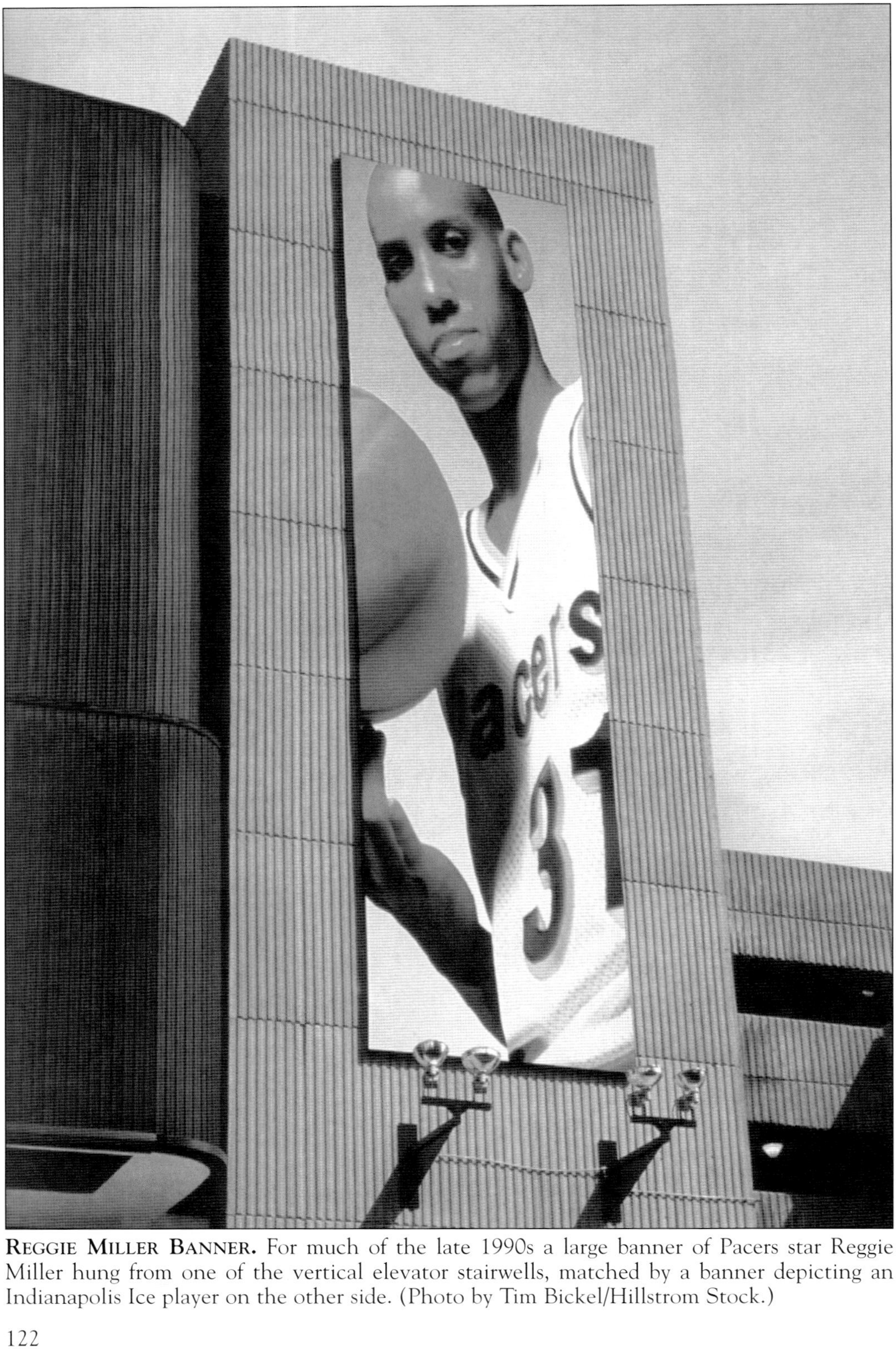

Reggie Miller Banner. For much of the late 1990s a large banner of Pacers star Reggie Miller hung from one of the vertical elevator stairwells, matched by a banner depicting an Indianapolis Ice player on the other side. (Photo by Tim Bickel/Hillstrom Stock.)

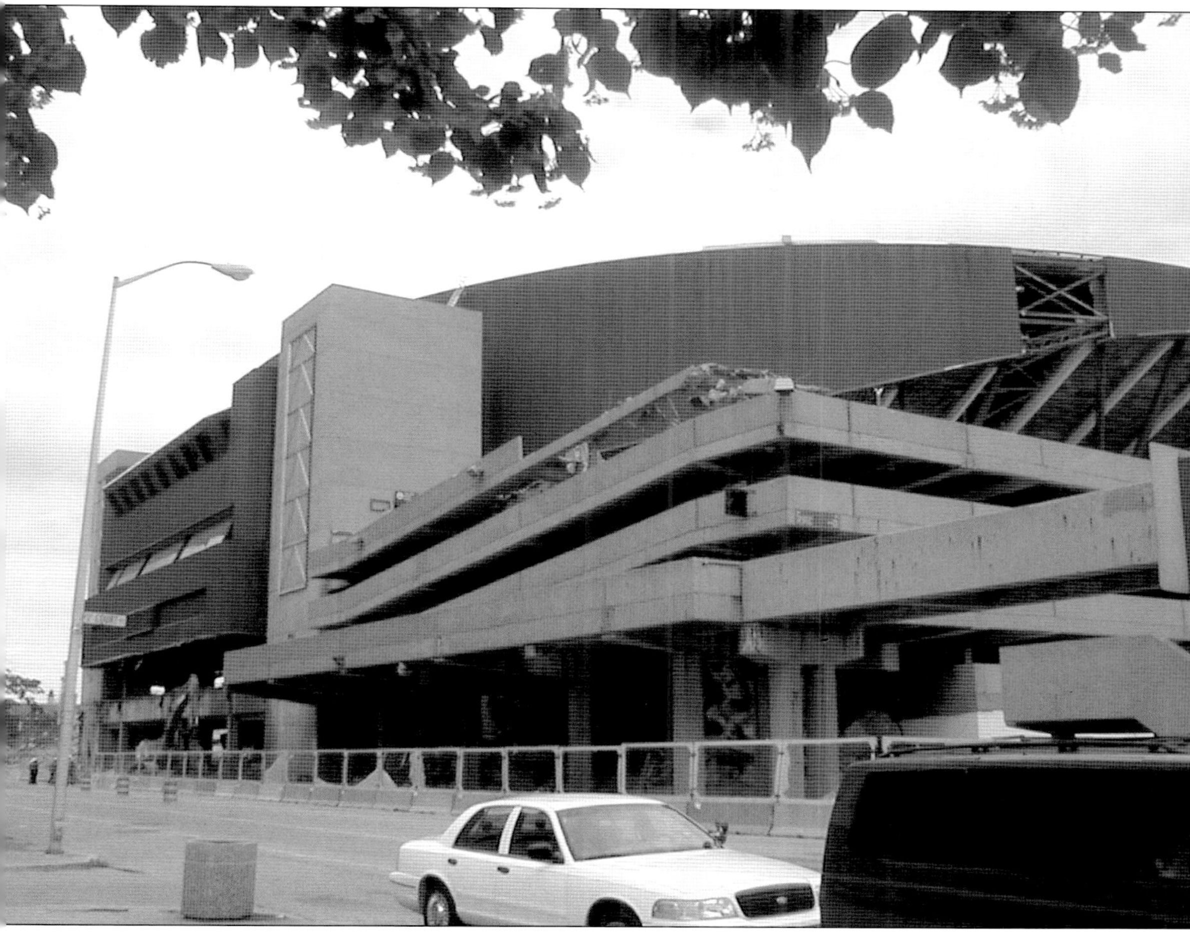

DEMOLITION BEGINS—APRIL 2001. Much of the parking garage is gone in this photo, as well as a section of the metal wall around the edge of the dome.

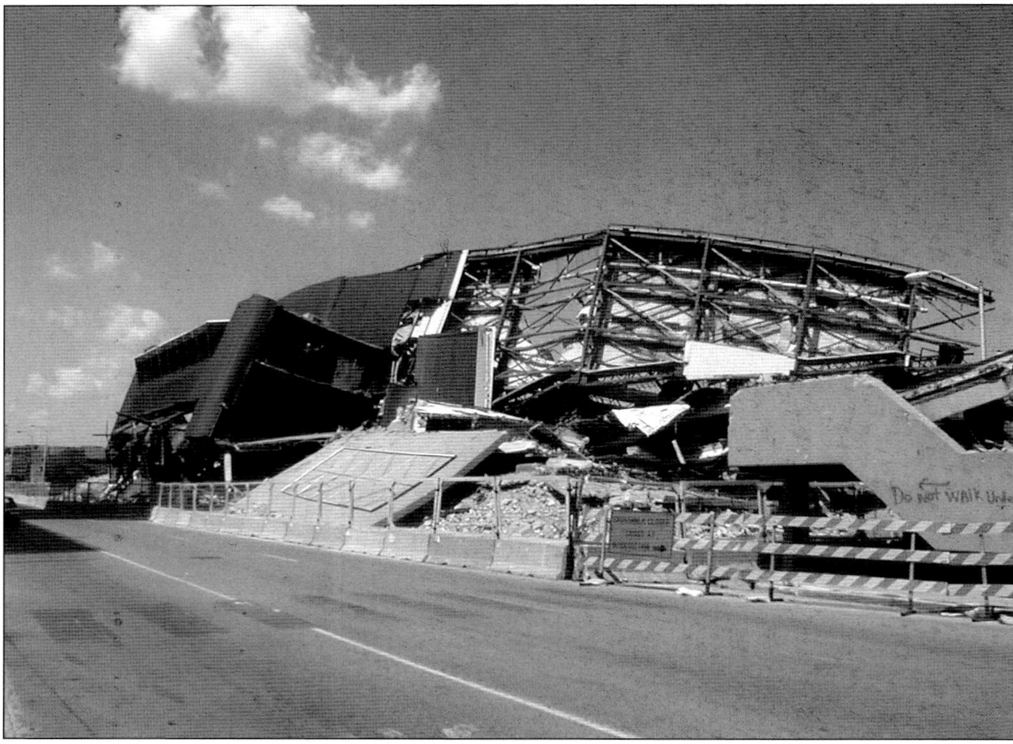
Do not WALK

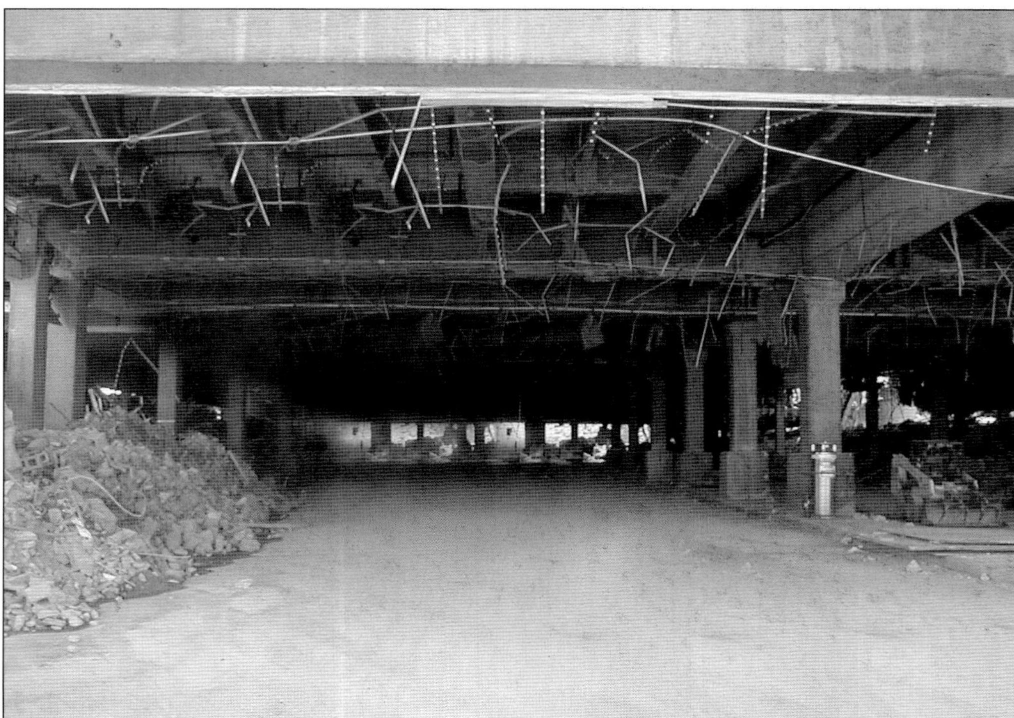

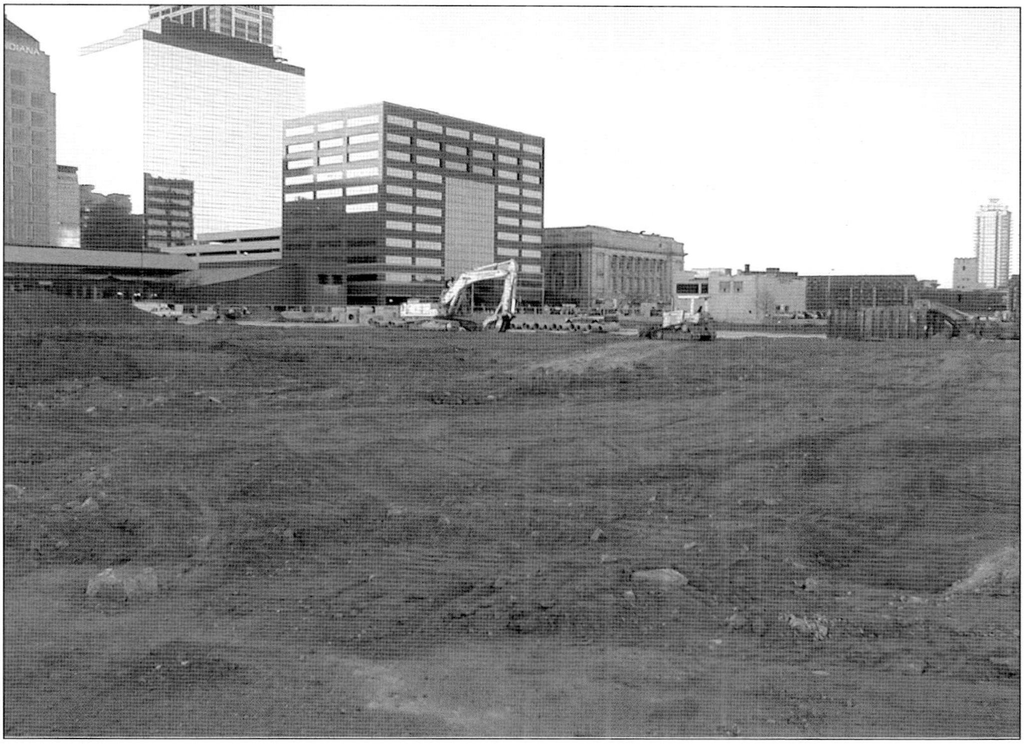

CLEARED SITE—DECEMBER 2001. The arena's location is nearly clear. A "wall" that once blocked neighborhoods east of downtown is now gone, and city officials were anxious to reuse the land for new purposes.

AFTER THE IMPLOSION—JULY 2001. The late Market Square Arena after the implosion, looking at the southwest corner next to the city/county building (opposite page, top). Amazingly, Market Street remains unblocked under the demolished building above it (opposite page, bottom), as rubble could not block a critical utility access panel for the east side of downtown, located under the arena. CDI expertly kept the bridge intact, still supporting an arena floor piled with millions of pounds of concrete and twisted metal.